Praise for
The Endowment Model of Investing

"This is a terrific book—required reading for any CIO. With their focus on beta-based analysis, Marty, Anthony and Brett have developed a sophisticated approach for how to exploit the power of diversification in the 21st century."

—Lyn Hutton, Chief Investment Officer, Commonfund

"Any fund sponsor or portfolio manager considering alternative assets should read this book. The authors show that alternative assets can increase a fund's risk exposure in the short term as their stress betas rise during market crises. When properly allocated, however, alternative assets can provide a central role in maximizing value over the long term."

—Bruce I. Jacobs, Principal, Jacobs Levy Equity Management, and editor of *Market Neutral Strategies*

"The key question is whether beta-based performance analysis and other novel mathematical modeling approaches can effectively deal with the triumvirate of return, risk and diversification in a portfolio. While that key question may be unresolved for, no group other than the authors have made such a rigorous and penetrating assessment of the problem. In my judgment—A MUST READ FOR EVERY CHIEF INVESTMENT OFFICER OR STRATEGIST."

—Allan S. Bufferd, Treasurer Emeritus, MIT

"The authors' frameworks shed needed light on the risks and return sources in non-traditional portfolios. Were this book previously available, many endowment fiduciaries might have understood better what was happening to their portfolios during the financial crisis, and why their pain was predictable, inevitable, and—curses to the Investment Deities—necessary for long-term success."

—Andrew K. Golden, President, Princeton University Investment Company

"This is a must read for every institutional investor concerned with portfolio risk management. Full of important insights and robust analyses, its deconstruction of equity risk exposure under conditions of stress is particularly valuable and would have saved endowment funds much grief (and money) had they digested its warnings before the markets crashed."

—Ian Kennedy, Former Global Director of Research at Cambridge Associates

"Every endowment will benefit by having its key people study this elegant, rigorous, and articulate examination of the endowment model's focus on achieving superior long-term returns—and why skillful implementation is always crucial."

—Charles D. Ellis, Author, *Winning the Loser's Game*

"Is the endowment model broken? The answer, is 'No, but you need to step up your game.' Their appealing mix of analysis and common sense will take you where you need to go."
—Jack R. Meyer, Managing Partner, CEO, Convexity Capital

"A solid analysis of the trend towards allocating into multiple asset classes that indicates when such diversification helps to control fund-level risk—and when it does not."
—Jim Simons, Chairman, Renaissance Technologies LLC

"A balanced book... neither coming to bury nor praising the model... takes us through problems like 'dragon risk.' All-in-all, a balanced and exceptionally thoughtful study of the endowment model that is sorely needed. Heartily recommended."
—Clifford Asness, Chairman, AQR Investments

"A valuable new approach that probes more deeply into the various forms of diversification."
—Frank J. Fabozzi, Professor in the Practice of Finance Yale School of Management and Editor, *Journal of Portfolio Management*

"The Endowment Model is a major advance in the science of investing for endowments. It provides a formal way to incorporate such difficult-to-handle concepts as investment 'alphas' into a risk/return framework... I think the book is great."
—David Booth, Chief Executive Officer, Dimensional Fund Advisors

"The authors have suggested a framework that is quite intuitive and relatively simple. Many institutional funds may find this framework insightful for asset allocation and risk management purposes."
—Roger Clarke, Chairman of Analytic Investors, Inc.

"Leibowitz, Bova and Hammond have collaborated in creating a compendium of insightful and actionable principles for the endowment space... (and) a significant proportion of institutional portfolios. This is an important contribution for developing a framework for success for many institutional portfolios."
—H. Gifford Fong, President, Gifford Fong Associates

"The endowment model is a tenet of institutional investing that the recent credit crisis calls into question. Leibowitz, Bova and Hammond have produced a must read for assessing the future of this trusted model. Their very readable book calls for maintaining the endowment model but adjusting our time horizons when applying it."
—Edgar Sullivan, Managing Director, Promark Global Advisors (formerly General Motors Asset Management)

The Endowment
Model of
Investing

Founded in 1807, John Wiley & Sons is the oldest independent publishing company in the United States. With offices in North America, Europe, Australia, and Asia, Wiley is globally committed to developing and marketing print and electronic products and services for our customers' professional and personal knowledge and understanding.

The Wiley Finance series contains books written specifically for finance and investment professionals as well as sophisticated individual investors and their financial advisers. Book topics range from portfolio management to e-commerce, risk management, financial engineering, valuation, and financial instrument analysis, as well as much more.

For a list of available titles, visit our Web site at www.WileyFinance.com.

The Endowment Model of Investing

Return, Risk, and Diversification

MARTIN L. LEIBOWITZ
ANTHONY BOVA
P. BRETT HAMMOND

WILEY

John Wiley & Sons, Inc.

Published by John Wiley & Sons, Inc., Hoboken, New Jersey.
Published simultaneously in Canada.

For general information on our other products and services or for technical support, please contact our Customer Care Department within the United States at (800) 762-2974, outside the United States at (317) 572-3993, or fax (317) 572-4002.

Wiley also publishes its books in a variety of electronic formats. Some content that appears in print may not be available in electronic books. For more information about Wiley products, visit our web site at www.wiley.com.

Library of Congress Cataloging-in-Publication Data:

Leibowitz, Martin L., 1936–
  The endowment model of investing : return, risk, and diversification / Martin L. Leibowitz, Anthony Bova, P. Brett Hammond.
      p. cm. – (Wiley finance series)
  Includes bibliographical references and index.
  ISBN 978-0-470-48176-9 (cloth)
  1. Institutional investments.   2. Portfolio management.   I. Bova, Anthony, 1978–
II. Hammond, P. Brett.   III. Title.
  HG4521.L346   2010
  332.67′253–dc22

                                                                2009041471

Printed in the United States of America.

10 9 8 7 6 5 4 3 2 1

Contents

Preface

The purpose of this volume is to focus on the endowment allocation model, to understand the source of its value to investors, to analytically examine its theoretical underpinnings and its empirical behavior, and finally, to reassess where and when it should be used given its benefits and limitations. It does so by adopting a new approach to describing the risk-and-return characteristics of individual asset classes and then exploring how this reformulation affects their role within a total portfolio.

U.S. equity turns out to be the primary risk factor in most institutional portfolios. A total portfolio's beta is derived by combining the explicit equity percentage with the correlation-based equity sensitivity that is implicitly present in all nonequity assets. This total beta approach suggests most U.S. institutional funds share three surprising characteristics:

1. A total portfolio volatility that is more than 90 percent dominated by equity volatility
2. Fund-level beta values that almost always lie between 0.55 and 0.65
3. Total projected volatilities of 10 to 11 percent in normal equity markets

The book is divided into four parts. Part One, "Alpha/Beta Building Blocks of Portfolio Management" (Chapters 1 and 2), demonstrates that asset classes and portfolios can be decomposed into equity-beta and beyond-beta components. Because of the dominance of the equity risk factor, the typical institutional allocation does not fit the common textbook definition of portfolio diversification as a means of reducing portfolio risk.

Part Two, "Beta-Based Asset Allocation" (Chapters 3 through 14), builds on this total beta framework to develop analytical tools that provide a deeper understanding of the risk-and-return dimensions of institutional portfolios. It also addresses the limitations of optimization techniques in the face of a proliferation of novel asset classes that have only a relatively brief historical performance record. The concepts of an equity-based beta and the corresponding beyond-beta alphas shine a fresh light on the process of incorporating new asset classes into the endowment model. One novel suggestion is to reverse the standard historical process of asset allocation where traditional assets form a base to which the nonstandard assets are added incrementally. By inverting this process, at least mentally, an alpha core of nonstandard assets is first formed that specifically focuses on the appropriate constraints for the nonstandard assets. The traditional equity and fixed income components are then incorporated as supplementary swing assets to obtain the desired level of total beta risk.

Part Three, "Theoretical and Empirical Stress Betas" (Chapters 15 through 19), examines both theoretical and actual portfolio behavior in selected regimes. Of particular interest are the implications during periods of significant market declines (such as 2008–2009) when correlations "go toward 1" (they cannot literally "go to 1" without driving an asset's residual risk to zero). In such environments, beta values can rise significantly and become *stress betas*. It is during these stress times that the endowment model—or any typical highly diversified allocation—may significantly underperform traditional 60/40 allocations.

Part Four, "Asset Allocation and Return Thresholds" (Chapters 20 and 21), develops implications for the future of the endowment model. One key conclusion is that the modern endowment model should not be viewed as a technique for reducing short-term volatility, but rather a strategy for accumulating incremental returns and achieving more divergent outcomes over the long term. The final chapter suggests a number of key takeaways for investors.

The endowment model should continue to be an attractive option for long term investors if they are truly long term and able to ride out bouts of significant short term volatility. At the same time, investors should be leery of accepting the endowment model's past periods of higher returns as a simplistic template for the future. Many of the more notable early successes were achieved by organizations that enjoyed special advantages in staff and analytical resources, highly committed sponsors, flexible funding needs, extensive access networks, and perhaps most important—early entry.

The dynamic nature of the financial markets means that they are always evolving. And just as nature abhors a vacuum, so financial markets abhor any easily followed source of excess return.

With all these caveats in mind, diversification still remains one of the most powerful risk-reducing and return-enhancing tools in the investor's arsenal. Beta-based analysis provides a simple and pragmatic approach for avoiding some common allocation problems and enabling diversification strategies to reap their full potential benefits.

Acknowledgments

This beta-based approach to asset allocation would not have been possible without the early work of Harry Markowitz and William Sharpe. These pioneers developed the fundamental principles of diversification and identified the central role of systematic beta measures that form the foundation for our studies.

We would also like to express our gratitude to the many clients who address allocation problems on a daily basis and who have been so generous in sharing their insights into the nature of these issues.

Finally, the authors would like to acknowledge Morgan Stanley and TIAA-CREF for their encouragement and support of this research.

Alpha/Beta Building Blocks of Portfolio Management

CHAPTER 1

The Modern Endowment Allocation Model

*O*ver the past two decades, many institutional investors, beginning with the larger ones, adopted a broadly diversified asset allocation with greatly reduced allocations of traditional U.S. equities and bonds. Endowments and foundations, in particular, adopted this allocation model.

TRULY LONG-TERM ORIENTATION

The traditional and widely used institutional asset allocation benchmark or policy portfolio commonly consisted of a majority of U.S. equities and a reciprocal proportion of U.S. bonds. Beginning in the 1990s, endowments increasingly took advantage of the nature of their liabilities to adopt a purposeful diversification directed toward long term outcomes and a much-reduced focus on the short term.

NOVEL ASSET CLASSES AND SPECIAL ACCESS

This (re)evolution was largely driven by a growing awareness of investable assets containing return premia derived from such nontraditional features as illiquidity, longer investment horizons, less-than-transparent valuation, and other factors. Leading endowments turned to nonstandard alternative assets and to managers with niche expertise, special flexibility, and unique market access. As shown in Exhibit 1.1, between 1992 and 2008, college and university endowment allocations to nonstandard assets—real estate, hedge funds, private equity, natural resources, venture capital, and other alternatives—rose from 3 percent to more than 25 percent, with a

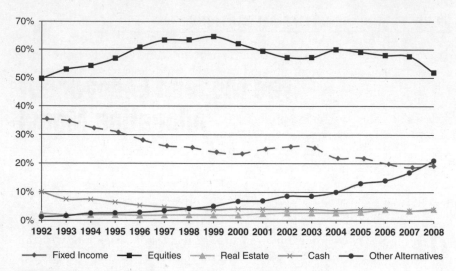

EXHIBIT 1.1   College and University Endowment Asset Allocation
(equally weighted)
Source: 1992–2008 NACUBO/TIAA-CREF Endowment Surveys

commensurate decrease in allocations to fixed income, cash, and public U.S. equity (National Endowment Surveys, hereafter NES).[1]

Dramatically, by the end of this period, the largest endowments and foundations—those over $1 billion in assets—had increased their commitment to nonstandard assets, on average, to 50 percent of the total portfolio.

REMAKING THE INVESTMENT MANAGER RELATIONSHIP

Endowments and foundations have traditionally depended on a successful selection of internal and external investment managers. The growing commitment to alternative assets as opposed to traditional assets has required a reworking of many of these processes, including far more intensive manager screening, vetting, and monitoring; significantly increased sensitivity to alignment of interests between the institution and its managers; and the need to incubate and nurture special investment talent (internally as well as externally). Specific mechanisms include direct support for investment startups and spinoffs, selected acceptance of lockups and performance fees, clawbacks, and a regular intensive analysis of manager performance and risk.

MORE MARKET-SENSITIVE ALLOCATIONS

The tradition of the long term policy portfolio with relatively fixed asset categories was at one point ubiquitous in the endowment and foundation world. The strategic policy portfolios and accompanying asset class buckets were intended to act as benchmarks against which actual allocations could be gauged. This system promoted rigid allocations, regular rebalancing, and adherence to the underlying asset buckets. However, increased market volatility and the appearance of attractive new asset classes called into question this tradition of overly rigid allocations and fixed asset buckets. Institutions were urged to work in a more flexible fashion with allocations (for example, establish wider allocation bands and more frequent policy portfolio reviews) and to use assets that did not necessarily fit into the traditional categories (Bernstein 2003; Leibowitz and Hammond 2004). The late Peter L. Bernstein was one of the earliest and most articulate authors arguing for a rethinking of the policy portfolio concept. Such an approach would, it was hoped, enable the endowment to deal with increased investment uncertainty as well as take advantage of new opportunities.

Beginning in the 1990s, this modern approach to endowment management paid off handsomely, providing returns that far surpassed traditional equity-and-bond portfolios. As shown in Exhibit 1.2, the largest endowment portfolios averaged an equally weighted return of 12.1 percent for the 19 years ending in June 2008, in contrast to 9 percent average annual return for a portfolio of 60 percent equities and 40 percent bonds (S&P 500 and Lehman Aggregate indexes, respectively). Over this period, the larger endowments' 12.1 percent return also far exceeded the 8.2 percent earned by the less diversified smaller endowments. These realized returns for the larger endowments were also far greater than the theoretical returns projected from the standard expected risk-and-return (covariance) models.

This success of the modern allocation model did not go unnoticed. The value of this approach was underscored in 2000, and then revised in 2009 by the publication of David Swenson's groundbreaking treatise, *Pioneering Portfolio Management*. Many endowments, foundations, and pension funds began to look for ways to emulate these allocations.

The apparent attractions of the modern endowment allocation model for institutions and individuals include the well-known benefits of diversification (for example, low correlations with traditional stocks and bonds), risk control (closer to bond-like volatility), and return enhancement (aiming for stock-like returns). For many, these attractions seemed obvious, especially during a period with some of the lowest interest rates on record and diminished expectations for the standard equity risk premia. As a

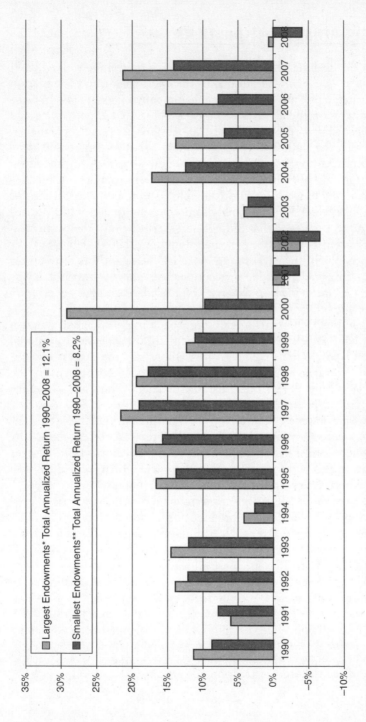

EXHIBIT 1.2 College and University Endowments' Annual Investment Returns

Source: 1990–2008 NACUBO/TIAA-CREF Endowment Surveys

*1990–1997 Size > $400 million; 1998–2008 Size > $1 billion
**1990–1997 Size < $25 million; 1998–1999 Size < $25 million; 2000–2001 Size < $75 million; 2002–2008 Size < $25 million

result, a fundamental shift seemed to be under way in what it meant to be well diversified. The new definition closely matched the modern allocation model, which offered upside return and a possibility for downside protection.

However, as dramatically illustrated by the 2008–2009 investment market meltdown, when equities underperformed, some of the diversification benefits of the modern allocation model seemed to evaporate. For the fiscal year ending in June 2009, many of the endowment returns fell as much as 30 percent, compared to –14 percent for a traditional 60/40 portfolio. These losses were far larger than anticipated, especially for fully diversified portfolios that included a significant percentage of assets that were suppose to provide an absolute return.

With the most recent results in mind, is the modern allocation model just an illusion in which anticipated returns can be undermined by additional risk compared to the more traditional model? Or, are the model's benefits a function of the larger institutions' ability to get in early, but ultimately prove transitory as the investment herd subsequently crowds in, thus driving down returns? Or, did the endowment model experience a stress period unlikely to be repeated when markets return to normal?

This book focuses on the modern allocation model, first to understand the source of its value to investors, then to analytically examine its theoretical and actual behavior, and finally to reassess where and when it should be used given its benefits and limitations. It does so by adopting a new approach to evaluating the risk-and-return characteristics of standard and nonstandard asset classes and their use in portfolios. This analysis is based on the observation that, despite the inclusion in institutional portfolios of a variety of asset classes well outside the traditional stock-bond orbit, *U.S. equities continue to act as the overwhelmingly dominant risk factor for most institutional portfolios.*

Our analysis indicates that the modern allocation model does not fit the textbook definition of portfolio diversification, whereby additional asset classes are used to bring the portfolio closer to the efficient frontier by reducing risk or increasing expected return. Instead, because of the dominance of U.S. equities as a risk factor, the risk of additional asset classes and portfolios containing them can be described using a *beta with respect to equities*. Similarly, asset class and portfolio returns can be decomposed into a component associated with the underlying equity exposure and a *beyond-beta alpha* that is more uniquely associated with the asset class itself.

Building on this insight, the book develops analytical tools for evaluating institutional portfolios and applies those tools to develop a deeper understanding of the risk-and-return dimensions of these portfolios.

ASSET ALLOCATION

The modern allocation model follows in the general tradition of portfolio theory first developed in the 1950s (particularly, but certainly not restricted to Markowitz 1952, 1991; Sharpe 1963, 1964; Ross 1976), but it poses certain challenges as well. The Capital Asset Pricing Model or CAPM (Sharpe 1964) initially focused primarily on individual securities and implications for portfolio formation. If the expected return of a single security is given by $E(R_i)$, the return of the market by $E(R_e)$, and the risk-free rate by r_f, then

$$E(R_i) = r_f + \beta_i[E(R_e) - r_f]$$

In this formulation, the CAPM says that, in equilibrium, idiosyncratic risk will be diversified away, leaving only the systematic effect of the market tempered by how much the individual security responds to market movements (that is, its beta, β_i, or the covariance of the individual security return and the market return divided by the market return variance.[2]

Since the relationship between the market return and the individual security return is linear, it is not surprising that subsequent practical and academic developments pointed out that the CAPM could be scaled up to the portfolio level and hence to asset selection and allocation (Brinson et al., 1991) with the following form:

$$E(R_p) = r_f + [E(R_e) - r_f]\sum_{i=1}^{n} \omega_i \beta_i$$

in which R_p is the portfolio return and ω_i and β_i are, respectively, the portfolio weight and market-related beta of the ith asset class.[3] Now portfolio formulation is done at the level of asset classes rather than individual securities, leaving security selection to a subsequent step. There is a large literature of helpful and appropriate approaches to portfolio construction in response to asset-class allocation, for example (Ross and Roll 1984; Campbell and Viceira 2002).

There are a couple of well-known implications of this simple characterization of asset allocation. First, it is the foundation of mean-variance optimization, which is the search for the set of portfolios—the efficient frontier—in which each portfolio maximizes return for a specified level of risk.

Second, asset allocation requires that asset classes under consideration are well defined, behave in predictable ways, and are widely available.

Inputs—expected future asset returns, volatilities, and covariances—must be specified in advance in order to do a formal static or dynamic mean-variance optimization.

The input estimation challenge is ubiquitous and ever-present, but its problems are magnified when using newer, nonstandard asset classes. Unlike traditional asset classes with century-long (or more) return histories (Ibbotson 2004; Dimson et al., 2002), most nonstandard asset classes do not enjoy a lengthy history of well-documented returns. The Goldman Sachs Commodities Index was created in 1991, but subsequently estimated back to 1970. The historical performance data on hedge funds, which now number over 8,000 in a wide variety of strategies, suffers from survivor bias, self-reporting, portfolio illiquidity, return backfilling, and secular versus cyclical trends in returns (Lo 2005; Schneeweis and Pescatore 1999; Rhodes-Kropf et al., 2004). Similar issues are said to affect published venture capital (Jones and Rhodes-Kropf 2002) and private equity returns (and in these latter cases, long holding periods and the use of IRR-based returns can result in return smoothing). Real estate performance suffers from all these problems and is notoriously unreliable as a guide to the future.

Modern allocation modeling can also be challenged by other characteristics of nonstandard assets, including asymmetric and fat-tail distributions, returns that are relatively more dependent on manager skill, illiquidity effects, and evolving return distributions. (In a subsequent chapter, we call these and other challenges that are exogenous to the model itself examples of *dragon risk*.)

The question for our purpose is not whether a given nonstandard asset is attractive or unattractive. Rather, the issue is how to value its relative attractiveness in a specific portfolio context in light of the special risks involved.

Furthermore, the increase in the number of asset classes considered in any portfolio formulation exercise can affect the confidence we have in the results. With only a few asset classes, especially when there is considerable confidence about expected returns, portfolio optimization modeling is fairly straightforward and stable. A change in the inputs that describe an asset will have a fairly predictable effect on the proportion of the portfolio assigned to that asset, so stress-testing an allocation model in those circumstances can proceed in a straightforward manner. On the other hand, as the number of asset classes proliferates, results become unstable and harder to anticipate. The inclusion or exclusion of a single asset class or change in that asset's inputs could have unpredictable or nonintuitive effects on the allocation assignments, not just for one asset class but for many.

For example, consider the following set of asset classes in Exhibit 1.3. Some, such as U.S. equities, U.S. bonds, and cash, are the standard assets

EXHIBIT 1.3 Asset Class Expected Real Return and Volatility

	Return	Volatility (Sigma)	Correlation with U.S. Equity
U.S. Equity	7.25	16.50	1
International Equity	7.25	19.50	0.65
Emerging Mkt Equity	9.25	28.00	0.45
Absolute Return	5.25	9.25	0.5
Equity Hedge Funds	5.75	12.75	0.85
Venture Capital	12.25	27.75	0.35
Private Equity	10.25	23.00	0.7
REITS	6.50	14.50	0.55
Real Estate	5.50	12.00	0.1
Commodities	5.25	19.00	−0.25
U.S. Bonds Govt	3.50	7.00	0.35
U.S. Bonds All	3.75	7.50	0.3
U.S. Bonds TIPS	3.25	6.50	0.35
Cash	1.50	2.00	0.35

Source: Morgan Stanley Research

used in what is often called *traditional asset allocation,* while others, such as hedge funds, private equity, and real estate, are considered to be nonstandard assets that are added in modern asset allocation.

These inputs—expected returns, sigmas, and an accompanying covariance matrix for the full set of standard and nonstandard assets—are supplied by a consulting firm that is deeply involved in institutional asset allocation.

Using these inputs, Exhibit 1.4 illustrates the challenges associated with modern asset allocation using nonstandard classes. The simplest allocation, Portfolio A, uses an allocation of just two standard assets, U.S. equities and cash. This point lies on the efficient frontier with an expected volatility (sigma) of 9.90 percent and an expected overall return of 4.95 percent. The Sharpe ratio for this portfolio is 0.35.

Portfolio B is similar to Portfolio A, except that U.S. bonds are substituted for the cash allocation. The resulting 60/40 mix is often referred to as the *traditional allocation.* Again, the results are plausible and unsurprising: the expected return rises to 5.85 percent, with an expected volatility (sigma) of 11.17 percent and a slightly improved Sharpe ratio of 0.39.

When we turn to the portfolio B′, things begin to change. For this portfolio, we allow the optimizer to include venture capital along with equities, bonds, and cash. At a preselected expected risk level chosen to

EXHIBIT 1.4 Portfolio Risk-and-Return Characteristics

	A	B	B′	C	C′	C″
U.S. Equity	60	60	19	20	0	0
International Equity	▲	▲	▲	15	0	0
Emerging Mkt Equity	▲	▲	▲	5	10	16
Absolute Return	▲	▲	▲	10	0	0
Equity Hedge Funds	▲	▲	▲	▲	0	0
Venture Capital	▲	▲	35	10	22	▲
Private Equity	▲	▲	▲	10	8	31
REITS	▲	▲	▲	▲	30	20
Real Estate	▲	▲	▲	10	22	21
Commodities	▲	▲	▲	▲	8	12
U.S. Bonds All	▲	40	46	20	0	0
Cash	40	▲	▲	▲	0	0
Expected Return	4.95	5.85	7.37	7.08	8.07	7.73
Standard Deviation	9.90	11.17	11.17	10.83	10.83	10.83
Sharpe Ratio	0.35	0.39	0.53	0.52	0.61	0.58

Source: Morgan Stanley Research

match the sigma of portfolio B, the resulting unconstrained allocation seems nonsensical, to say the least. Portfolio B′ allocates a whopping 35 percent to the nonstandard asset. This result is clearly unacceptable in the real world, even though the expected return and Sharpe ratio represent significant improvements over the first two portfolios.

With the trend toward using a broader array of asset classes in an attempt to diversify risk, a number of institutions have embraced the more modern type of allocation represented by Portfolio C. In Portfolio C, the direct exposure to U.S. equities is reduced to only 20 percent. There is a significant 15 percent exposure to international equities, as well as a 5 percent exposure to emerging markets. Absolute return, reflecting certain categories of hedge funds, amounts to 10 percent. This 10 percent weighting is also applied to venture capital, private equity, and real estate. As with equities, bonds have been reduced to 20 percent, far lower than in traditional portfolios. Given the assumptions contained in the covariance matrix, Portfolio C turns out to have a volatility of 10.83 percent and an expected return of about 7.08 percent, surprisingly close to the 11.17 percent volatility of the traditional Portfolio B. Portfolio C appears more diversified in regard to asset classes and sources of return—but in fact, is not really much different from the traditional Portfolio B in regard to this form of risk.

For the fifth portfolio, Portfolio C′, we throw out all the constraints and throw in the kitchen sink, that is, all of the available asset classes. We then pick the point on the efficient frontier where the sigma matches the volatility level of Portfolio C. Note that this unconstrained optimization produces an allocation with *all* nonstandard assets and *no* standard assets. Most of the portfolio statistics are highly attractive—compared to Portfolio C, expected return rises by more than a percentage point and the Sharpe ratio improves by nearly 0.10. However, the elimination of standard assets from the mix is counterintuitive, to say the least.

Finally, Portfolio C″ is similar to Portfolio C′, except that it removes venture capital from the mix. Once again, the unconstrained optimizer assigns no weight to standard assets. Even more, changes to the asset weights relative to Portfolio C′ are difficult to understand without deeper analysis. In sum, neither B′, C′, nor C″ would make sense in most institutional settings, nor would they be easy to explain to an investment committee.

As we will see in subsequent chapters, one way to deal with the challenges of asset-class inputs, portfolio stability, and other issues is to torture the modeling process by imposing piecemeal constraints, adjusting inputs, and other fixes that make the resulting portfolios more palatable. It would be far more satisfying and understandable to find a simple, transparent approach to the problem, one that reveals the critical risk and return characteristics of the underlying assets as well as the portfolio itself. For many institutional portfolios, the total beta approach can provide greater clarity as well as a more intuitive perspective on the most important determinants of total portfolio risk.

BETA-BASED RISK AND RETURN: THE SIGMA AND BETA LINES

Returning to the standard CAPM model, the third and most important implication is that the portfolio return depends on the sum of the various asset class betas scaled by the asset class weights.

What follows from this notion is that the beta sensitivity to equities is the parameter that captures about 90 percent or more of the volatility risk for most allocations seen in the U.S. institutional market. This single parameter is a value that lurks hidden within virtually every asset class, and that, in aggregate, accumulates to become the portfolio's overall exposure to the equity market. Once these underlying beta values are uncovered, it becomes clear that while the traditional 60/40 appears quite different from the highly diversified endowment model, they in fact share certain common risk characteristics. This analysis suggests that portfolio betas can

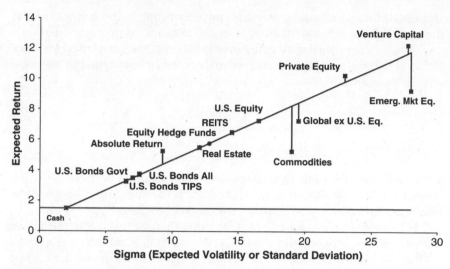

EXHIBIT 1.5 Expected Returns and the Cash-Equity Sigma Line
Data Source: Cambridge Associates Data

be used, within limits, to determine the likelihood of adverse events that fundamentally set the risk limits for a wide range of the asset allocations seen in practice.

A simple way to understand these conclusions is to start with the more familiar volatility measure and then see how introducing beta can add to our understanding. Exhibit 1.5 uses the asset class inputs from Exhibit 1.4 to display each asset's expected return relative to a sigma line that intersects the cash and U.S. equity returns.

The majority of asset risk-and-return dots lie near or on the line, indicating that their return assumptions appear to be in direct linear proportion to their relative expected volatility.[4]

At the heart of this book lies the proposition that by looking at asset class and portfolio risk in a different way—through the beta lens—we can simplify the analysis of portfolio risk and find hidden meaning that will improve our understanding of complex asset class and portfolio behavior and help us build better tools for asset allocation and portfolio construction. It can also help us better measure the sources of volatility, how risk relates to return, and the decomposition of asset class and portfolio return in their fundamental building blocks.

To begin this journey, we can review the beta risk measure and compare it to the total volatility measure. In the most basic terms, beta indicates how much we would expect a particular asset to move in response to a 1 percent change in the overall equity market. One way to think about it is that it is the coefficient of the regression of asset class returns on the equity market.[5]

An equivalent way to describe beta is that it is the correlation between the asset (or portfolio) return and the market return, multiplied by the ratio of their volatilities,

$$\beta_p = \frac{Cov\ p,e}{\sigma_e^2} = \rho_{pe} \frac{\sigma_p}{\sigma_e}$$

where p is still the individual asset class or investment portfolio, e is the market portfolio (or an equivalent), and ρ_{pe} is the correlation between the asset class/investment portfolio and the market portfolio.[6]

In this formulation, we can see that, other things being equal, the higher the correlation between the asset class (or portfolio) returns and market returns, the higher the beta. But in thinking about beta, we should not neglect the other terms. Like the correlation, the relationship between portfolio or asset class volatility and beta is linear and positive. Not so with *market* volatility, however, which has a powerful inverse and nonlinear effect on beta. As market volatility rises, beta will fall, all other things being equal (which itself would probably be a rare event!).[7]

So what does this mean in practical terms? First, in our terms, each asset class beta is a measure of that asset's risk with respect to domestic equities. Second, a widely cited advantage of nonstandard assets is their supposedly low correlations and betas with respect to traditional equities. Whether or not this is true in all cases, we can see that a low beta can result from three nonexclusive conditions: (1) low correlation between an asset class and the market; (2) low asset class volatility; or (3) high equity market volatility, or any combination of 1, 2, or 3. So, we are reminded that asset class beta and correlation are not the same thing, and the respective volatilities also play a major role. Thus, an asset class may have a low correlation with U.S. equity, but still have a relatively significant beta sensitivity.

The beta measure is useful for a number of reasons. First, it incorporates both the correlation and volatility effects described earlier. Unlike sigma, betas can be related to a common risk factor such as the S&P 500 and therefore become comparable, scalable, and additive. Moreover, within the portfolio context, it is the total beta that is typically the overwhelmingly dominant source of risk. As long as the residuals are not themselves highly correlated, the total portfolio beta is simply a weighted sum of the individual asset class or security betas. Thus, an asset's beta provides a far more accurate measure of its contribution to the overall portfolio risk than the asset's volatility alone.

EXHIBIT 1.6 Structural Betas and Alphas

	Return	Sigma	Beta	Alpha
U.S. Equity	7.25	16.50	1.00	0.00
International Equity	7.25	19.50	0.77	1.39
Emerging Mkt Equity	9.25	28.00	0.76	3.42
Absolute Return	5.25	9.25	0.28	2.32
Equity Hedge Funds	5.75	12.75	0.66	0.56
Venture Capital	12.25	27.75	0.59	7.47
Private Equity	10.25	23.00	0.98	3.15
REITS	6.50	14.50	0.48	2.35
Real Estate	5.50	12.00	0.07	3.82
Commodities	5.25	19.00	−0.29	5.73
U.S. Bonds Govt	3.50	7.00	0.15	1.36
U.S. Bonds All	3.75	7.50	0.14	1.69
U.S. Bonds TIPS	3.25	6.50	0.14	1.18
Cash	1.50	2.00	0.04	0.00

Data Source: Cambridge Associates Data

Exhibit 1.6 now uses the market assumptions in Exhibit 1.3 but displays the asset class betas and beyond-beta alpha returns.

With these derived betas and the associated returns, Exhibit 1.7 replaces Exhibit 1.5's sigma volatility with a beta risk measure on the horizontal axis and displays a *beta line* intersecting cash and U.S. equities.

In contrast to the sigma cash-equity line, most of the asset class returns now lie above the beta line. As such, expected total return consists of three components as illustrated in the exhibit by the decomposition of the expected return assumed for venture capital (12.25 percent). First, all asset classes build on the foundation represented by the risk-free rate ($r_f = 1.50$ percent), the cash-equivalent return. The second return component (3.27 percent)—the return between the risk-free return line and the beta line—is a direct linear function of an asset class's beta and could, in theory, be replicated by a combination of equities and cash.

The third component is the return in excess of the beta line (7.47 percent). This last component, which we call beta-based or *structural alpha,* is a function of the unique risk-and-return profile of the individual asset class. The three return components sum to the total return for the asset class (1.50 percent + 3.27 percent + 7.47 percent = 12.25 percent). And, as we will see in the next chapter, each component has its own associated risk.

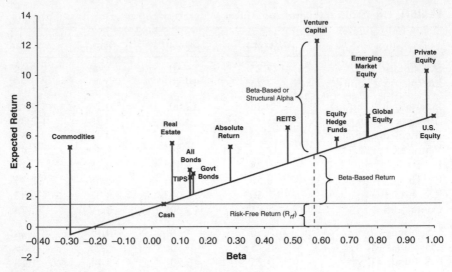

EXHIBIT 1.7   The Beta Line and Structural Alphas
Data Source: Cambridge Associates Data

The remainder of this book builds on these simple concepts of a structural beta and beta-based alpha to illuminate the endowment model and to handle the inclusion of newer forms of asset classes in institutional portfolio construction. First, we examine the nature and use of structural beta and alpha, where it becomes clear that many portfolios that appear quite different on the surface in fact share common risk characteristics. The consequence is that many portfolios containing nonstandard assets seem to be designed to pursue extra return rather than reduced risk. In contrast, we find that identifying and using structural alphas to design portfolios can enhance returns with only modest levels of additional risk at the fund level. These hidden sources of excess return can be uncovered by analyzing the fundamental risk structure of standard return assumptions.

We then turn more directly to the role of structural alpha and beta in asset allocation and portfolio construction. By reversing the usual asset allocation process in which traditional assets form the base, an *alpha core* of nonstandard assets can be used along with supplementary traditional *swing* assets to better relate a portfolio's risk to its expected return.

Drawing on our theoretical analysis of beta and alpha-based asset allocation, we then consider actual portfolio behavior in selected regimes. Of particular interest are the implications of *stress betas* during significant market declines, when betas can rise significantly and portfolios can fail, at least for a time, to provide the expected risk protection.

In a concluding chapter, we offer suggestions for the future of the endowment model in light of our theoretical and applied findings. The modern endowment model is not a magic potion that will smooth returns and lower short-term volatility, but rather a strategy for accumulating incremental returns and achieving more divergent outcomes—over the long term. One critical implication is that the endowment model should continue to be an attractive option for long term investors that are able to ride out periods of significant short term volatility. Another is that institutional leaders and individual investors should not be lulled by the prospect of incremental excess returns into thinking that these will be available during each and every investment period. A third implication is the unexpected challenge for any modern portfolio of obtaining excess returns above the risk-free rate. Finally, a deeper and more exact analysis of the sources of portfolio risk and return can assist institutions in constructing and managing assets in a way that will better reflect their investment objectives and related needs.

NOTES

1. We use college and university endowments as an example and recognize that they are a subset of the world of nonprofit institutional asset management, including independent foundations, public pensions, and, arguably, private pensions. Unless specified, all annual figures here refer to fiscal years rather than calendar years.
2. Or $\beta_i = \frac{\text{cov}(R_i, R_e)}{\sigma_e^2}$.
3. At the time, this shift in the level of analysis was a significant step (and is still being debated today (Ibbotson and Kaplan 2000; Kritzman and Page 2003).
4. Notable exceptions are commodities and emerging market equities, both of which lie below the line. These are the result of the inputs, which were supplied by an independent source.
5. In formal terms, $y_i = \alpha_i + \beta_i x_e$, where y_i is the return of an individual security or asset class, β_i is the coefficient that describes the effect of the market return, x_m, on the individual security or asset class return, and α_i is the excess return of the security or asset class over the market portfolio. For a portfolio of securities or asset classes, $y_p = \sum_{i=1}^{n} \alpha_i \omega_i + x_m \sum_{i=1}^{n} \beta_i \omega_i$, in which ω_i is the weight of the ith security or asset class in the portfolio.
6. In recent years, the term *beta* has also been used to refer to gaining exposure to individual asset classes of all types through index-like portfolios, such as how well a fixed-income fund represents the behavior of the overall bond market. Moreover, in theory, the market can be defined most broadly as the sum of all available world investment opportunities (or more narrowly as all of a country's investable securities). For this analysis, the reference market is U.S. equity.

7. In other words, a change in beta with respect to correlation is given as $\frac{d\beta_p}{d\rho_{pe}} = \frac{\sigma_p}{\sigma_e}$, while a change in beta with respect to sigma is given as $\frac{d\beta_p}{d\sigma_e} = -\frac{\rho_{pe}\sigma_p}{\sigma_e^2}$.

REFERENCES

Bernstein, P. L. 2003. "Which policy do you mean?" *Economics and portfolio strategy*. New York: Peter L. Bernstein, Inc.

Brinson, G. P., B. D. Singer, and G. L. Beebower. 1991. "Determinants of portfolio performance II: An update." *Financial Analysts Journal* 47 (3): 40–48.

Campbell, J. Y., and L. M. Viceira. 2002. *Strategic asset allocation: Portfolio choice for long-term investors*. New York: Oxford University Press.

Dimson, E., P. Marsh, and M. Staunton. 2002. *Triumph of the optimists: 101 years of global investment return*. Princeton, NJ: Princeton University Press.

Ibbotson, R. 2004. *Stocks, bonds, bills and inflation yearbook: 1983*. Chicago: Ibbotson Associates.

Ibbotson, R., and P. Kaplan. 2000. "Does asset allocation explain 40, 90 or 100 percent of performance?" *Financial Analysts Journal* 56 (1): 26–33.

Jones, C., and M. Rhodes-Kropf. 2002. *The price of diversifiable risk in venture capital and private equity*. Columbia University Working Paper.

Kritzman, M., and S. Page. 2003. "The hierarchy of investment choice." *Journal of Portfolio Management* 29 (4): 11–23.

Leibowitz, M. L., and P. B. Hammond. 2004. "The changing mosaic of investment patterns." *Journal of Portfolio Management* 30 (3): 10–25.

Lo, A. 2005. *The dynamics of the hedge fund industry*. Charlottesville, VA: Research Foundation of the CFA Institute.

Markowitz, H. M. 1952. "Portfolio selection." *Journal of Finance* 7 (1): 77–91.

———. 1991. "Foundations of portfolio theory." *Journal of Finance* 46 (2): 469–477.

National Endowment Surveys (NES). National Association of College and University Business Officers 1992–2008.

Rhodes-Kropf, M., A. Ang, and R. Zhao. 2004. *Do funds of funds deserve their extra fees?* Columbia University Working Paper.

Ross, S. A. 1976. "The arbitrage theory of capital asset pricing." *Journal of Economic Theory* 13: 341–360.

Ross, S. A., and R. Roll. 1984. "The arbitrage pricing theory approach to strategic portfolio planning." *Financial Analysts Journal*, May-June: 14–26.

Schneeweis, T., and J. F. Pescatore. 1999. *The handbook of alternative investment strategies*. New York: Institutional Investor, Inc.

Sharpe, W. F. 1963. "A simplified model for portfolio analysis." *Management Science* 9 (2): 277–293.

———. 1964. "Capital asset prices: A theory of market equilibrium under conditions of risk." *Journal of Finance* 19 (3): 425–442.

Swenson, D. F. Revised 2009. *Pioneering portfolio management: An unconventional approach to institutional investment*. New York: The Free Press.

CHAPTER 2

Structural Betas and Alphas

*T*here is one parameter that captures about 90 percent or more of the volatility risk for most allocations seen in the U.S. institutional market. This single parameter is the beta sensitivity to U.S. equities, a value that lurks hidden within virtually every asset class, and that, in aggregate, accumulates to become the portfolio's overall exposure to the equity market. Once these underlying beta values are uncovered, it becomes clear that many portfolios that appear quite different on the surface in fact share common risk characteristics. This analysis suggests that portfolio betas can be used, within limits, to determine the likelihood of adverse events that fundamentally set the risk limits for many asset allocations.

    Structural alphas can enhance returns with relatively little added risk. These hidden sources of excess return can be uncovered by analyzing the fundamental risk structure of standard return assumptions. Structural alphas do not depend on special manager selection or asset management skills, but they can create the opportunity for higher expected returns without a material increase in overall portfolio risk. Identifying structural alphas at the portfolio level is particularly helpful in untangling the returns in more modern portfolios with their high levels of diversification.

FINDING THE BETA IN THE BLACK BOX

Over the last several decades, characterizing the volatility of a portfolio mix has grown increasingly sophisticated. Starting with variance, covariance, and standard deviation, moving to value-at-risk (VAR), expected shortfall (or conditional VAR), factor exposure, and on to robust and Bayesian estimation, computer packages are available to carry out calculations that have modernized our understanding of portfolio risk. Unsurprisingly, with sophistication comes complexity. And complexity can challenge understanding. These approaches share a *black box* character that can obscure the allocation's fundamental structure.

Even if the theory is relatively clear, the practical task of relating a portfolio's return to its risk can add additional complexity and the need for heroic assumptions to achieve sensible results. Optimization studies behind asset allocations for many pension funds, endowments, foundations, and even individuals, often use a process described as a tortured optimization technique. Based on the simple, insightful mean-variance approach, first suggested by Harry Markowitz in the 1950s, it uses a covariance matrix to characterize the volatility behavior among various asset classes. This procedure generates an efficient frontier representing the highest portfolio return from various asset mixtures that can be achieved across a range of volatilities. This efficient frontier is, of course, highly dependent on both the assumptions in the covariance matrix and the constraints established for each asset class. *Torturing* refers to the common practice of sequentially manipulating the constraints to achieve portfolios that are theoretically optimal, but that also satisfy the more ephemeral criterion of being palatable.

Fortunately, there is a way to simplify the problem of risk control: by finding the hidden beta.

THE STRUCTURAL BETA

The beta concept is firmly grounded in financial market theory and practice. Traditionally, it is commonly used for risk-adjusting stock portfolios or individual stocks with respect to a broad equity market portfolio. More recently, beta has been used to refer to the index-like returns of any asset class. A manager can receive a beta return through low-cost passive exposure to an individual asset class, in contrast to the higher-cost alpha return associated with active management of that asset class. In this context, beta refers not to the market, but rather to individual asset class behavior.

The market beta concept is seldom applied to individual asset classes, especially in the context of asset allocation. This neglect is all the more curious since, as we found in Chapter 1, the underlying covariance matrix actually contains all the information needed to tease out these hidden betas, or *structural betas* as we will call them here to differentiate them from other uses of the beta concept. Moreover, as we have seen, the structural beta calculation is quite simple (beta equals the correlation between an asset class and U.S. equities multiplied by the ratio of the two asset class volatilities).

Recalling the return, risk, and covariance characteristics of the standard and nonstandard asset classes we introduced in Chapter 1, Exhibit 1.6, we can illustrate the beta calculation using the matrix values of 0.65 for the correlation between U.S. equity and international equity, and 16.50 percent and 19.50 percent for their respective volatilities. The projected beta for international equities then consists of the 0.65 correlation multiplied by the ratio of 19.50 divided by 16.50, leading to a beta of 0.77. Similarly, the expected beta for bonds is the 0.30 correlation between bonds and U.S. equities multiplied by the ratio of their volatilities (7.50 divided by 16.50), the result being a beta of 0.14. Similar calculations produce the structural betas for all of the asset classes. (Note that commodities, because of their negative correlation, actually have a negative beta of –0.3.)

Using that same reasoning, in moving from a standard sigma volatility line in Chapter 1, Exhibit 1.5 to the beta line repeated in Exhibit 2.1, *all* the asset classes now shift to positions *above* the cash-equity line. The explanation for this rather striking transformation is that beta captures only one component of total risk. Therefore, the move to beta values leads to a lower risk measure and creates a left-hand shift from the full risk embedded in the standard volatility diagram. This effect has important implications for portfolio construction and risk control that we explore in subsequent chapters.

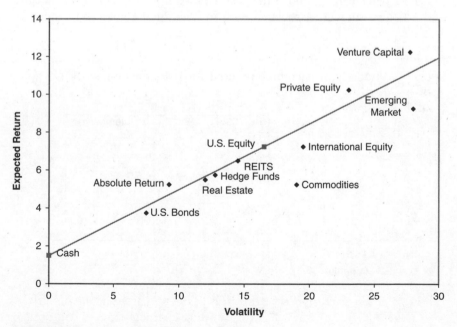

EXHIBIT 2.1 Expected Returns versus Beta
Source: Morgan Stanley Research

RETURN COMPONENTS OF ASSET CLASSES

In Exhibit 2.2, to show the portion of the total volatility (σ_i) derived from international equity's beta—its beta-based volatility (or $\beta_i\sigma_e$)—we shift the risk point for international equity to 12.68 percent, a figure computed by multiplying international's β of 0.77 by the 16.50 percent volatility of U.S. equity.

Turning from our structural beta and beta-based volatility measures to a consideration of expected return, we can separate international equity's expected return by decomposing into the following components:

- The first is the risk-free rate (r_f) of 1.50 percent.
- The second is the β-based expected return (βr_p) from a combination of U.S. equities and cash formed into a portfolio having a beta of 0.77 and the associated β-based volatility of 12.68 percent. Exhibit 2.2 shows this β-based expected return as 4.42 percent, which is the product of international's $\beta = 0.77$ and the 5.75 percent risk premium (r_p) assumed for U.S. equity.
- The third is the hidden structural alpha (α), the remaining return of 1.33 percent lying above the cash-U.S. equity line. This 1.33 percent, which is uniquely associated with international equity and cannot be

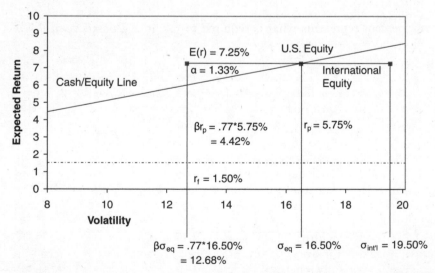

EXHIBIT 2.2   Expected Return from International Equity
Source: Morgan Stanley Research

replicated by a combination of U.S. equities and cash, is derived from sources other than U.S. equity risk. It captures the primary diversifying benefit of an asset class such as international equity, with its less-than-perfect correlation with U.S. equities.

In this analysis, alpha is structural, in that it refers neither to managerial skill (for example, excess return), the equity risk premium, nor a more general return over the risk-free rate. Instead, it is the return above the cash-equity line. Since both U.S. and international equity have exactly the same expected return of 7.25 percent, they have the same excess return of 5.75 percent relative to cash. However, since our separation is based on the cash-equity line, we obtain a zero structural alpha for U.S. equities versus 1.33 percent for international equities. (A return, if any, associated with active management of international equities would be in addition to the structural alpha.)

RISK COMPONENTS OF ASSET CLASSES

Of course, the incremental structural alpha of 1.33 percent is not without its own sources of volatility, in which total risk, like expected return, is a function of three components: the risk-free rate (in which volatility, by definition, is zero), β-based risk, and α-based risk. The structural alpha risk of 14.82 percent represents what is required to take the β-based volatility of 12.68 percent to the 19.50 percent total volatility for international equity (that is, $[14.82]^2 + [12.68]^2 = [19.50]^2$).[1] Structural alpha risk, which has zero correlation with U.S. equity, reflects other risk factors, such as currencies, interest rates, liquidity concerns, and so forth. In certain contexts, these other risk factors must be explicitly taken into account, for example, in an asset and liability framework. We demonstrated in the preceding chapter, however, that the risks of most institutional portfolios are dominated by their beta-based exposure to U.S. equity. This risk dominance dwarfs the incremental risk associated with structural alphas. Hence, structural alpha represent a significant source of return with a potentially diversifiable risk, especially when U.S. equity comprises the overriding factor in a portfolio's overall risk.

For example, with typical policy portfolios, the beta relative to U.S. equities accounts for over 90 percent of the total volatility. The remaining 10 percent of volatility is derived from the embedded alphas. For such portfolios, the return benefits from these alphas at the portfolio level can clearly be more valuable than the modest 10 percent cost in incremental α-based risk.

EXHIBIT 2.3 Return Breakdown by Asset Class

Asset Class	Total Expected Return $E(r_i)$	β Relative to U.S. Equity β	Expected r_f	Return βr_p	Component α
Venture Capital	12.25	0.59	1.50	3.38	7.37
Commodities	5.25	−0.29	1.50	−1.66	5.41
Real Estate	5.50	0.07	1.50	0.42	3.58
Emerging Mkt Equity	9.25	0.76	1.50	4.39	3.36
Private Equity	10.25	0.98	1.50	5.61	3.14
REITS	6.50	0.48	1.50	2.78	2.22
Absolute Return	5.25	0.28	1.50	1.61	2.14
U.S. Bonds	3.75	0.14	1.50	0.78	1.47
International Equity	7.25	0.77	1.50	4.42	1.33
Equity Hedge Funds	5.75	0.66	1.50	3.78	0.47
U.S. Equity	7.25	1.00	1.50	5.75	0.00
Cash	1.50	0.00	1.50	0.00	0.00

Source: Morgan Stanley Research

Of course, these alphas are an intrinsic component of the total expected return from the asset class, and as such would be incorporated in any standard optimization procedure. By carving out these alphas, we can gain greater insight into how these sources of incremental return interact with a portfolio's overall risk profile. With more clarity on these fundamental risk-and-return tradeoffs, the portfolio manager may see options for return enhancement that might otherwise be obscured in a black box optimization.

In Exhibit 2.3, we separate the returns of the 12 asset classes, listed in order of decreasing alpha. As discussed earlier, the total return for international equities of 7.25 percent decomposes into a risk-free return of 1.50 percent that applies to all asset classes, a beta-based return of 4.42 percent, and a 1.33 percent alpha. With a beta value of 1.00, U.S. equity's return has a 1.50 percent risk-free component and a beta-based return of 5.75 percent. From our method of defining alpha, the U.S. equity alpha will always be zero. The other alphas range from over 7 percent for venture capital down to zero for cash.

Exhibit 2.4 shows the α-returns and α-risks associated with each of the asset classes involved in our illustrative allocation. Exhibit 2.5 is a plot of these asset classes in a α-return/α-risk diagram. Note that both cash and

EXHIBIT 2.4 Asset Level α-Risks and α-Returns

Asset Class	α	β	Exact σ	$\beta\sigma$	σ_α
Venture Capital	7.37	0.59	27.75	9.71	25.99
Commodities	5.41	−0.29	19.00	−4.75	18.40
Real Estate	3.58	0.07	12.00	1.20	11.94
Emerging Mkt Equity	3.36	0.76	28.00	12.60	25.00
Private Equity	3.14	0.98	23.00	16.10	16.43
REITS	2.22	0.48	14.50	7.98	12.11
Absolute Return	2.14	0.28	9.25	4.63	8.01
U.S. Bonds	1.47	0.14	7.50	2.25	7.15
International Equity	**1.33**	**0.77**	**19.50**	**12.68**	**14.82**
Equity Hedge Funds	0.47	0.66	12.75	10.84	6.72
U.S. Equity	0.00	1.00	16.50	16.50	0.00
Cash	0.00	0.00	0.00	0.00	0.00

Source: Morgan Stanley Research

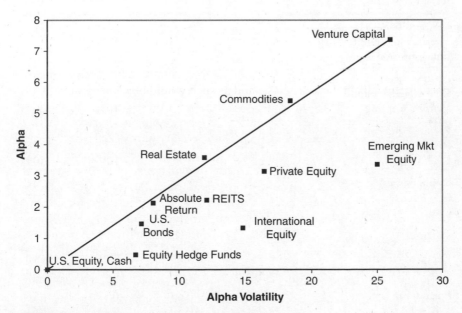

EXHIBIT 2.5 Asset Classes in α Risk-and-Return Space
Source: Morgan Stanley Research

U.S. equities have zero α-return and α-risk. For many of the other asset classes, the α-return and the α-risks can loom quite large. It is curious, but perhaps coincidental, that four asset classes—venture capital, commodities, real estate, and absolute return—fall on a straight line, implying that they all have the same very high α-risk-and-α-return ratio.

PORTFOLIO BETA VALUES

The asset class betas can now be weighted and added together to determine the overall structural beta for any given mixture of asset classes, that is, for any given asset allocation. Exhibit 2.6 displays four allocations covering a wide range of complexity, the first three of which are the same portfolios introduced in the preceding chapter. Recalling the simplest allocation,

EXHIBIT 2.6 Model Portfolios

Asset Class	A	B	C	D
U.S. Equity	60%	60%	20%	
International Equity			15%	
Emerging Mkt Equity			5%	
Absolute Return			10%	20%
Equity Hedge Funds				
Venture Capital			10%	20%
Private Equity			10%	
REITS				
Real Estate			10%	20%
Commodities				20%
U.S. Bonds		40%	20%	20%
Cash	40%			
Total	100%	100%	100%	
Expected Return	4.95	5.85	7.08	6.40
Exact σ	9.90	11.17	10.83	8.04
Portfolio β	0.60	0.65	0.57	0.16
β-Based σ	9.90	10.80	9.45	2.61
β-Based σ/Exact σ Ratio	100.0%	96.7%	87.2%	32.4%

Source: Morgan Stanley Research

Portfolio A, it consists of just 60 percent U.S. equity and 40 percent cash, and its structural beta is a combination of 60 percent of $\beta = 1$ for U.S. equities and 40 percent of $\beta = 0$ for cash, netting to $\beta_A = 0.6$ for the overall portfolio. On this basis, Portfolio A has a projected volatility ($\beta_A \sigma_e$) of 9.90 percent, due solely to its 60 percent equity exposure multiplied by the equity volatility of 16.50 percent. In this trivial case, the β-based volatility estimate corresponds precisely to the far more complex calculation of the *exact* volatility (or σ_A) derived from a computer computation incorporating the entire covariance matrix.

A more interesting situation is presented by the traditional asset allocation in Portfolio B, which is the same as Portfolio A in having 60 percent equities, but now has 40 percent bonds replacing A's 40 percent cash. As noted earlier, bonds have a $\beta = 0.14$. When 40 percent of this $\beta = 0.14$ is added to the beta contribution of 0.6 from the direct equity exposure, we obtain an overall $\beta_B = 0.65$ for this portfolio, slightly greater than that of Portfolio A. The exact volatility of Portfolio B (σ_B) derived from the covariance matrix is 11.17 percent. The simple product of the beta of 0.65 and the equity volatility of 16.50 percent gives a β-based volatility approximation (or $\beta_B \sigma_e$) of 10.80 percent, accounting for 97 percent of the exact volatility figure.

MODERN ALLOCATIONS WITH ALTERNATIVES

With the trend toward using a broader array of asset classes in an attempt to diversify risk, a number of institutions have embraced the more modern type of allocation represented by Portfolio C. As we saw in the preceding chapter, in Portfolio C, the direct exposure to U.S. equities is 20 percent, with a 15 percent exposure to international equities and a 5 percent exposure to emerging markets. Absolute return, venture capital, private equity, and real estate each receive a 10 percent weighting and bonds are reduced to 20 percent. Given the assumptions contained in the covariance matrix, Portfolio C turns out to have an exact volatility (σ_C) of 10.83 percent, surprisingly close to the 11.17 percent exact volatility of the traditional Portfolio B. Portfolio C appears more diversified in terms of asset classes and sources of return—but in fact, is not really much different from the traditional Portfolio B in terms of volatility.

Most allocations seen in practice fall somewhere within the bounds set by the simplicity of the traditional Portfolio B and the broad diversity of the modern Portfolio C. Consequently, one typically sees exact volatilities that cluster around the 10- to 11-percent level, a somewhat curious result given the wide variety of financial situations and purposes served by institutional portfolios.

Turning to the beta-based calculation, we again note that Portfolio C has a greatly reduced exposure to U.S. equities of only 20 percent. Each asset class comprising the remaining 80 percent weight, however, has some correlation with U.S. equities, thereby creating an *implicit* equity exposure that is reflected in their respective β_i values. Using the individual asset class betas together with the weights comprising Portfolio C, we obtain the portfolio beta (β_C) of 0.57 shown in Exhibit 2.6. Again, Portfolio C's β_C, even with its much broader diversification of asset classes, remains surprisingly close to the traditional Portfolio B's $\beta_B = 0.65$. The closeness of these two beta values again demonstrates that, in spite of its diversification across a wider range of asset classes, Portfolio C remains quite similar to the traditional Portfolio B in its basic risk characteristics.

As an approximation to the overall volatility, Portfolio C's β-based volatility ($\beta_C\sigma_e$) is 0.57×16.50 percent $= 9.45$ percent. This β-based estimate is not quite as good an approximation as with Portfolio B, but it still captures 87 percent of the exact volatility. Given that the covariance matrix itself is at best an approximation for describing the projected behavior of these markets, the β-based measure seems like an attractive summary measure.

THE EXTREME ALLOCATION

It is also possible to present extreme portfolio allocations in which virtually none of the earlier results holds. Portfolio D represents an extreme portfolio with characteristics that differ greatly from the preceding three. It has no direct exposure to U.S. equities, international equities, emerging market equities, or private equities. Only five asset classes are included, with a 20 percent weight for each. Note that its exact volatility (σ_D) of 8.04 percent is significantly lower than the 10- to 11-percent volatilities of Portfolios A–C. It also has a very low projected $\beta_D = 0.16$, and its beta-based volatility ($\beta_D\sigma_e$) estimate of 2.61 percent accounts for only 32 percent of the exact volatility of 8.04 percent. Clearly, most of the comments regarding the first three portfolios do not apply to Portfolio D. Moreover, Portfolio D is not one likely to be encountered in practice.

RETURN COMPONENTS AT THE PORTFOLIO LEVEL

We now show how these return components can be projected from the asset class level to the four sample portfolios. Portfolio A, chosen for simplicity, consists solely of 60 percent U.S. equity and 40 percent cash. Exhibit 2.7

EXHIBIT 2.7 Return Components: Portfolio A

| Asset Class | Weight | β Contribution | Return Contribution | | | Total |
			r_f	β	α	
U.S. Equity	60%	0.60	0.90	3.45	0.00	4.35
Cash	40%	0.00	0.60	0.00	0.00	0.60
Total	100%	0.60	1.50	3.45	0.00	4.95

Source: Morgan Stanley Research

shows the equity return contribution of 0.60×1.50 percent $= 0.90$ percent from the 1.50 percent risk-free rate and a beta-based contribution of 0.60×5.75 percent $= 3.45$ percent.

The 40 percent cash adds only a risk-free-based return of 0.60 percent, or 0.4×1.50 percent. Thus, Portfolio A's total return can be separated into a risk-free component of 1.50 percent, a beta-based return of 3.45 percent, and in this particular case, no alpha from the two asset classes.

Portfolio B reflects a traditional asset allocation with 40 percent in U.S. bonds. Exhibit 2.8 shows that the $\beta = 0.14$ for bonds leads to a β-based return of 0.14×5.75 percent $= 0.78$ percent, and the 40 percent weight in bonds leads to a portfolio contribution of 0.40×0.78 percent $= 0.31$ percent.

Drawing on Exhibit 2.3, we know that bonds have a 1.47 percent alpha, resulting in an alpha-based contribution of 0.4×1.47 percent $= 0.59$ percent. In aggregate, triaging Portfolio B's traditional 60/40 equity/bond ratio yields a beta of 0.65, a beta-based return of 3.76 percent, an alpha of 0.59 percent, and, of course, a risk-free return of 1.50 percent, for a total expected return of 5.85 percent.

EXHIBIT 2.8 Return Components: Portfolio B

| Asset Class | Weight | β Contribution | Return Contribution | | | Total |
			r_f	β	α	
U.S. Bonds	40%	0.05	0.60	0.31	0.59	1.50
U.S. Equity	60%	0.60	0.90	3.45	0.00	4.35
Total	100%	0.65	1.50	3.76	0.59	5.85

Source: Morgan Stanley Research

EXHIBIT 2.9 Return Components: Portfolio C

Asset Class	Weight	β Contribution	Return Contribution			
			r_f	β	α	Total
Venture Capital	10%	0.06	0.15	0.34	0.74	1.23
Real Estate	10%	0.01	0.15	0.04	0.36	0.55
Emerging Mkt Equity	5%	0.04	0.08	0.22	0.17	0.46
Private Equity	10%	0.10	0.15	0.56	0.31	1.03
Absolute Return	10%	0.03	0.15	0.16	0.21	0.53
U.S. Bonds	20%	0.03	0.30	0.16	0.29	0.75
International Equity	15%	0.12	0.23	0.66	0.20	1.09
U.S. Equity	20%	0.20	0.30	1.15	0.00	1.45
Total	100%	0.57	1.50	3.29	2.28	7.08

Source: Morgan Stanley Research

Using the same analysis with the more broadly diversified and more modern-looking Portfolio C in Exhibit 2.9, we calculate a beta of 0.57, a beta-based return of 3.29 percent, and an alpha of 2.28 percent.

Exhibit 2.10 represents the extreme Portfolio D consisting of 20 percent distributed across five asset classes, none of which is U.S. or international equity.

Portfolio D has a very low beta of 0.16, and it is not too surprising that its beta return contribution is only 0.91 percent. The majority of D's return comes from its alpha of 3.99 percent. Its total return is fairly significant at

EXHIBIT 2.10 Return Components: Portfolio D

Asset Class	Weight	β Contribution	Return Contribution			
			r_f	β	α	Total
Venture Capital	20%	0.12	0.30	0.68	1.47	2.45
Commodities	20%	−0.06	0.30	−0.33	1.08	1.05
Real Estate	20%	0.01	0.30	0.08	0.72	1.10
Absolute Return	20%	0.06	0.30	0.32	0.43	1.05
U.S. Bonds	20%	0.03	0.30	0.16	0.29	0.75
Total	100%	0.16	1.50	0.91	3.99	6.40

Source: Morgan Stanley Research

6.40 percent, but the composition of this return is vastly different from the preceding three portfolios.

COMPARISON OF PORTFOLIOS' RISKS AND RETURNS

Returning to our four portfolios, Exhibit 2.11 summarizes their returns with their β-based risk characteristics. These risk measures provide a valuable prism for examining the return components. Portfolio A has an exact volatility of 9.90 percent, representing its beta of 0.6 multiplied by the equity volatility of 16.50 percent.

The exact volatility of Portfolio B is somewhat greater, at 11.17 percent, and its 0.65 beta value is slightly above A's. When applied to the 16.50 percent equity volatility, this 0.65 beta yields a β-based volatility estimate of 10.80 percent. B's somewhat higher beta provides a slightly increased beta return, and there is a further lift from the 0.59 percent alpha.

In Portfolio C, the alpha leaps to 2.28 percent, while the beta-based return declines somewhat to 3.29 percent, as the beta value drops to 0.57 from Portfolio B's 0.65. However, it is worth noting that C's exact volatility of 10.83 percent is only slightly different from that of Portfolio B. Thus, if we accept all the assumptions in the return-covariance matrix, Portfolio C is a superior portfolio to B, providing an extra 1.23 percent of return for a roughly comparable level of risk.

Even though C has a much broader array of asset classes, its real diversification is in the sources of alpha return, not in the basic risk factors.

EXHIBIT 2.11 Portfolio Risk/Return Summary

	A	B	C	D
r_f	1.50	1.50	1.50	1.50
β-Return	3.45	3.76	3.29	0.91
α-Return	0.00	0.59	2.28	3.99
Total Return	4.95	5.85	7.08	6.40
Exact σ	9.90	11.17	10.83	8.04
β	0.60	0.65	0.57	0.16
β-Based σ	9.90	10.80	9.45	2.61
β-Based σ/Exact σ Ratio	100.0%	96.7%	87.2%	32.4%

Source: Morgan Stanley Research

Portfolio D, by contrast, has a vastly different risk structure, with a beta value of only 0.16 and a beta-based volatility of 2.61 percent. D's return is overwhelmingly due to its alpha return, accounting for almost 4 percent out of the total 6.40 percent return. While Portfolio D has many theoretically desirable characteristics, most institutional portfolio managers would view it as an extreme case well outside the bounds of practicality.

IMPLICATIONS FOR INSTITUTIONAL PORTFOLIOS

To summarize the surprises found in the more practically relevant examples of the traditional Portfolio B and the modern Portfolio C, first, the exact volatilities of the traditional and the modern portfolio turn out to be pretty close. Second, the beta values of these two portfolios, which look so vastly different, also turn out to be quite close. Third, and perhaps most striking, the beta-based volatility is a good approximation to the exact volatility in both cases. Moreover, since these portfolios span the spectrum of most U.S. allocations, one can expect these three observations to apply quite broadly. (This analysis addresses the asset-only problem, however. When liabilities are explicitly included in what is sometimes called a surplus optimization procedure, interest rates and other factors may emerge as important additional dimensions of risk.)

A single-minded pursuit of active management alphas can lead to the neglect of other activities that could be also characterized as alpha-seeking. Additional opportunities for exploiting structural alphas can easily be derived from the standard market assumptions forming the basis for a given asset allocation. We see both good news and bad news in these findings. On the one hand, the bad news is that standard diversification really does not meaningfully reduce the primary β-factor in a portfolio (although the target level of β-risk *is* controllable). On the other hand, the good news is that, even for portfolios with comparable levels of underlying risk, there are structural alphas that can supply significantly enhanced returns.

Both the return and the risk dimensions can be separated into risk-free, β-based, and α components. Most importantly, this breakdown demonstrates that there are structural alphas that derive from the market assumptions embedded in any return-covariance matrix. These structural alphas have nothing to do with any assumed special skills that the sponsor or the manager can bring to selecting or managing a given asset class. Rather, these structural alphas arise from the typical allocation risk structure in which the overriding β-risk swamps the α-risks associated with the implied α-return. The net result is that, given the assumed covariances, there exist sources of significant incremental return that come with very little marginal risk at the portfolio level.

These structural alphas offer a superb risk-and-reward relationship that should be exploited to the extent that there are no major exogenous considerations or factors (such as those present in various asset or liability frameworks), that these asset classes are available in sufficient size and liquidity, and, perhaps most critically, that one has faith in the market assumptions embedded in the return-covariance matrix.

BETA AS THE KEY RISK FACTOR

Focusing on the role of betas as a risk factor, one can ask about the most serious situation that might confront an institution with a long-term investment plan. In our view, it is not volatility *per se,* but rather the prospect of a market deterioration so severe and so prolonged that it overrides the institution's investment fortitude and forces a fundamental reconsideration of its basic investment philosophy. In virtually all conceivable cases, and as we have seen, such a dire situation would almost surely be created by, or at least associated with, a dramatic movement in U.S. equities. The beta value reflects the portfolio's sensitivity to equity movements. Consequently, the portfolio beta may well prove more effective than the standard volatility measure in assessing the probability of such a philosophy-changing event.

The beta values are derived from a covariance matrix that typically reflects historical results over both normal and abnormal time periods. It is well known that correlations tighten when there is a sudden move in the market, either up or down. Such short-term spikes, if followed by a relatively quick rebound, may not represent a real threat. However, over a longer period of serious underperformance, tightening of correlations would probably also occur. Recall that beta is the product of the correlation (ρ_{pe}) and a ratio of the selected portfolio volatility and equity market volatility (σ_e/σ_p). If correlations are tightening at the same time as market volatility is rising, then even if portfolio volatility remains relatively low, the portfolio beta will increase significantly.[2]

Tighter correlations and increased market volatility generally imply increased betas, reinforcing our argument that beta is the dominant factor characterizing those stress scenarios most feared by institutional managers.

An institution typically strives to develop an allocation that maximizes expected return within acceptable risk limits. If the beta value represents the best gauge of the probability of those risk events having the most overriding significance, then the portfolio beta should play a key role in setting risk limits for the allocation process.

NOTES

1. In other words, $\sigma_{eq}^2 - \left(\beta_p \sigma_p\right)^2 = \sigma_\alpha^2$, in which the last term is the variance associated with the structural alpha.
2. *Ceteris paribus,* if correlation increases, then beta will increase. Similarly, if market volatility increases in relation to portfolio volatility, then beta will increase. If both are increasing, then the increase in beta is multiplied: $\uparrow\uparrow \beta_p = \uparrow \rho_{pe} \frac{\uparrow \sigma_e}{\sigma_p}$.

Beta-Based Asset Allocation

CHAPTER 3

Beyond Diversification:
Dragon Risk

*T*heoretically efficient portfolios tend to be highly concentrated when gen-erated by an optimization model without constraints. The pure opti-mization process often concentrates significant weight in nonstandard asset classes that yield high risk-and-return ratios. Modern allocations, however, typically place piecemeal limits of 5 to 10 percent on each individual non-standard asset class. We have called this portfolio torturing, which goes well beyond the level of diversification needed to achieve reasonable reductions in modeled risk. Such torturing also lowers the return below what is the-oretically achievable by unconstrained efficient portfolios that are free to concentrate in the higher-returning asset classes.

These piecemeal limits are really intended to address nonstandard as-set dragon risks—those beyond-model concerns that surround deployments into nonstandard assets. This fundamental uncertainty is very different from the probability distributions that conventional models of risk assign to tra-ditional asset classes. By imposing piecemeal limits to address dragon risks, portfolio managers free themselves to assign sizable weights to a broad range of nonstandard assets. The resulting reduction in formal model risk can be small, suggesting that diversification enables portfolios to pursue return en-hancement with a more sizable commitment of the fund's assets than might otherwise be made available.

THE NATURE OF DIVERSIFICATION

Portfolio diversification in modern times can be comforting or unsettling, depending on the asset classes chosen and their recent performance. Building on our new understanding of structural beta and alpha, we can examine the

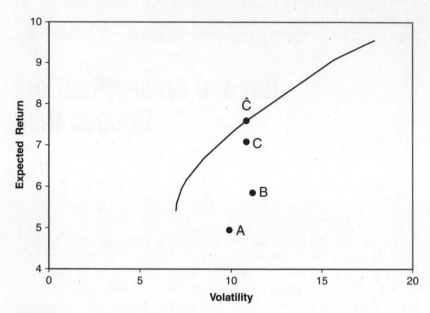

EXHIBIT 3.1 Unconstrained Efficient Frontier
Source: Morgan Stanley Research

implications of modern portfolios using nonstandard asset classes in light of their nonstandard risks. Exhibit 3.1 plots our various sample portfolios in standard risk-and-return space, including *simplistic* Portfolio A, *standard* Portfolio B, and *modern* Portfolio C. In addition, Portfolio Ĉ is a new portfolio that is on the efficient frontier, representing the highest-return portfolio having the same volatility as C. The weightings and characteristics of these four portfolios are detailed in Exhibit 3.2.

Portfolios B and C form the endpoints of the spectrum of portfolios likely to be encountered in practice. The volatility of these two portfolios is quite close in spite of Portfolio C's far greater diversification and its return increment of 123 basis points over Portfolio B. However, the more efficient portfolio, Portfolio Ĉ, manages to add a further 50 basis points of return by being more concentrated than its counterpart C with its broader diversification.

Portfolio Ĉ tells us that a higher return with comparable risk could be obtained through a greater concentration in just the two or three highest-alpha classes.

This strongly suggests that the purpose of excess diversification as is illustrated in Portfolio C is to address *dragon risk*—the bundle of concerns

EXHIBIT 3.2 Portfolio Asset Weights and Characteristics

Asset Class	A	B	C	C^
U.S. Equity	60%	60%	20%	20%
International Equity			15%	
Emerging Mkt Equity			5%	10%
Absolute Return Equity Hedge Funds			10%	
Venture Capital			10%	24%
Private Equity REITS			10%	2%
Real Estate			10%	24%
Commodities U.S. Bonds		40%	20%	20%
Cash	40%			
Total	100%	100%	100%	100%
Expected Return	4.95	5.85	7.08	7.59
Exact σ	9.90	11.17	10.83	10.83
Portfolio β	0.60	0.65	0.57	0.55
β-Based σ	9.90	10.80	9.45	7.92

Source: Morgan Stanley Research

and trepidations that lie outside a formal model but naturally arise when moving into uncharted territory. Without these limits on the maximum exposure for each nonstandard single asset class, it would be difficult to justify having 60 percent of the portfolio weight deployed in nonstandard assets even if they, as a group, promise significantly higher returns. Thus, one could say that the primary goal of Portfolio C's high level of diversification is to achieve higher returns rather than to reduce modelable risk.

DRAGON RISK

The term *dragon risk* strikes us as a poignant way to distinguish modelable risk from the more fundamental uncertainty about the validity of any model. This critical distinction has been discussed at some length in the work of Peter Bernstein (1996) and Frank Knight (1921). We take the term from a paper by Cliff Asness (2002), referring to the medieval mapmaker's characterization of uncharted territories as places where dragons might dwell. Dragon risk includes a range of concerns relating to nonstandard asset classes:

1. The mean-variance model may be misspecified
2. The risk of asymmetries and fat tails
3. The potential perils of relatively new investment vehicles
4. The wider range of performance outcomes for less-efficient assets that depend more on a manager's skill
5. Potential material shifts away from historical results as a novel asset class becomes more fashionable and finds itself in a more crowded space
6. The greater headline and embarrassment risks
7. The possibility of singularly sour outcomes that may not be widely shared among peer institutions

The truth is that most practitioners harbor some appropriate skepticism regarding any modeled market assumptions. This skepticism is particularly intense as it relates to the more nonstandard asset classes. Relative to nonstandard assets, we think we understand the risk-and-return dynamics in the fixed-income markets. We even think we know how the risk characteristics of U.S. equity behave; equity volatility has been reasonably stable, within certain ranges, over long periods of time. We are much less secure about the long-term behavior of asset classes or strategies that lie outside of these relatively well-charted waters. This insecurity is exacerbated for relatively new asset classes and situations in which the dynamics may be changing as the asset classes become more popular in the institutional marketplace. In other words, some forms of risk are viewed differently regardless of how they may be characterized in a formal covariance model. For those asset classes in which the market assumptions are subject to doubt regarding their validity or stability over time, it is perfectly rational to overdiversify and superimpose intuitively chosen constraints on how large a weight will be tolerated in a given portfolio.

For these reasons, the modern allocation extends diversification beyond that needed to control explicit model risk to a piecemeal level that brings the less explicit dragon risks within digestible bounds.

A DIVERSIFICATION MODEL

To shed further light on this issue, we explore how diversification functions within an artificially simplistic model in which the β-value is assumed to be fixed at some target value. We then devote 60 percent of the portfolio weight to a single nonstandard asset class having a structural α-based risk of 12 percent. The resulting α-risk contributed to the portfolio then becomes

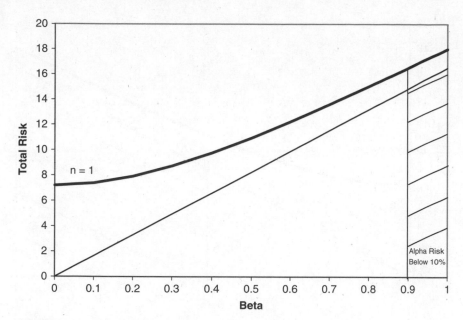

EXHIBIT 3.3 Total Risk versus Beta with 1 Nonstandard Asset
Source: Morgan Stanley Research

.6 × 12 = 7.20 percent. As illustrated in Exhibit 3.3, the fund's total volatility then depends on the chosen β-value. At the outset, for $\beta = 0$, the total volatility is determined by the 7.20 percent α-risk. As the target β-value rises, the total volatility increases, but the incremental role of the α-risk declines. For a sufficiently large β-value, in this case $\beta = .9$, the α-risk drops to less than 10 percent of the total risk. At some such threshold, the role of the α-risk becomes negligible, especially if one accepts the argument that any serious stress scenario would be associated with a major down move in U.S. equities.

Under these simplified conditions, the portfolio's total volatility is determined by the α-risk and the target β-value. In turn, the basic α-risk itself is a function of how many independent asset classes are represented in the 60 percent nonstandard allocation. This model enables us to focus clearly on the diversification effect itself.

In Exhibit 3.4, the 60 percent weight is totally concentrated in a single nonstandard asset. If we were to diversify beyond one nonstandard asset class into three or four, each having the same 12 percent α-risk, the portfolio level alpha risk would be reduced. The alpha risks, being essentially independent of one another, are self-moderating because they accumulate as the sum of squares. In contrast, we know that the beta risks are additive,

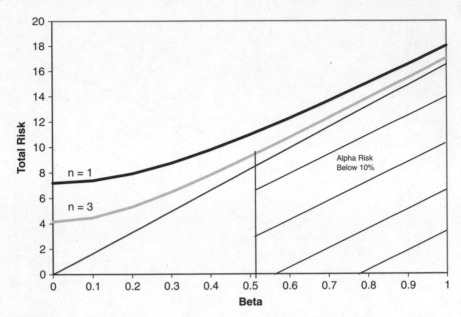

EXHIBIT 3.4   Total Risk versus Beta with 1 and 3 Nonstandard Assets
Source: Morgan Stanley Research

and therefore every increment counts. Thus, by distributing the nonstandard 60 percent weight across three or four nonstandard asset classes, one obtains a reduction in cumulative alpha risk. Exhibit 3.4 shows the results when the 60 percent nonstandard weight is allocated across three 20 percent classes, all presumed to be uncorrelated and each having an α-risk of 12 percent. One can see that the α-risk is reduced to a level where the 10 percent threshold is attained at the $\beta = .52$ mark.

Continuing this approach, we can ascertain how many equally sized asset classes are needed to achieve the 10 percent threshold as a function of the portfolio's target β. This required level of diversification is displayed in Exhibit 3.5.

As we saw earlier, for a portfolio β of .52. only three nonstandard asset classes are needed, each with a 20 percent weight. Any diversification beyond the threshold level is essentially optional and, from a purely theoretical viewpoint, actually represents overdiversification. As we well know, there may be exogenous reasons for pursuing apparent overdiversification, but it certainly comes with an associated cost in portfolio return given that the added classes provide lower expected return.

Finally, Exhibit 3.6 adopts a β-target of .6 and shows the percentage of α-risk remaining in the portfolio at various levels of diversification.

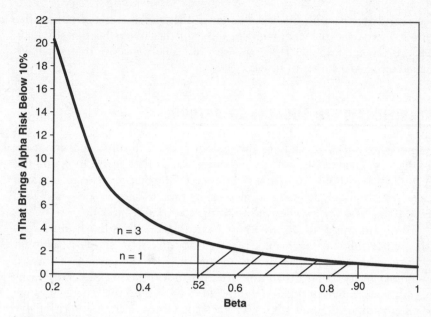

EXHIBIT 3.5 Diversification Levels Needed to Bring Alpha Risk Below 10 percent
Source: Morgan Stanley Research

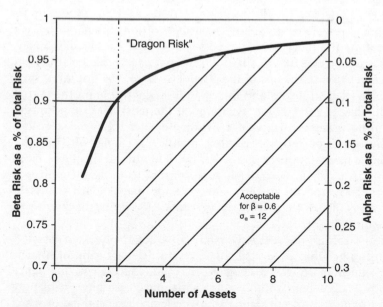

EXHIBIT 3.6 Alpha and Beta Risks at Various Levels of Diversification
Source: Morgan Stanley Research

Piecemeal diversification beyond this level does not materially reduce the portfolio's *modeled* risk characteristics. But further diversification does address the less-quantifiable risks and the multiple concerns that we have grouped under the rubric of dragon risk.

DIVERSIFICATION IN SOURCES OF RETURN

The preceding analysis leads to different numerical results, depending on the values assigned to the individual α-risks, the level of portfolio β, and the negligibility threshold for α-risks. However, the basic message remains intact. The levels of diversification seen in practice go well beyond that needed to address the risk derived from the covariance model.

From common practice, we know that dragon risk is taken quite seriously. As portfolio managers and sponsors move from the simple traditional allocation with its heavy weightings in two or three standard asset classes, they almost always deploy their nonstandard allocations in a piecemeal fashion, with most individual class weightings falling in the 5 to 10 percent range and perhaps an occasional 15 to 20 percent. Concern over dragon risk plays a key (but arguably appropriate) role in how these modern portfolios are constructed.

For these reasons, many managers set limits of 5 percent for emerging markets, 10 to 20 percent for absolute return strategies, 10 to 15 percent for venture cap and private equity (either separately or in combination). But if the argument for absolute return is so powerful—if one could really achieve reliable returns in excess of Treasury bill rates with very little volatility and very little correlation to the rest of the portfolio—then why not invest large percentages in such strategies and then add leverage to obtain the desired level of volatility? At this point, even among the most avid supporters of absolute return strategies, one finds few takers for such leveraged strategies.

Overdiversification provides comfort relative to a range of issues that fall outside the basic optimization model. Indeed, without this more piecemeal approach, it would be difficult for sponsors to bring themselves to make sizable commitments to the higher-yielding nonstandard classes. In this sense, one could say that piecemeal diversification opens the door to the serious pursuit of higher returns.

As we saw earlier, the real issue is not so much the question of *modeled risk* but rather the *model* itself. The broad diversification of modern portfolios is aimed more at increasing returns than reducing risk. In essence, the added asset class breadth allows for a significant assignment of portfolio weight to a series of nonstandard, α-producing assets, none of which could comfortably accommodate a large weighting on a stand-alone basis.

Within the context of a mean-variance optimization, this high level of diversification is typically forced by establishing relatively tight constraints on the maximum weight allowed for each nonstandard asset class. By providing a degree of fundamental comfort, this seeming overdiversification enables a more significant portfolio weight to be assigned to high return, nonstandard asset classes. From this vantage point, such overdiversification may be both reasonable and prudent.

POTENTIAL DIVERSIFICATION COSTS

However, overdiversification does bear a cost in return—and perhaps even in risk control. In regard to return, there will always be some hierarchy of α-returns associated with nonstandard asset classes. By definition, mandated diversification always forces more portfolio weight into the lower-return classes. The resulting allocation may reflect a reasonable risk-and-reward tradeoff, but it should be recognized that such diversification does extract a certain return penalty.

In regard to risk control, overdiversification can also create a certain danger insofar as it encourages moving beyond nonstandard asset classes with fairly well-known performance characteristics (that is, international equity and real estate) into more novel asset classes with greater levels of uncertainty. In addition to the danger of performance blowups and other surprise events, these asset classes may exhibit β exposures that are far greater than anticipated under certain stress scenarios. As we saw in earlier chapters, it is just such β exposure that represents the most serious risk for institutional portfolios.

Although, the dragon risk fears that lead to overdiversification are understandable, they do create opportunities for bolder knights. Reducing overdiversification in certain nonstandard asset classes can lead to significant improvements in portfolio return—*if* the α-risk can be more securely modeled, *if* there is a reasonable assurance of a positive α-return, and *if* the manager is willing to move out ahead of his peers.

OVERDIVERSIFICATION VERSUS DRAGON RISK

In formal optimizations, broad diversification is often forced by setting constraints on the maximum weight that can be allocated to each nonstandard asset class. For larger funds, these constraints may be justified in regard to availability limits or (sometimes exaggerated) liquidity requirements. However, one way or another, such constraints reflect a form of intuitive diversification, with the intended effect that the portfolio achieves risk control along two dimensions—the explicitly modeled risks and the implicit dragon risk of unknown dangers.

The key takeaway from this thinking is that diversification is often more piecemeal and thus more tortured than is needed to control a fund's formally modeled risk. However, excess diversification does open the door to putting a significant allocation into higher-returning nonstandard assets while controlling the dragon risk that would arise from having too much weight in any one such asset class.

CHAPTER 4

Reverse Asset Allocation Using Alpha Cores

*T*he *structural alpha-beta framework provides an opportunity to greatly simplify the optimization process. The complexities involved in standard optimization can obscure the more intuitive decision process that, in the final analysis, ends up defining the structure of the policy portfolio. Using the alpha-beta framework, we can develop a simpler approach that may better reflect how such portfolios are really constructed.*

The key is to decompose a portfolio's assets in two groups: swing assets and an alpha core. Swing assets are the traditional liquid assets—U.S. equity, U.S. bonds, and cash—while an alpha core consists of all other assets— non-U.S. equity, real estate, hedge funds, private equities, and so forth—that are subject to relatively tight portfolio constraints. The risk-and-return characteristics of an alpha core can be abstracted from any specific assets and transformed into basic alpha and beta terms.

The allocation process can be viewed as a three-step process that essentially reverses the usual approach in which traditional assets form the core and additional assets are added, within limits. Instead of using traditional assets as the starting point, the alpha-beta framework first calls for determining the maximum acceptable limits for each nontraditional asset class. Second, these assets are combined into a subportfolio—the alpha core. The third step is to add the traditional swing assets to achieve the desired risk level for the overall portfolio. The resulting efficient frontier then takes on a relatively simple three-part shape determined by the alpha core-based return uplift: a cash-equity line, a fixed core segment, and an equity extension to 100 percent equity.

SIMPLIFYING THE PORTFOLIO OPTIMIZATION PROCESS

The concept of an efficient frontier is the subject of a rich literature dating back to the mean-variance methodology first developed by Markowitz in the 1950s (Markowitz 1959). In Exhibit 4.1, we display a long-only efficient frontier based on a hypothetical return-covariance matrix. Risk-and-return positions are also denoted for the Portfolios A, B, and C that previously served as representative allocations.

As we saw in Chapter 2, one problem with any formal mean-variance analysis is that it often devolves into a tortured optimization process. Starting with the better-known standard asset classes (for example, equities and fixed income), modern portfolio analysis may add additional asset classes in a sequential step-wise fashion or even all at once. Using the raw input of returns, volatilities, and correlations for different asset classes, the initial computer-based solution will almost always be unacceptable. Certain asset classes will be given weights that far exceed their credible limits. The typical next step is to impose a sequence of piecemeal constraints, until repeated optimization produces a portfolio that has been tortured into palatability.

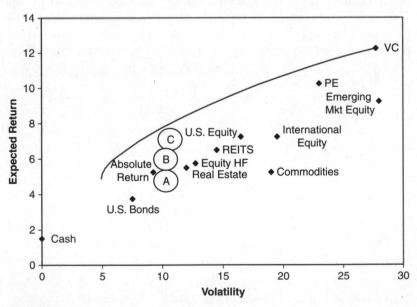

EXHIBIT 4.1 An Unconstrained, Efficient Frontier
Source: Morgan Stanley Research

There is nothing fundamentally wrong with this procedure when a reasonable portfolio is the final outcome. However, the mathematical and computer complexities involved in the standard optimization can obscure the more intuitive decision process that should play a fundamental role in the final outcome. One way to address this problem is to accept some approximations in order to obtain a simpler and more naturally intuitive framework. The structural alpha-beta framework can provide a path to this simplification. Moreover, this alpha-beta approach may even better reflect how portfolios are structured in practice.

The underlying philosophy here is that any set of market assumptions is inherently imprecise—at best! Therefore, it is far better to develop approximate guidelines than to become enmeshed in complex methodology that promises theoretically refined solutions, but obscures the role that should be played by intuition, judgment, and common sense.

THE ALPHA CORE

The key is to use the alpha-beta approach to decompose a portfolio's assets into two groups, which we refer to as the swing assets and the alpha core. Swing assets are the traditional liquid assets—U.S. equity, U.S. bonds, and cash—that are used relatively freely to help shape the portfolio's overall risk structure. The second group—the alpha core—consists of all other assets that are subject to relatively tight position limits for one reason or another.

These limits may be based on regulatory or organizational constraints, difficulty of access to satisfactory investment vehicles or managers, underdeveloped financial markets, excessive transaction costs, problematic fee structures, liquidity concerns of various sorts, peer-based standards, headline risk, insufficient or unreliable performance data, and so forth. Many of these issues will fall under the category that we have called dragon risk, that is, legitimate fears about moving into uncharted waters where unknown dangers lurk. In essence, one may not be able to trust the risk-and-return assumptions for these nontraditional assets to the same extent as estimates for the more traditional asset classes. (And even for U.S. bonds and equities, there are always plenty of fundamental issues, given any model of their prospective returns!)

Markets and institutional positions clearly evolve over time, but today's alpha cores generally include assets such as international equity, emerging market equity, real estate, natural resources, and more recently, different forms of private equity and hedge funds (and sometimes even commodity funds). In spite of their position constraints, these asset classes can aggregate to serve as a valuable source of incremental alpha return. Alpha is defined here as that component of expected return that lies above and beyond the return that can be associated with the asset's implicitly embedded U.S. equity exposure.

The alpha core is often viewed as serving to diversify and moderate the volatility of the basic swing assets. However, in practice, most institutional portfolios are beta-dominated, with total U.S. equity exposure accounting for roughly 90 percent of the total risk. This overwhelming beta risk tends to swamp any volatility reduction from the alpha core. Thus, rather than the often-cited diversification argument, the alpha core's real benefit is return enhancement (although there may be some less-quantifiable diversification benefits other than those captured by the standard volatility measure).

The alpha core approach reverses the traditional view of how asset allocation modeling proceeds. Instead of starting with the standard swing assets and adding more exotic investments until an acceptable portfolio is reached, the alpha core approach reverses the process by presuming that the fund will first determine the maximum acceptable limits for each asset class outside the basic swing assets. The next decision is to combine these asset choices into a coherent subportfolio—the alpha core. The composition of this subportfolio will generally involve both intuitive and qualitative considerations that go well beyond the explicit quantitative characteristics embedded in the return-covariance matrix. For modern portfolios, structuring the alpha core is appropriately demanding of concentrated research, judgment, and deliberation, both by fund sponsors and by their managers. While they might not use the term *alpha core,* we believe that sizable funds already do devote major effort to this decision, both at the allocation *and* the implementation levels.

Once an acceptable alpha core has been formed, its return and risk characteristics can be transformed into basic alpha and beta terms. One (admittedly heroic) assumption is then needed to achieve an enormous simplification: that the fund will try to include this specific alpha core at some maximum allowed percentage within the final portfolio. When the desired overall risk falls outside the range in which this maximum percentage can be sustained, it is assumed that the fund will maintain the alpha core's internal structure even as its percentage within the overall portfolio has to be reduced.

The basic idea here is that the fund has already made a qualitative determination as to how much of the alpha core assets can be accommodated within the overall portfolio. Since the core acts as a return enhancer, the fund would like to maintain the maximum acceptable core contribution whenever possible.

A second key assumption is that, regardless of the detailed asset composition of the core subportfolio, its performance characteristics can be summarized in terms of an aggregate alpha return, an alpha volatility, and a beta value. To the extent that these three parameters are sufficient for allocation purposes, the problem of constructing the alpha core can be separated from the development of an efficient frontier.

Taken together, these core assumptions then allow the allocation problem to be decomposed into three basic steps: determining the size limits for asset classes that can be used to form the alpha core, developing an optimal alpha core given these constraints, and incorporating the swing assets to form a portfolio that best represents the desired balance of return and risk.

THE SWING ASSETS

In most cases, the primary determinant of the total portfolio risk will be the swing assets—equity, bonds, and cash. Here again, we must make another assumption to attain the desired degree of intuitiveness and simplification: that the fund will prefer to have a mixture of equity and bonds as the basic swing assets whenever possible, thereby avoiding a significant allocation to cash except when needed to achieve very low risk levels.

This assumption seems to accord quite well with what one sees in practice. Even when short-term interest rates are quite high, long-term funds tend to view cash allocations more as a temporary tactical move rather than as a permanent strategic allocation.

Given these respective roles for the alpha core and the swing assets, the entire efficient frontier takes on a relatively simple form:

- A basic, fixed alpha core segment consisting of the core at its maximum weight, with portfolio risk levels determined by varying mixtures of bonds and equity
- A lower-risk cash line segment with varying levels of cash
- A higher-risk equity extension segment that trades off the alpha core weight for greater equity exposure

In practice, most allocations will fall within the middle-risk segment, that is, the fixed alpha core segment, which is then mixed with bonds and equity.

THE FIXED ALPHA CORE SEGMENT

In Exhibits 4.2 and 4.3, we have used the assets contained in our familiar modern Portfolio C to show how a portfolio can be decomposed into an alpha core and a set of swing assets. The 100 percent core case is particularly interesting because it displays the fundamental character of the core, even

EXHIBIT 4.2 Portfolios with Various Alpha Core Percentages

Core Assets in Overall Portfolio Alpha Core %	100%	60.0%	80.0%	40.0%
International Equity	25.0	15.0	20.0	10.0
Emerging Mkt Equity	8.3	5.0	6.7	3.3
Absolute Return	16.7	10.0	13.3	6.7
Venture Capital	16.7	10.0	13.3	6.7
Private Equity	16.7	10.0	13.3	6.7
Real Estate	16.7	10.0	13.3	6.7
Expected Return	8.13	4.88	6.50	3.25
β	0.58	0.35	0.46	0.23
β-Return	3.31	1.98	2.65	1.32
α	3.32	1.99	2.65	1.33
r_f	1.50	0.90	1.50	1.50
σ_α	7.08	4.25	5.66	2.83
σ	11.84	7.10	9.47	4.74

Swing Assets in Overall Portfolio Swing Assets %	0.0%	40.0%	20.0%	60.0%
U.S. Equity	0.0	20.0	10.0	30.0
U.S. Bonds	0.0	20.0	10.0	30.0
Cash	0.0	0.0	0.0	0.0
Expected Return	0.00	2.20	1.10	3.30
β	0.00	0.23	0.11	0.34
β-Return	0.00	1.31	0.65	1.96
α	0.00	0.29	0.15	0.44
r_f	1.50	1.50	1.50	1.50
σ_α	0.00	1.43	0.72	2.15
σ	0.00	4.01	2.01	6.02

Overall Portfolio				
Expected Return	8.13	7.08	7.60	6.55
β	0.58	0.57	0.57	0.57
β-Return	3.31	3.29	3.30	3.28
α	3.32	2.28	2.80	1.77
r_f	1.50	1.50	1.50	1.50
σ_α	7.08	4.48	5.71	3.55
σ	11.84	10.45	11.05	10.07

Source: Morgan Stanley Research

EXHIBIT 4.3 Portfolios with Fixed 60 Percent Alpha Core and Varying Bond and Equity Mixtures

Core Assets in Overall Portfolio					
Alpha Core %	60.0%	60.0%	60.0%	60.0%	60.0%
International Equity	15.00	15.00	15.00	15.00	15.00
Emerging Mkt Equity	5.00	5.00	5.00	5.00	5.00
Absolute Return	10.00	10.00	10.00	10.00	10.00
Venture Capital	10.00	10.00	10.00	10.00	10.00
Private Equity	10.00	10.00	10.00	10.00	10.00
Real Estate	10.00	10.00	10.00	10.00	10.00
Expected Return	4.88	4.88	4.88	4.88	4.88
β	0.35	0.35	0.35	0.35	0.35
β-Return	1.98	1.98	1.98	1.98	1.98
α	1.99	1.99	1.99	1.99	1.99
r_f	1.50	1.50	1.50	1.50	1.50
σ_α	4.25	4.25	4.25	4.25	4.25
σ	7.10	7.10	7.10	7.10	7.10

Swing Assets in Overall Portfolio					
Swing Assets %	40.0%	40.0%	40.0%	40.0%	40.0%
U.S. Equity	0.00	10.00	20.00	30.00	40.00
U.S. Bonds	40.00	30.00	20.00	10.00	0.00
Cash	0.00	0.00	0.00	0.00	0.00
Expected Return	1.50	1.85	2.20	2.55	2.90
β	0.05	0.14	0.23	0.31	0.40
β-Return	0.31	0.81	1.31	1.80	2.30
α	0.59	0.44	0.29	0.15	0.00
r_f	0.60	1.50	0.60	1.50	0.60
σ_α	2.86	2.15	1.43	0.72	0.00
σ	3.00	3.16	4.01	5.22	6.60

Overall Portfolio					
Expected Return	6.38	6.73	7.08	7.43	7.78
β	0.40	0.49	0.57	0.66	0.75
β-Return	2.30	2.79	3.29	3.79	4.28
α	2.58	2.43	2.28	2.14	1.99
r_f	1.50	1.50	1.50	1.50	1.50
σ_α	5.12	4.76	4.48	4.31	4.25
σ	8.35	9.32	10.45	11.69	13.01

Source: Morgan Stanley Research

though in practice a lower core percentage is actually used within any given portfolio. Exhibit 4.2 shows the portfolios derived from the various core percentages, with bonds and equity sharing equal roles in completing the overall portfolio. We can see that the alpha core portfolios have superior alphas to the swing assets, but their drawback is the limited weight that they can accommodate. The shaded column of each exhibit corresponds to the parameters associated with the original Portfolio C.

In Exhibit 4.3, the alpha core percentage is fixed at 60 percent, and the columns depict varying proportions of equity and bonds in the remaining 40 percent. In essence, the lower panel of Exhibit 4.3 depicts the series of portfolios that determine a portion of the efficient frontier that we shall refer to as the *fixed core segment*.

GENERALITY OF THE ALPHA CORE REPRESENTATION

For concreteness, Portfolio C's core is used as a base case. However, it should be noted that the analysis makes use of only three of the C core's parameters: beta, alpha, and the alpha risk. Any alpha core, no matter what its underlying asset class structure, can be approximately modeled using these alpha and beta parameters. While this model will not be theoretically exact, it will be a reasonable approximation for most allocation problems. Our goal is to achieve greater simplicity and intuitiveness, consistent with the intrinsically approximate nature of the market assumptions themselves.

We believe that most allocation situations, especially those falling within the relevant region, can be analyzed using a fixed alpha core characterized solely by these alpha and beta parameters. The discussion can then have a generality that goes beyond specific assets, and the findings can apply to any alpha core having the indicated parameter values. Indeed, it is this generality that enables the alpha core concept to be applicable to a very wide spectrum of asset class constraints and portfolio situations.

Exhibit 4.4 is a graph of the fixed alpha core segment of an efficient frontier based on Exhibit 4.3's fixed 60 percent core.

Our total risk calculations assume that the alpha and beta-based volatilities are independent of each other. At the 40 percent bonds point in Exhibit 4.4—corresponding to the first column in Exhibit 4.3—the return is 6.38 percent and the total volatility is 8.35 percent, with the volatility being derived from a combination of the alpha- and beta-based volatilities of the 60 percent core and the 40 percent bonds. As we move along the frontier from left to right, equities replace bonds until at the far right the equity concentration reaches 40 percent. At this right-most point, the expected

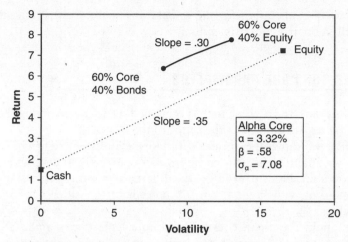

EXHIBIT 4.4 Alpha Core Fixed at 60 Percent Weight
Source: Morgan Stanley Research

return is 7.78 percent and the volatility is 13.01 percent, as shown in the fifth column in Exhibit 4.3. (Note that in between the frontier's two endpoints is a 20 percent equity–20 percent bond point that reflects the position of the original Portfolio C.)

Comparing the two endpoints of this segment, the return rises by 1.40 percent, reflecting equity's return advantage over bonds. The volatility difference is 4.66 percent, so the average slope of this fixed core segment is

$$\frac{1.40}{4.66} = .30$$

Moreover, by inspection, it appears that the slope is roughly constant across the entire segment, that is, there is no evidence of the downward curl typically portrayed in standard efficient frontier diagrams.

As a base of comparison, Exhibit 4.4 also shows the straight line representing all long-only, unlevered portfolios consisting of cash and U.S. equities. The slope of this straight line is 0.35, corresponding to the Sharpe ratio for equities. Thus, roughly speaking, the fixed core segment with its 0.30 slope can be viewed basically as carving out a portion of the cash-equity line, raising its return by the core's alpha contribution, and tilting the orientation to a slightly lower slope. This slight downward slope relative to the cash-equity line results from several factors, but it is primarily due to the lost return from the progressive removal of the bond's alpha return. (A more mathematical explanation for the orientation of the fixed core segment is presented in the technical appendix.)

VARYING THE CORE PARAMETERS

Up to this point, the alpha core has remained static. By changing the core's characteristics, we can affect the shape of the frontier.

Exhibit 4.5 shows the frontier with a lower core alpha return of 2.00 percent. As we might expect, the entire frontier essentially undergoes a parallel downward shift. Not surprisingly, the difference in returns at each risk level is 0.79 percent, which equates to 60 percent of the difference in the two alpha values.

If we hold the alpha constant and adjust the core's alpha risk from 7.08 percent to 10.00 percent, the segment shifts to the right and we obtain the graph in Exhibit 4.6. At the right-most location, both curves are far more beta-dominated, thereby reducing the impact of any difference in their alpha volatilities. However, it is worth noting that while this effect raises the slope of the lower curve, the effect is so slight that it still appears to be roughly parallel to the cash-equity line.

In Exhibit 4.7, we make the assumption that the alpha core has a beta of zero, quite an extreme assumption, since most alpha cores will have at least a moderate implicit beta value. A zero beta leads to a downward diagonal

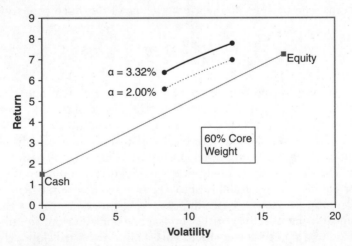

EXHIBIT 4.5 The Alpha Return Effect
Source: Morgan Stanley Research

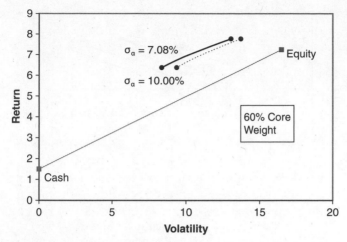

EXHIBIT 4.6 The Alpha Volatility Effect
Source: Morgan Stanley Research

shift to account for the loss of both beta-related return and risk. We also get a curve with more of the standard downward curl at the beginning. With less beta dominance at this left-most point, the curl reflects a more significant diversification effect from the alpha-based volatility of both bonds and the alpha core. This diversification effect also leads to a somewhat shorter fixed

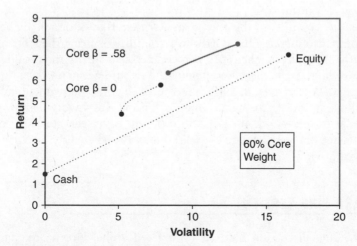

EXHIBIT 4.7 The Core Beta Effect
Source: Morgan Stanley Research

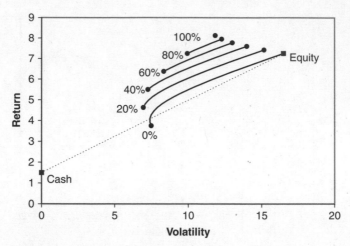

EXHIBIT 4.8   The Core Weight Effect
Source: Morgan Stanley Research

core segment. However, once the risk level progresses beyond the short span of the curl, the segment's slope once again becomes roughly comparable to that of cash-equity line.

Exhibit 4.8 shows how different fixed percentages of the alpha core affect the frontier's position and orientation. Higher core percentages increase the portfolio's alpha return and naturally raise the level of the segment, just as we saw in Exhibit 4.5.

Since the volatility of the core is greater than that of bonds, higher core percentages also increase the portfolio's volatility, shifting the start of each segment to the right. Higher core percentages also shrink the residual allocation to swing assets, thereby reducing the risk range spanned by the fixed core segment. Ultimately, at a 100 percent fixed core, the segment collapses into a single point. At the same time, as Exhibit 4.8 vividly demonstrates, all these segments—with their vastly different core weights—are roughly parallel (once one gets beyond the initial downward curl that occurs at the lower weights).

THE CASH LINE SEGMENT

The preceding discussion focused on a fixed alpha core percentage with only equity and bonds as swing assets. While cash is not typically used in long-term portfolios, it can function as a swing asset for funds seeking

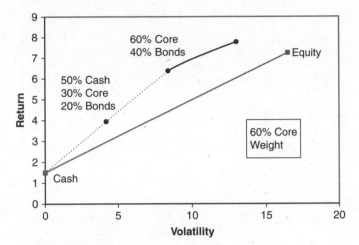

EXHIBIT 4.9   The Cash Line Segment
Source: Morgan Stanley Research

low-risk portfolios. Moreover, cash can sometimes become a significant swing asset in those (generally narrow) risk regions in which the bond-equity mix generates a pronounced downward curl.

Exhibit 4.9 displays the basic 60 percent fixed core segment, but with an added line that extends from the cash position (with its zero percent volatility and its return of 1.50 percent) to the initial point of the fixed core segment. Portfolios along this cash line will be composed of cash, the alpha core, and bonds—that is, no explicit equity. The inclusion of this cash line creates a frontier with two distinct segments.

In general, the cash line can touch the fixed core segment at three different places: a literal point of internal tangency within the body of the segment, the beginning of the segment (as in Exhibit 4.9), or in rare situations, at the end of the curve. This point of tangency represents a portfolio that can be combined with varying proportions of cash to achieve the optimal allocations at lower-risk levels. (Although this chapter does not consider short sales, leverage, or financial futures, it is worth noting that this cash line and its extension would become the entire efficient frontier if leverage were to be allowed.)

An internal point of tangency is illustrated in Exhibit 4.10 for the case of a 20 percent core weight. The point of tangency corresponds to a portfolio consisting of the 20 percent core, a bond weight of 60 percent, and 20 percent equity. Note that the efficient frontier now consists of the cash line together with the fixed core segment that lies to the right of the tangency point. This

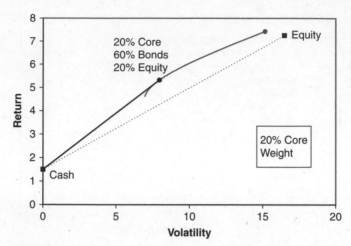

EXHIBIT 4.10   The Cash Line Segment: An Internal Point of Tangency
Source: Morgan Stanley Research

part of the 20 percent segment also has a roughly constant slope, although it is somewhat more downward tilting than in the 60 percent base case.

THE BOND BRIDGE

In the preceding discussion, the initial point on the core segment was assumed to be a portfolio with the fixed core weight and the remaining weight in bonds. In theory, more general frontiers would allow the core weight to range down to zero, with the slack taken up by a combination of bonds and equity. Such flexibility would generally result in more of a front-end curl. Theoretically, this curl could lead to another frontier component—a bridge from the fixed core segment to the tangency point with the cash line.

However, with cores having typical values, these bridges will either be nonexistent or tend to be virtually indistinguishable from the cash line itself. Exhibit 4.11 provides an illustration of this situation for the case of the 80 percent maximum core weight, in which the core is replaced by bonds to achieve lower-risk levels. The cash line touches this frontier at a 65 percent core weight, creating a bond bridge from the cash line to the initial point of the 80 percent fixed core segment. However, even for this extreme case of an 80 percent maximum core, the bridge shown in Exhibit 4.11 appears to be little more than an extension of the cash line.

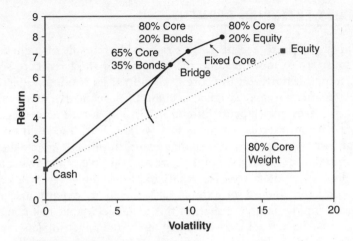

EXHIBIT 4.11   The Bond Bridge
Source: Morgan Stanley Research

Exhibit 4.12 presents the fixed core segments for core weights from zero percent to 100 percent together with the front end extensions generated by the full range of cash and bond mixtures. It can be shown that in all cases with maximum core weights at or below 60 percent, there is no need for a bond bridge. Since this covers most realistic cases, we can overlook the bond bridge.

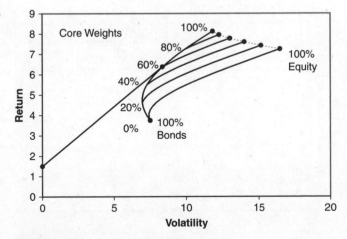

EXHIBIT 4.12   A Spectrum of Frontiers
Source: Morgan Stanley Research

THE EQUITY EXTENSION SEGMENT

If a fund is willing to accept greater risk in the pursuit of higher return, then it must try to move beyond the endpoint of the fixed core segment. At this endpoint, however, the core is already at its maximum percentage, with the remaining weight assigned to equity. Consequently, in moving onto this equity extension segment (Exhibit 4.13), lower core percentages must be mixed with an ever-increasing equity weight. With the addition of this extension, we now have a frontier that spans all possible portfolios, given our assumptions regarding the alpha core and the role of the swing assets.

Trading away alpha core for equity exposure, however, will generally not be productive. Indeed, in Exhibit 4.13, the equity extension segment is downward sloping, implying that, in this instance, higher risk comes with lower returns. Since few funds would be interested in getting less return for more risk, it follows that this particular third segment is essentially vestigial in nature. The equity extension will be of value only when the core's alpha return is sufficiently lower than the equity risk premium.

THE THREE-SEGMENT FRONTIER

For our maximum core base case, we obtain a simple three-segment efficient frontier. Exhibit 4.13 displays this frontier in risk-and-return space, while Exhibit 4.14 shows how the corresponding asset weights vary across the

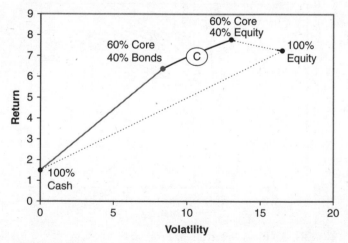

EXHIBIT 4.13 The Equity Extension Segment
Source: Morgan Stanley Research

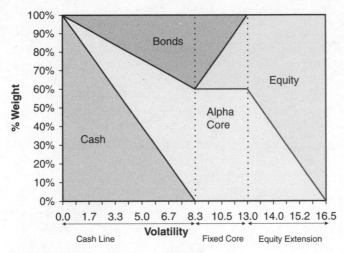

EXHIBIT 4.14 Allocations across the Frontier
Source: Morgan Stanley Research

risk spectrum. At low levels of risk, varying levels of cash are mixed with the 60 percent core–40 percent bond portfolio. At the initial point of the fixed core segment, the core rises to 60 percent of the total portfolio, with the remaining 40 percent first in bonds, and then with an increasing weight assigned to equities. At the end of the fixed core segment, the portfolio has 60 percent core and 40 percent equity. To attain higher risk levels, the frontier moves into the equity extension, where the equity replaces the alpha core until reaching the 100 percent equity portfolio.

THE FRONTIER SLOPE

Most institutional funds end up at more or less the same risk level, that is, an overall volatility of 10.50 ± 1 percent. Many considerations could theoretically enter into the determination of the appropriate risk level for a given fund. One such factor is the return incentive for accepting an incremental level of risk, a measure closely related to the slope of the efficient frontier.

In Exhibit 4.15, we show this slope function for our base case example. The cash line has a very high and constant slope. (After all, this would be the entire optimal frontier *if* leverage were available at the cash rate!) With this high incentive to extend, and given the aversion to having significant cash in long-term allocations, it is little wonder that few portfolios are located on this cash line. As the frontier moves into the fixed core segment, the slope

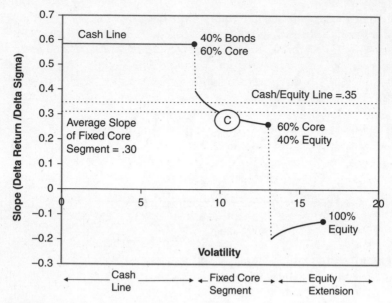

EXHIBIT 4.15   Slopes along the Frontier
Source: Morgan Stanley Research

moderates toward lower values, indicating a decreasing (but still positive) incentive to taking on more risk.

The average slope of this fixed core segment is indicated by the lower horizontal dotted line. It can be seen that once into the body of this fixed core segment, the incremental slope deviates relatively little from its overall average value, consistent with our earlier observations that the segment is close to a straight line. Moreover, we also see that the segment's average slope is only slightly lower than that of the cash-equity line. The proximity of these two slopes underlies the near-parallel appearance of the segment to the cash-equity line. It is also interesting that the original Portfolio C is nestled near the center of the fixed case segment.

Finally, upon entering the equity risk extension, the slope drops dramatically to a negative value, indicating that additional risk is not rewarded in this particular case.

THE UPLIFTED FRONTIER

The assumption of a fixed alpha core is seen to generally lead toward a three-part efficient frontier: a cash-equity line, the fixed core segment itself, and an equity extension to 100 percent equity (which may or may not be truly productive). The cash line is quite literally a straight line by construction. In most cases, the fixed core segment is nearly a straight line. Moreover, it is almost parallel to the cash-equity line, having only a slightly lower slope. And finally, while the equity extension will always have some curvature, it will also be very close to a straight line because the beta effect dominates the risk in this region.

Thus, the efficient frontier virtually devolves into a piecewise linear form with three segments. For all practical purposes, both the first and third segments are tied to the fixed points of 100 percent cash and 100 percent equity, respectively. Consequently, the entire shape of the efficient frontier is determined by the fixed core segment.

Now consider the right-most point of the fixed core segment, which in our base case, consists of the maximum core weight of 60 percent and the remaining 40 percent in equity. The core is the only source of alpha at this point and hence the alpha return advantage over the cash-equity line is the core's contribution of 1.99 percent (the alpha value in the last column of Exhibit 4.3). As shown in Exhibit 4.16, this alpha increment determines the height of this endpoint above the cash-equity line. At the segment's left-most point, the 40 percent bond position contributes an added alpha of .58 percent, leading to a total alpha of 2.58 percent (the alpha value in the first column in Exhibit 4.3). This higher alpha return is the source of the moderate downward tilt in the fixed core segment relative to the cash-equity line.

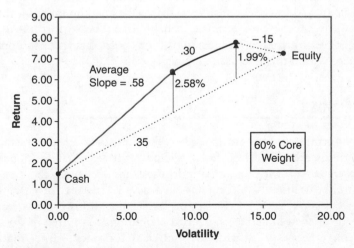

EXHIBIT 4.16 The Alpha Uplift Model
Source: Morgan Stanley Research

This analysis suggests that the entire efficient frontier is essentially defined by the core's maximum weight and alpha return that sets the return height above the cash-equity line, and the core's beta, which plays a major role in locating the segment's position along the risk spectrum. Thus, the efficient frontier can be viewed as a sort of tectonic uplifting of the cash-equity line to a plateau having an altitude set by the core's alpha return. The plateau's location along the risk spectrum is determined largely by the core's beta. The key here is the alpha return, since without a sufficient alpha boost, the efficient frontier would just collapse onto the cash-equity line.

The risk position of many portfolios is also illuminated by this model. As noted earlier, there are numerous reasons to move to risk positions beyond the cash line. However, once within the fixed core segment, the incentive to take on increased risk declines to a lower and relatively constant level. And when moving onto the equity extension, the risk-and-return incentive drops quite dramatically, often becoming negative, as in our base case example. Thus, in regard to risk-and-return tradeoffs, there is a seemingly irresistible incentive for long-term funds to move beyond the cash line, but an equally strong basis for not going further into the equity extension.

Broadly speaking, this three-part form describes the incremental slope structure of many efficient frontiers, even those developed with fewer heroic assumptions and having a more pronounced curvature. These boundaries establish the midsection of the fixed core segment in our example as forming a sweet spot on the efficient frontier. Within this region, the incremental risk-and-return tradeoff is a moderate incentive, but not a compelling basis, for seeking additional risk. Consequently, within this region, a more forceful role can be played by other considerations such as maximum allowable risk, peer group pressures, broad market benchmarks, and so forth. And so we should not be surprised to see most allocations nestled at risk positions lying somewhere within this fixed core segment.

CHANNEL RISK

Three important caveats are in order. The first is to clearly restate that these findings are all derived from a fixed return–covariance matrix that was chosen *strictly* for illustrative purposes only. As such, these expected return numbers should not be construed as any sort of forecast of asset class performance. And, of course, the asset allocations used as examples should not be viewed as recommended weightings. As noted at the outset, our objective here is to develop an analytical approach, rather than to be prescriptive in any way.

The second caveat is closely related to the dragon risk problem we examined in Chapter 3. Market assumptions for alpha core–type assets are generally more problematic than the return models for traditional swing assets. For many core-type asset classes, there can be special problems in projecting future returns on the basis of historical performance statistics. Since such asset classes may be in the process of becoming more institutionally accessed or increasingly securitized, it may even be arguable as to whether their basic return characteristics can be viewed as stable over time. In addition, survivorship and reporting biases can create artificial positive tilts. Moreover, with highly unstable return patterns, it can be quite difficult to differentiate alpha returns from beta-sourced returns. And then, for those assets in which the returns are intentionally asymmetric, any covariance-based methodology will be inherently misleading.

The third caveat is more subtle. The assets that comprise alpha cores often do not have liquid, investable vehicles that reliably reflect the fundamental returns of their asset class as a whole. The risk assessment for such assets should therefore include the channel uncertainty associated with the choice of the specific investment vehicle or management team that implements them (see Swensen 2000). This channel risk should be distinguished from the intrinsic volatility of the asset returns themselves in that added vehicle and manager risk will generally not be captured in a given covariance matrix.

RISK MITIGATION AND ASSET CLASS INCLUSION

The key point here is that the intrinsic random volatility of the asset class can usually be dealt with by its inclusion as only one component of an alpha core, a limit on the size of the alpha core, the alpha risk diversification from the other assets within the core, and the usual submergence of all alpha risk within a typically beta-dominated institutional portfolio. Thus, at the level of the overall portfolio, an individual asset's alpha volatility per se is not likely to become a major issue on either a long term or even a short term basis.

The optimal Sharpe ratio is attained when the portfolio contains some portion of *every* independent asset having a positive expected return, regardless of how large its volatility may be (Treynor and Fischer 1973). However, the key condition here is that any such asset class must have a truly positive expected return. In our framework, this means that the expected alpha return must be credibly positive.

Unfortunately, the vehicle and manager channel risk essentially reflects uncertainty regarding these expected alphas themselves. As such, some of this uncertainty will undoubtedly incorporate the prospect of ending up with a vehicle or a manager that may actually have negative expected alpha returns. This facet of risk is more complex than simple random-walk-like volatility. And this channel risk cannot be diversified or dominated away in the same fashion as the intrinsic volatility. If the expected expectation is either negative or positive but too low compared with the potential for negative outcomes, then there will be serious questions as to how much (or even whether) this asset class should be included in an alpha core. Obviously, a given sponsor may have some structural advantages relating to special knowledge, technical expertise, size (both larger and smaller size funds have certain advantages and disadvantages) and so forth, that could help shape this channel risk into a more favorable distribution. (Other sponsors may find themselves on the less fortunate side of such distributions.)

In any case, the basic message is that it is well worth devoting effort to try to peel apart these two different facets of risk. Since portfolio value is derived from positive alphas, it is well worth devoting considerable effort to improving the process of vehicle and manager vetting and selection. In the final analysis, individual fund sponsors would be well advised to be as realistic as possible in evaluating their ability to access a vehicle-and-manager combination that can credibly deliver, with sufficient assurance, that holy grail of a reliably positive alpha.

CONCLUSION

The complexities involved in the standard optimization can obscure the more intuitive decision process that should play a role in asset allocation. We believe our structural alpha-beta framework provides an opportunity to greatly simplify this decision process.

The key is to separate a portfolio's assets in two groups: swing assets and an alpha core. Swing assets are traditional liquid assets—U.S. equity, U.S. bonds, and cash—while the alpha core consists of all other assets that are subject to relatively tight portfolio constraints. Although the alpha core is often viewed as serving to diversify the volatility of the swing assets, its real benefit tends to be return enhancement.

After a fund determines the maximum acceptable limits for the nontraditional assets, these asset choices can be combined in some fashion into an alpha core. The composition of the alpha core will generally involve both intuitive and qualitative considerations that go well beyond the explicit quantitative characteristics embedded in the return-covariance matrix.

Once an acceptable alpha core has been formed, its risk-and-return characteristics can be transformed into basic alpha and beta terms. An important point is that any alpha core, regardless of its underlying asset class structure, can be approximately modeled using these alpha and beta parameters. While this model will not be theoretically exact, it will be a reasonable approximation for most allocation problems.

Since its basic role is to enhance return, the fund will typically try to keep the core at its predetermined maximum percentage. The final step in this process is to adjust the swing assets to attain the desired risk level for the overall fund.

These assumptions lead to a three-part efficient frontier: a cash-equity line, a fixed core segment itself, and an equity extension to 100 percent equity. Both the first and third segments are tied to the fixed points of cash and 100 percent equity, respectively. Consequently, the entire shape of the frontier is determined by the fixed core segment.

Not surprisingly, most allocations fall within the fixed core segment. One of the reasons for this has to do with the slope of the efficient frontier, which is essentially a measure of the incremental return per unit of risk. There appears to be an incentive for long-term funds to move beyond the cash line, and an equally strong basis for not pursuing the equity extension. These boundaries establish the fixed core segment as forming a sweet spot on the efficient frontier, where most real-life portfolios are likely to cluster.

The assets in the alpha core often do not have investment channels available that reliably reflect the fundamental returns of the asset class as a whole. Thus, in addition to the intrinsic return volatility embedded within these assets, there exists the channel uncertainty associated with the selection of the investment vehicle and the management team. At the overall portfolio level, any truly random volatility is likely to be dominated by the portfolio's beta effect. However, channel risk reflects an uncertainty regarding these expected alphas themselves and thus cannot be diversified away in the same way. Consequently, it is critically important to recognize that the same alpha returns may not be available, as passive investments, to all funds. Individual funds should try to be as realistic as possible in assessing their ability to evaluate, access, implement, and then effectively monitor any prospective sources of alpha return.

APPENDIX

Alpha Independence

The covariance σ_{ij}^2 between any two distinct assets, with random returns, $\tilde{r}_i$ and $\tilde{r}_j$, and mean returns, $\bar{r}_i$ and $\bar{r}_j$, can be expressed as

$$\sigma_{ij}^2 = E\left\{(\tilde{r}_i - \bar{r}_i)(\tilde{r}_j - \bar{r}_j)\right\} - E\left\{\tilde{r}_i - \bar{r}_i\right\} E\left\{\tilde{r}_j - \bar{r}_j\right\}$$

$$= E\left\{(\tilde{r}_i - \bar{r}_i)(\tilde{r}_j - \bar{r}_j)\right\}$$

If we let r_f be the risk-free rate, $\tilde{r}_e$ the return of the equity market, and $\tilde{\varepsilon}_i$ an orthogonal residual with $\bar{\varepsilon}_i = 0$, then

$$\sigma_{ij}^2 = E\left[(\alpha_i + \beta_i(\tilde{r}_e - r_f) + r_f + \tilde{\varepsilon}_i - \bar{r}_i)(\alpha_j + \beta_j(\tilde{r}_e - r_f) + r_f + \tilde{\varepsilon}_j - \bar{r}_j)\right]$$

$$\sigma_{ij}^2 = E\left[(\beta_i(\tilde{r}_e - r_f) + \tilde{\varepsilon}_i)(\beta_j(\tilde{r}_e - r_f) + \tilde{\varepsilon}_j)\right]$$

$$\sigma_{ij}^2 = E\left[(\beta_i(\tilde{r}_e - r_f)\tilde{\varepsilon}_j + \beta_j(\tilde{r}_e - r_f)\tilde{\varepsilon}_i + \beta_i\beta_j(\tilde{r}_e - \bar{r}_e)^2 + \tilde{\varepsilon}_i\tilde{\varepsilon}_j)\right]$$

$$= \beta_i E(\tilde{r}_e\tilde{\varepsilon}_j) + \beta_j E(\tilde{r}_e\tilde{\varepsilon}_i) + \beta_i\beta_j\sigma_e^2 + E(\tilde{\varepsilon}_i\tilde{\varepsilon}_j)$$

$$= \beta_i\beta_j\sigma_e^2 + \rho_{\varepsilon_i\varepsilon_j}\sigma_{\varepsilon_i}\sigma_{\varepsilon_j}$$

$$= \rho_{ie}\rho_{je}\sigma_{r_i}\sigma_{r_j} + \rho_{\varepsilon_i\varepsilon_j}\sigma_{\varepsilon_i}\sigma_{\varepsilon_j}$$

But since $\tilde{r}_e$ and $\tilde{\varepsilon}_i$ are orthogonal by construction,

$$\sigma_{r_i} = \sqrt{(\beta_i\sigma_e)^2 + \sigma_{\varepsilon_i}^2}$$

$$= \sqrt{(\rho_{ie}\sigma_{r_i})^2 + \sigma_{\varepsilon_i}^2}$$

and

$$\sigma_{\varepsilon_i} = \sqrt{\sigma_{r_i}^2 - \rho_{ie}^2\sigma_{r_i}^2}$$

$$= \sigma_{r_i}\sqrt{1 - \rho_{ie}^2}$$

We can express this result as

$$\sigma_{ij}^2 = \sigma_{r_i}\sigma_{r_j}\left[\rho_{ie}\rho_{je} + \rho_{\varepsilon_i\varepsilon_j}\sqrt{1 - \rho_{ie}^2}\sqrt{1 - \rho_{je}^2}\right]$$

and the correlation between r_i and r_j becomes

$$\rho_{ij} = \frac{\sigma_{ij}^2}{\sigma_{r_i}\sigma_{r_j}}$$

$$= \rho_{ie}\rho_{je} + \rho_{\varepsilon_i\varepsilon_j}\sqrt{1 - \rho_{ie}^2}\sqrt{1 - \rho_{je}^2}$$

From this formulation, one can see that even nonzero cross-correlations $\rho_{\varepsilon_i\varepsilon_j}$ will have relatively little effect on ρ_{ij} when either ρ_{ie} or ρ_{je} are high, that is, when either of the assets have a sufficiently large beta. Since this result holds for portfolios as well as individual assets, it suggests that the cross-correlations are not likely to play a major role when dealing with beta-dominated portfolios.

The Beta-Plus Volatility Approximation

The above result also has some interesting implications for the variance σ_p of mixtures of two assets (or two portfolios),

$$
\begin{aligned}
\sigma_p^2 &= \omega^2\sigma_i^2 + (1-\omega)^2\sigma_j^2 + 2\omega(1-\omega)\rho_{ij}\sigma_i\sigma_j \\
&= \omega^2\sigma_i^2 + (1-\omega)^2\sigma_j^2 + 2\omega(1-\omega)\sigma_i\sigma_j\left[\rho_{ie}\rho_{je} + \rho_{\varepsilon_i\varepsilon_j}\sqrt{1-\rho_{ie}^2}\sqrt{1-\rho_{je}^2}\right] \\
&= \omega^2\sigma_i^2 + (1-\omega)^2\sigma_j^2 + 2\omega(1-\omega)\left[\beta_i\beta_j\sigma_e^2 + \rho_{\varepsilon_i\varepsilon_j}\sigma_i\sigma_j\sqrt{1-\rho_{ie}^2}\sqrt{1-\rho_{je}^2}\right] \\
&= \omega^2\left[\beta_i^2\sigma_e^2 + \sigma_{\varepsilon_i}^2\right] + (1-\omega)^2\left[\beta_j^2\sigma_e^2 + \sigma_{\varepsilon_j}^2\right] \\
&\quad + 2\omega(1-\omega)\left[\beta_i\beta_j\sigma_e^2 + \rho_{\varepsilon_i\varepsilon_j}\sigma_{\varepsilon_i}\sigma_{\varepsilon_j}\right] \\
&= \left[\omega^2\beta_i^2 + 2\omega(1-\omega)\beta_i\beta_j + (1-\omega)^2\beta_j^2\right]\sigma_e^2 + \omega^2\sigma_{\varepsilon_i}^2 + (1-\omega)^2\sigma_{\varepsilon_j}^2 \\
&\quad + 2\omega(1-\omega)\rho_{\varepsilon_i\varepsilon_j}\sigma_{\varepsilon_i}\sigma_{\varepsilon_j} \\
&= \left[\omega\beta_i + (1-\omega)\beta_j\right]^2\sigma_e^2 + \omega^2\sigma_{\varepsilon_i}^2 + (1-\omega)^2\sigma_{\varepsilon_j}^2 + 2\omega(1-\omega)\rho_{\varepsilon_i\varepsilon_j}\sigma_{\varepsilon_i}\sigma_{\varepsilon_j} \\
&= \beta_p^2\sigma_e^2 + \omega^2\sigma_{\varepsilon_i}^2 + (1-\omega)^2\sigma_{\varepsilon_j}^2 + 2\omega(1-\omega)\rho_{\varepsilon_i\varepsilon_j}\sigma_{\varepsilon_i}\sigma_{\varepsilon_j}
\end{aligned}
$$

in which

$$
\beta_p = \omega\beta_i + (1-\omega)\beta_j
$$

And with beta-domination in either asset, that is, with either

$$
\sigma_{\varepsilon_i} \ll \beta_i\sigma_e \qquad or \qquad \sigma_{\varepsilon_j} \ll \beta_j\sigma_e
$$

we can use the beta-plus approximation

$$
\sigma_p^2 \cong \beta_p^2\sigma_e^2 + \omega^2\sigma_{\varepsilon_i}^2 + (1-\omega)^2\sigma_{\varepsilon_j}^2
$$

More generally, consider a portfolio with asset holdings having weight ω_i, beta β_i, and residual σ_{α_i}

We can define

$$\beta_p = \sum_i \omega_i \beta_i$$

and

$$\sigma_{\alpha_p}^2 = \sum_i \omega_i^2 \sigma_{\alpha_i}^2$$

The beta-plus approximation then becomes

$$\sigma_p^2 \cong \beta_p^2 \sigma_e^2 + \sigma_{\alpha_p}^2$$

corresponding to the assumption that $\rho_{\varepsilon_i \varepsilon_j} \cong 0$

The Efficient Frontier with a Fixed Alpha Core

Applying this approach to an alpha core with maximum weights ω and parameters α_c, β_c and σ_c, we can identify the risk-and-return location of the fixed core segment. The ending point of this segment will have the weight ω_c assigned to the core and $(1 - \omega_c)$ in equity. The return at this point will be:

$$r_{end} = \omega \left[\alpha_c + \beta_c (r_p) \right] + (1 - \omega)(r_p) + r_f$$
$$= \omega \alpha_c + (\omega \beta_c + 1 - \omega)(r_p) + r_f$$
$$= \omega \alpha_c + \beta_{end}(r_p) + r_f$$

in which $\beta_{end} = \omega \beta_c + (1 - \omega)$, (r_p) is the risk premium of equities and r_f is the cash return. For our base case values,

$$r_{end} = .6 * 3.32 + [.6 * .58 + 1 - .6] (5.75) + 1.50$$
$$= 7.78$$

Similarly, the risk at this endpoint will just be

$$\sigma_{end}^2 = \omega^2 \sigma_{\alpha_c}^2 + [\omega \beta_c + (1 - \omega)]^2 \sigma_e^2$$
$$= \omega^2 \sigma_{\alpha_c}^2 + [\beta_{end} \sigma_e]^2$$
$$= (.6)^2 (7.08)^2 + (.75)^2 (16.50)^2$$
$$\sigma_{end} = 13.01$$

The return at the starting point of the fixed core segment will be

$$r_{start} = \omega\left[\alpha_c + \beta_c(r_p)\right] + (1-\omega)(\alpha_B + \beta_B r_p) + r_f$$
$$= [\omega\alpha_c + (1-\omega)\alpha_B] + [\omega\beta_c + (1-\omega)\beta_B](r_p) + r_f$$
$$= [\omega\alpha_c + (1-\omega)\alpha_B] + \beta_{start}(r_p) + r_f$$

in which the subscript B refers to parameters for U.S. bonds and β_{start} is defined as $\omega\beta_c + (1-\omega)\beta_B$.

Thus,

$$r_{start} = [.6*3.32 + .4*1.47] + [.6*.58 + .4*.14](5.75) + 1.50$$
$$= 6.38$$

We can also calculate the risk at the starting point as

$$\sigma_{start}^2 = \omega^2\sigma_{\alpha_c}^2 + (1-\omega)^2\sigma_{\alpha_B}^2 + [\omega\beta_c + (1-\omega)\beta_B]^2\,\sigma_e^2$$
$$= \omega^2\sigma_{\alpha_c}^2 + (1-\omega)^2\sigma_{\alpha_B}^2 + [\beta_{start}\sigma_e]^2$$
$$= (.6)^2(7.08)^2 + (.4)^2(7.15)^2 + (.4)^2(16.5)^2$$
$$\sigma_{start} = 8.35$$

We can calculate the average slope of the fixed core segment as follows:

$$\frac{\Delta r}{\Delta\sigma} = \frac{r_{end} - r_{start}}{\sigma_{end} - \sigma_{start}}$$

In our base case, we obtain the following:

$$\frac{\Delta r}{\Delta\sigma} = \frac{7.78 - 6.38}{13.01 - 8.35}$$
$$= \frac{1.40}{4.66}$$
$$= .30$$

which is slightly less than the slope of the cash-equity line,

$$\frac{r_{end} - r_f}{\sigma_e - 0} = \frac{r_p}{\sigma_e}$$
$$= \frac{5.75}{16.50}$$
$$= .35$$

The equity extension starts with (σ_{end}, r_{end}), the ending point of the fixed core segment, and terminates at (σ_e, r_e), the 100 percent equity point. Thus, the average slope for the equity extension is:

$$\frac{\Delta r}{\Delta \sigma} = \frac{r_e - r_{end}}{\sigma_e - \sigma_{end}}$$

$$= \frac{7.25 - 7.78}{16.5 - 13.01}$$

$$= -\frac{.53}{3.49}$$

$$= -.15$$

Thus, in this particular case, the equity extension line has a negative slope and hence would not really be a viable component of the efficient frontier. More generally, one could have equity extensions with positive slopes. It turns out that the beta-leveraging factor can play a role in determining the α/β combination that leads to a positive or negative sloped equity extension. The extension's return difference is

$$\Delta r = r_e - r_{end}$$

A positive slope will occur only when $\Delta r > 0$,

$$r_e - r_{end} > 0$$
$$[r_p + r_f] - [\omega\alpha_c + (\omega\beta_c + 1 - \omega)(r_p) + r_f] > 0$$
$$r_p - [\omega\alpha_c + (\omega\beta_c + 1 - \omega)(r_p)] > 0$$
$$-\omega\alpha_c - \omega\beta_c(r_p) + \omega(r_p) > 0$$
$$\omega(r_p) > \omega(\alpha_c + \beta_c(r_p))$$
$$(r_p) - \beta_c(r_p) > \alpha_c$$
$$r_p > \frac{\alpha_c}{1 - \beta_c}$$

or, finally, for the equity extension to have a positive slope, we must have

$$r_p > BLF - \alpha_c$$

in which $BLF - \alpha_c = \dfrac{\alpha_c}{1 - \beta_c}$ is the beta-leveraging factor.

For our base case,

$$\alpha_c = 3.32 \quad \text{and} \quad \beta_c = .58 \text{ so that}$$

$$BLF - \alpha_c = \frac{3.32}{1 - .58}$$
$$= 7.81$$

which is considerably greater than the $(r_p) = 5.75$. Consequently, the equity extension is nonproductive in this particular case.

For alpha cores with lower values of α_c and/or β_c, this situation could well be reversed and the equity extension would then become a viable component of the efficient frontier.

The cash line extends from the cash point $(0, r_f)$ to the point of tangency with the fixed core segment. As noted in the text, this tangency could occur at either the beginning, the middle, or at the end of the fixed core segment. Because of the constraints, when the tangency is internal, it may not be always easy to find an analytical expression for the cash line. However, when the point of tangency is at the beginning (as in our base case) or at the end, the cash line's slope can be quickly found.

For our base case, the slope is simply found,

$$\frac{\Delta r}{\Delta \sigma} = \frac{r_{start} - r_f}{\sigma_{start} - 0}$$
$$= \frac{6.38 - 1.50}{8.35 - 0}$$
$$= \frac{4.88}{8.35}$$
$$= .58$$

REFERENCES

Markowitz, H. 1959. *Portfolio Selection: Efficient Diversification of Investments.* Hoboken, N.J.: John Wiley & Sons.

Swensen, D. F. 2000. *Pioneering Portfolio Management.* New York: The Free Press.

Treynor, J., and F. Black. 1973, January. "How to Use Security Analysis to Improve Portfolio Selection," *Journal of Business.*

CHAPTER 5

The Efficient Frontier with Bonds as the Risk-Free Base

*F*or good reasons, many long-term portfolios eschew cash in favor of bonds. Therefore, it may be useful to examine U.S. bonds as the alternative baseline to cash. A return-covariance matrix can be transformed into an alternative matrix, which describes returns and risks in a bond-relative framework.

A number of key findings follow from this transformation process. Because of bonds' relatively low volatility, there is little change in the risk characteristics of the nonbond assets. Overall volatility, revised beta value, and alpha-based volatility remain surprisingly close to the original cash-based values. There are major shifts, however, in the structural alpha-beta decomposition of the expected returns. The return premium for equity is significantly reduced when measured in relation to bonds, resulting in a much lower beta-related return for all higher-beta assets. This effect leads to a corresponding revision in the alphas, with the lower-beta assets having more significant alpha reductions. The net effect is that all the assets have lower risk-related returns, occurring in either the alpha or the beta component, depending on the asset's original beta value. Since the risk characteristics remain basically unchanged, and the return to each component is generally lower, the net result is a significantly flatter efficient frontier.

All these interactions lead to an interesting finding regarding the structure of alpha cores. Cores with high beta values will undergo less alpha compression under the move to bond-relative space. The volatility contribution of these higher-beta cores can be offset with a lower beta within the swing assets. Hence, all else being equal, for portfolios with prescribed volatility targets, one might want to tilt toward higher-beta alpha cores.

THE EQUITY RISK PREMIUM

The equity risk premium has, in recent years, been subject to particularly intense scrutiny. These discussions have been focused on diverse facets of the risk premium issue: its size, the relation of *ex post* experience to reasonable future expectations, the question of stability, the impact of liquidity and capital availability, the puzzle as to how large a premium investors should demand, the related issue of the premium's possible term structure over various horizons, the equity duration or sensitivity to changing interest rates—and the even more fundamental question of the baseline from which to measure the premium. In regard to this baseline measurement, numerous candidates have been put forward: short term cash, intermediate corporate bonds, Treasury bonds of various maturities, Treasury strips, inflation-linked bonds, some combination of various points along the yield curve, or even a base that could shift from high short rates in some years to higher long term rates in other years.

In this discussion, we strive to avoid taking a position on *any* of these important issues. And perhaps even more to the point, we do not express a view on the fundamental economic relationships that determine the premium's size or drive changes in its structure. Rather, our purpose here is simply to explore the structural alpha and beta analytics involved in moving from cash to the U.S. bond asset class as an alternative baseline. Our motivation here is simply knowing that some form of bonds is viewed by practitioners as the alternative lower-risk asset to equities, and thus long-term strategic allocations rarely entail the use of significant amounts of cash. Our purpose is simply to explore the alpha and beta effects implied by this common practice of having bonds serve as the fundamental baseline asset.

We have gone to some length, as stated in our initial caveat, to make it clear that our results are intended only to illustrate the methodology, and should not be taken as market forecasts or portfolio prescriptions.

BOND-RELATIVE ALPHAS AND BETAS

The first step is to transform the original return-covariance matrix into bond-relative terms. The details of this mathematical procedure are presented in the technical appendix to this chapter.

In its essence, the total return of every asset is now partitioned into the basic bond return plus a return premium relative to bonds. In this relative return space, bonds bear no risk, so that all risks are loaded onto the relative returns. For example, the total expected return for equity is 7.25 percent,

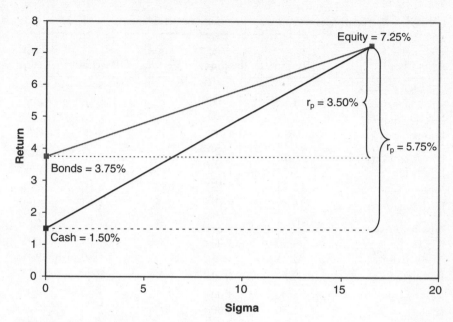

EXHIBIT 5.1 The Equity Risk Premium Relative to Bonds
Source: Morgan Stanley Research

which now leads to an expected relative return of 3.50 percent after deducting the baseline bond return of 3.75 percent. Since this relative return bears all the risk, the 3.50 percent difference will now serve as the equity risk premium (versus a premium of 5.75 percent in our original cash-based case, as shown in Exhibit 5.1). This 2.25 percent decline also extends across all the other asset classes (Exhibit 5.2), leading to major shifts in the premium percentage of each asset's total return (Exhibit 5.2).

The next step is to derive a revised beta reflecting the sensitivity of an asset's bond-relative return to this bond-relative equity. We designate the bond-relative values by a "*" so that β^* is the bond-relative analog to our original structural β. (Again, see the technical appendix.) With this transformation, the β^* of U.S. equity remains at 1, the β^* of U.S. bonds becomes zero, and it turns out that the β^* values of all other assets are only slightly changed (Exhibit 5.3).

While the betas themselves are little changed, there are major shifts in the beta-related returns as a result of the dramatic lowering of the equity risk premium. The percentage of the total return that is attributed to the beta return is reduced as well, with the reduction being much more significant for the higher-beta assets. However, because the higher-beta assets tend to have

EXHIBIT 5.2 Return Associated with Premium over Baseline

Asset Class	Return	Baseline	Total Return	Baseline	Total Return
High Beta Assets					
U.S. Equity	7.25	5.75	79%	3.50	48%
Private Equity	10.25	8.75	85%	6.50	63%
International Equity	7.25	5.75	79%	3.50	48%
Emerging Mkt Equity	9.25	7.75	84%	5.50	59%
Equity HF	5.75	4.25	74%	2.00	35%
Venture Capital	12.25	10.75	88%	8.50	69%
High Beta Average	**8.67**	**7.17**	**82%**	**4.92**	**54%**
Low Beta Assets					
REITS	6.50	5.00	77%	2.75	42%
Absolute Return	5.25	3.75	71%	1.50	29%
U.S. Bonds	3.75	2.25	60%	0.00	0%
Real Estate	5.50	4.00	73%	1.75	32%
Cash	1.50	0.00	0%	−2.25	NM
Commodities	5.25	3.75	71%	1.50	29%
Low Beta Average	**4.63**	**3.13**	**59%**	**0.88**	**26%**
Overall Average	**6.65**	**5.15**	**70%**	**2.90**	**41%**

Source: Morgan Stanley Research

greater total returns, this effect is more muted when viewed as a percentage of total return.

To help explain these results, the technical appendix develops a simple approximation for this change in beta return:

$$\text{Beta Return Change} = \beta \times (\text{Cash Return} - \text{Bond Return})$$

For the example of REITS, the difference in the β-return is a drop of $1.83 - 2.78 = -.95$ percent. Using the approximation formula, we obtain a reasonably close result,

$$\text{Beta Return Change} = (.48) \times (1.50 - 3.75)$$
$$= (.48) \times (-2.25)$$
$$= -1.02 \text{ percent}$$

EXHIBIT 5.3 Beta versus Beta*

Asset Class	β	β^*	β Ret	β^* Ret	β Ret/ Tot Ret	β^* Ret/ Tot Ret
High Beta Assets						
U.S. Equity	1.00	1.00	5.75	3.50	79%	48%
Private Equity	0.98	0.98	5.61	3.42	55%	33%
International Equity	0.77	0.79	4.42	2.75	61%	38%
Emerging Mkt Equity	0.76	0.78	4.39	2.73	47%	30%
Equity HF	0.66	0.68	3.78	2.39	66%	42%
Venture Capital	0.59	0.62	3.38	2.17	28%	18%
High Beta Average	**0.79**	**0.81**	**4.55**	**2.83**	**56%**	**35%**
Low Beta Assets						
REITS	0.48	0.52	2.78	1.83	43%	28%
Absolute Return	0.28	0.33	1.61	1.17	31%	22%
U.S. Bonds	0.14	0.00	0.78	0.00	21%	0%
Real Estate	0.07	0.14	0.42	0.50	8%	9%
Cash	0.00	0.08	0.00	0.26	0%	18%
Commodities	−0.29	−0.19	−1.66	−0.67	−32%	−13%
Low Beta Average	**0.11**	**0.15**	**0.66**	**0.52**	**12%**	**11%**
Overall Average	**0.45**	**0.48**	**2.61**	**1.67**	**34%**	**23%**

Source: Morgan Stanley Research

The original structural alphas referred to the returns above the cash-equity line. The new α^*s will now signify returns above the bond-equity line in bond-relative space. Exhibit 5.4 compares each original alpha with its bond-relative adjusted α^*.

The α^*s are lower than the original αs for all of the asset classes, with the size of the decrement dependent on the original beta. We get a negative α^* for two of the asset classes that previously had nonnegative αs. As with the β^* returns, the α^* returns now account for a smaller percentage of the total returns.

In contrast with the beta-return result, assets with lower betas now experience a bigger drop in their α^*s than assets with higher betas. As an example, Exhibit 5.5 displays the effects for private equity ($\beta = .98$) and real estate ($\beta = .07$). The alpha for private equity declines only slightly from 3.14 percent to 3.08 percent, while real estate incurs a major drop from 3.58 percent to 1.25 percent.

EXHIBIT 5.4 Alpha versus Alpha*

Asset Class	α	α^*	α/Tot Ret	α^*/Tot Ret
High Beta Assets				
U.S. Equity	0.00	0.00	0%	0%
Private Equity	3.14	3.08	31%	30%
International Equity	1.33	0.75	18%	10%
Emerging Mkt Equity	3.36	2.77	36%	30%
Equity HF	0.47	−0.39	8%	−7%
Venture Capital	7.37	6.33	60%	52%
High Beta Average	**2.61**	**2.09**	**26%**	**19%**
Low Beta Assets				
REITS	2.22	0.92	34%	14%
Absolute Return	2.14	0.33	41%	6%
U.S. Bonds	1.47	0.00	39%	0%
Real Estate	3.58	1.25	65%	23%
Cash	0.00	−2.51	0%	NM
Commodities	5.41	2.17	103%	41%
Low Beta Average	**2.47**	**0.36**	**47%**	**17%**
Overall Average	**2.54**	**1.22**	**36%**	**18%**

Source: Morgan Stanley Research

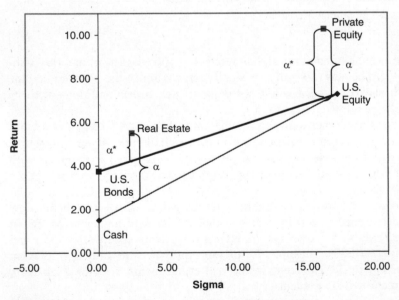

EXHIBIT 5.5 Private Equity and Real Estate Alpha Effect
Source: Morgan Stanley Research

Mathematically, this result follows immediately from the fact that, for all assets, the expected return premiums have all been reduced by exactly the same amount—the 2.25 percent difference between the returns from bonds and cash. These reduced premiums are then decomposed into an alpha component and a beta-related component. As we saw from Exhibit 5.3, the beta-related returns are more severely reduced for those assets having the higher betas. Since the combined reduction in the risk premium is the same for all assets, it follows that these high-beta assets must then have smaller declines in their α^* returns.

Indeed, it turns out that the alpha decline can be approximated by the formula,

$$\alpha^* - \alpha = (1 - \beta) \times (\text{Cash Return} - \text{Bond Return})$$

When this approximation is combined with the earlier one for the change in the β-related return, we have

$$(\alpha^* - \alpha) + (\beta^*_{\text{return}} - \beta_{\text{return}}) = [(1 - \beta) + \beta][\text{Cash Return} - \text{Bond Return}]$$

or

$$(\alpha^* + \beta^*_{\text{return}}) - (\alpha + \beta_{\text{return}}) = [\text{Cash Return} - \text{Bond Return}]$$

and finally,

$$(\text{Premium over Bonds}) - (\text{Premium over Cash})$$
$$= [\text{Cash Return} - \text{Bonds Return}]$$

Exhibit 5.6 demonstrates how the changes in the alpha and beta returns all add to the difference between the two baseline assets.

A more intuitive explanation is possible when the α^*s are interpreted as spreads over bonds or equities. Low-beta assets tend to be viewed as spread instruments over some fixed-income maturity. With U.S. bonds becoming the baseline asset and forming a more attractive substitute, these low-beta assets are now less desirable. In contrast, high-beta asset returns are viewed more as spreads over the underlying equity return and therefore largely retain their original alpha spreads.

RISK ANALYSIS

In the original cash-based space, we had the simplifying assumption that all assets are correlated with one another solely through their joint correlation

EXHIBIT 5.6 Change in Return Components

Asset Class	β Ret	β^* Ret	β Ret Change	α	α^*	α Ret Change	Tot Ret Change
High Beta Assets							
U.S. Equity	5.75	3.50	−2.25	0.00	0.00	0.00	−2.25
Private Equity	5.61	3.42	−2.19	3.14	3.08	−0.06	−2.25
International Equity	4.42	2.75	−1.67	1.33	0.75	−0.58	−2.25
Emerging Mkt Equity	4.39	2.73	−1.66	3.36	2.77	−0.59	−2.25
Equity HF	3.78	2.39	−1.39	0.47	−0.39	−0.86	−2.25
Venture Capital	3.38	2.17	−1.22	7.37	6.33	−1.03	−2.25
High Beta Average	**4.55**	**2.83**	**−1.73**	**2.61**	**2.09**	**−0.52**	**−2.25**
Low Beta Assets							
REITS	2.78	1.83	−0.95	2.22	0.92	−1.30	−2.25
Absolute Return	1.61	1.17	−0.44	2.14	0.33	−1.81	−2.25
U.S. Bonds	0.78	0.00	−0.78	1.47	0.00	−1.47	−2.25
Real Estate	0.42	0.50	0.08	3.58	1.25	−2.33	−2.25
Cash	0.00	0.26	0.26	0.00	−2.51	−2.51	−2.25
Commodities	−1.66	−0.67	0.99	5.41	2.17	−3.24	−2.25
Low Beta Average	**0.66**	**0.52**	**−0.14**	**2.47**	**0.36**	**−2.11**	**−2.25**
Overall Average	**2.61**	**1.67**	**−0.93**	**2.54**	**1.22**	**−1.32**	**−2.25**

Source: Morgan Stanley Research

with equities. In bond-relative space, the relative return measure is an asset's return less that of bonds. Consequently, the new variance must incorporate the variance introduced by bonds. (Again, see the technical appendix for the detailed formulation.) The net results are presented in Exhibit 5.7, and one can see that the shift from σ to σ^* may be sometimes positive and sometimes negative. The shift, in any case, however, is generally quite modest. The two exceptions are bonds and cash. Because the bond return is deducted from the asset return in this new space, cash takes on bond's volatility while the volatility of bonds relative to themselves is just zero.

With the estimates for β^* and σ^*, we can determine the risk σ_α^* associated with α^* from the completion formula,

$$\sigma_\alpha^{*2} = \sqrt{(\sigma^*)^2 - (\beta^* \sigma_e^*)^2}$$

As shown in Exhibit 5.8, σ_α^* increases for all of the assets. The effect is somewhat more pronounced for assets with low betas.

EXHIBIT 5.7 Volatility versus Volatility*

Asset Class	σ	σ*	% Change
High Beta Assets			
U.S. Equity	16.50	15.95	−3.4%
Private Equity	23.00	22.65	−1.5%
International Equity	19.50	19.48	−0.1%
Emerging Mkt Equity	28.00	27.99	0.0%
Equity HF	12.75	13.04	2.3%
Venture Capital	27.75	27.98	0.8%
High Beta Average	**21.25**	**21.18**	**−0.3%**
Low Beta Assets			
REITS	14.50	15.19	4.7%
Absolute Return	9.25	11.00	18.9%
U.S. Bonds	7.50	0.00	NM
Real Estate	12.00	13.96	16.3%
Cash	0.00	7.50	NM
Commodities	19.00	20.94	10.2%
Low Beta Average	**10.38**	**11.43**	**12.6%**
Overall Average	**15.81**	**16.31**	**4.8%**

Source: Morgan Stanley Research

We have previously used the alpha Sharpe ratios as a gauge of incremental return per level of risk. Since our adjusted numbers result in generally lower values for α^* and higher values for σ_α^*, the alpha Sharpe ratios will obviously all be reduced (Exhibit 5.9). For low-beta assets such as absolute return, real estate, and commodities, the decline in Sharpe ratios is quite severe. On the other hand, for high-beta assets such as Private Equity, the α-Sharpe ratio remains virtually unchanged (Exhibit 5.10).

PORTFOLIO LEVEL ANALYSIS

With the asset classes now decomposed in terms of their individual risk-and-return characteristics, we can apply this analysis to the portfolio level.

We can see from Exhibit 5.11 that the risk structure of the portfolios remains relatively the same in the new space: There is little change in the portfolio betas or the portfolio sigmas. Even with the assumed independence

EXHIBIT 5.8 Alpha Volatility versus Alpha Volatility*

Asset Class	σ_α	$\sigma_\alpha{}^*$	% Change
High Beta Assets			
U.S. Equity	0.00	0.00	NM
Private Equity	16.43	16.43	0.0%
International Equity	14.82	14.92	0.7%
Emerging Mkt Equity	25.00	25.07	0.2%
Equity HF	6.72	7.18	6.9%
Venture Capital	25.99	26.17	0.7%
High Beta Average	**14.83**	**14.96**	**1.7%**
Low Beta Assets			
REITS	12.11	12.70	4.9%
Absolute Return	8.01	9.62	20.1%
U.S. Bonds	7.15	0.00	NM
Real Estate	11.94	13.77	15.4%
Cash	0.00	7.40	NM
Commodities	18.40	20.72	12.6%
Low Beta Average	**9.60**	**10.70**	**13.2%**
Overall Average	**12.21**	**12.83**	**6.8%**

Source: Morgan Stanley Research

of residuals in the original cash-based framework, the asset residuals will now be correlated in bond-relative space. This residual correlation could theoretically complicate the portfolio analysis. It turns out, however, that the beta-based volatility continues to be the overwhelmingly dominant source of risk for all portfolios. Thus, even the now-correlated alpha risks remain small and, at the portfolio level, are still swamped by the beta risk.

The absolute level of return is not changed, but there are major shifts in the composition of returns. The alpha and beta returns have become a much smaller percentage of total return, with the baseline return of bonds accounting for a higher percentage.

THE ALPHA CORE

Exhibit 5.12 focuses on Portfolio C, abstracts its alpha core, expands it to a 100 percent-level portfolio, and then analyzes how its parameters change in a bond-relative space.

EXHIBIT 5.9 The Effect on Sharpe Ratios

Asset Class	Sharpe Ratio	Sharpe Ratio*	Change
High Beta Assets			
U.S. Equity	0.35	0.22	−0.13
Private Equity	0.19	0.19	0.00
International Equity	0.09	0.05	−0.04
Emerging Mkt Equity	0.13	0.11	−0.02
Equity HF	0.07	−0.05	−0.12
Venture Capital	0.28	0.24	−0.04
High Beta Average	**0.19**	**0.13**	**−0.06**
Low Beta Assets			
REITS	0.18	0.07	−0.11
Absolute Return	0.27	0.03	−0.23
U.S. Bonds	0.20	NM	NM
Real Estate	0.30	0.09	−0.21
Cash	NA	−0.34	NM
Commodities	0.29	0.10	−0.19
Low Beta Average	**0.25**	**−0.01**	**−0.26**
Overall Average	**0.22**	**0.07**	**−0.15**

Source: Morgan Stanley Research

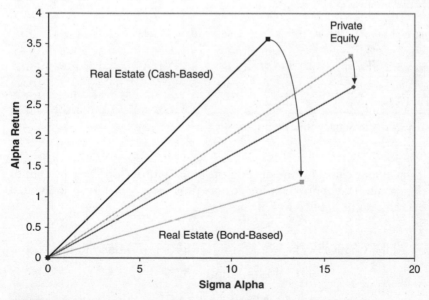

EXHIBIT 5.10 Sharpe Ratio Effect: Private Equity and Real Estate
Source: Morgan Stanley Research

EXHIBIT 5.11 Portfolio Summary

	A	A*	B	B*	S	S*	C	C*
Core Assets								
International Equity					20%	20%	15%	15%
Emerging Mkt Equity							5%	5%
Absolute Return							10%	10%
Venture Capital							10%	10%
Private Equity							10%	10%
Real Estate							10%	10%
Total Core Assets %	0%	0%	0%	0%	20%	20%	60%	60%
Swing Assets								
U.S. Equity	60%	60%	60%	60%	45%	45%	20%	20%
U.S. Bonds			40%	40%	35%	35%	20%	20%
Cash	40%	40%						
Total Swing Assets %	100%	100%	100%	100%	80%	80%	40%	40%
Expected Return	4.95	4.95	5.85	5.85	6.03	6.03	7.08	7.08
Beta (β^*)	0.60	0.63	0.65	0.60	0.65	0.61	0.57	0.56
Baseline Rate	1.50	3.75	1.50	3.75	1.50	3.75	1.50	3.75
Beta Return	3.45	2.21	3.76	2.10	3.75	2.12	3.29	1.98
Alpha (α^*)	0.00	−1.01	0.59	0.00	0.78	0.15	2.28	1.35
Baseline Return %	30%	76%	26%	64%	25%	62%	21%	53%
Beta Return %	70%	45%	64%	36%	62%	35%	46%	28%
Alpha Return %	0%	−20%	10%	0%	13%	2%	32%	19%
Sigma Alpha ($\sigma_\alpha{}^*$)	0.00	2.96	2.86	0.00	3.88	2.98	4.48	4.35
Beta Sigma ($\beta^*\sigma_e{}^*$)	9.90	10.05	10.80	9.57	10.75	9.68	9.45	9.00
Exact Sigma (σ^*)	9.90	10.47	11.17	9.57	11.43	9.69	10.83	9.19
Beta Sigma as % of Total Risk	100.0%	95.9%	96.7%	100.0%	94.0%	100.0%	87.3%	97.9%

Source: Morgan Stanley Research

One major change is the drop in the alpha return from 3.32 percent to 2.25 percent. The approximation formula for the α^* change in individual assets can also be applied to C's core,

$$\text{Alpha Change} = (1 - \beta_{\text{original}}) \times (\text{Cash Return} - \text{Bond Return})$$
$$= (1 - .58) \times (1.50 - 3.75)$$
$$= -.96 \text{ percent}$$

EXHIBIT 5.12 Alpha Core Analysis

	β	β^*	α	α^*	C	C*	Change
Core Assets							
International Equity	0.77	0.79	1.33	0.75	25%	25%	0%
Emerging Mkt Equity	0.76	0.78	3.36	2.77	8%	8%	0%
Absolute Return	0.28	0.33	2.14	0.33	17%	17%	0%
Venture Capital	0.59	0.62	7.37	6.33	17%	17%	0%
Private Equity	0.98	0.98	3.14	3.08	17%	17%	0%
Real Estate	0.07	0.14	3.58	1.25	17%	17%	0%
					100%	100%	
Expected Return					8.13	8.13	0.00
Beta (β^*)					0.58	0.61	0.03
Baseline Rate					1.50	3.75	2.25
Beta Return					3.31	2.13	−1.18
Alpha (α^*)					3.32	2.25	−1.07
Baseline Return %					18%	46%	28%
Beta Return %					41%	26%	−15%
Alpha Return %					41%	28%	−13%
Sigma Alpha ($\sigma_\alpha{}^*$)					7.08	7.26	0.18
Beta Sigma ($\beta^*\sigma_e{}^*$)					9.49	9.68	0.19
Exact Sigma (σ^*)					11.84	12.10	0.26
Beta Sigma as % of Total Risk					80.2%	80.0%	−0.1%
Return Contribution from High Beta Assets							
Beta Return					2.97	1.85	−1.12
Alpha					2.36	1.99	−0.38
Return Contribution from Low Beta Assets							
Beta Return					0.34	0.28	−0.06
Alpha					0.95	0.26	−0.69

Source: Morgan Stanley Research

which is very close to the exact value of 1.07 percent. Similarly, the approximation formula for the beta return provides an estimate of

$$\text{Beta-Return Change} = \beta \times (\text{Cash Return-Bond Return})$$
$$= .55 \times (-2.25)$$
$$= -1.31 \text{ percent}$$

versus the exact decline of –1.18 percent. (The deviation is due to the β values not coinciding exactly with the β^* values.)

By separating the alpha core into two groups—the high-beta assets (IE, EME, VC, and PE) and low-beta assets (AR, RE)—we can observe the changes that occur in the respective components of their return. The high-beta assets are responsible for almost all of the decline in total beta return, while the low-beta assets account for the majority of the drop in the alpha return.

EFFICIENT FRONTIER ANALYSIS

In Exhibit 5.13, we show how the effective efficient frontier could be portrayed as a three-part segment, with the middle portion representing a fixed alpha core together with varying percentages of equity and bonds. The alpha level embedded in the fixed core plays an important role in determining the distance that this segment is uplifted above the cash/equity line.

Exhibit 5.14 depicts the efficient frontier in bond-relative space. Overall, the frontier is flatter, reflecting a decreased payoff for taking risk beyond the bond baseline. In particular, there is no incentive for using cash, since cash

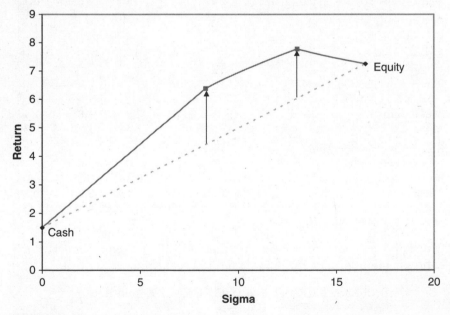

EXHIBIT 5.13 The Alpha Uplift Frontier with Cash as Risk-Free Base
Source: Morgan Stanley Research

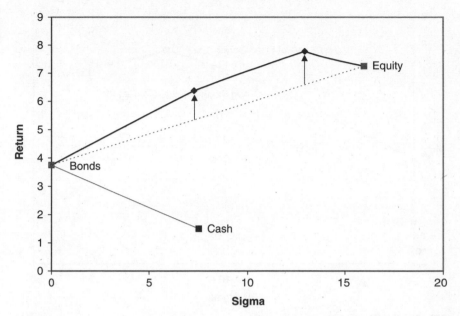

EXHIBIT 5.14   The Alpha Uplift Frontier with Bonds as Risk-Free Base
Source: Morgan Stanley Research

is now burdened with an unappetizing combination of a lower return *and* a significant risk exposure (relative to bonds). In essence, this means that cash drops off the efficient frontier (literally, as well as figuratively!).

In Exhibit 5.15, the cash-based and bond-based frontiers are plotted together. The two frontiers are remarkably close once one moves on to the fixed core segment. This convergence is simply a reflection of the re-basing having left each asset's *total* return unchanged and led to only modest changes in their beta-related risk. Along the fixed-core segment, the beta-related risk continues to be the dominant component of the total risk. It is this combination of the unchanged total return and the roughly similar total risk that drives this part of the frontier into near coincidence.

The major divergence between the two frontiers occurs in the first segment, and this effect basically reflects the replacement of cash with bonds as the minimum-risk baseline asset. There is also a leftward shift in the starting point of the fixed core segment. This shift to a lower-risk position arises from the risk reduction in the 40 percent bond portfolio as one moves into the bond-relative framework.

Exhibit 5.15's plot of the two frontiers unfortunately tends to obscure the significant differences in the risk-and-return incentives. In Exhibit 5.16,

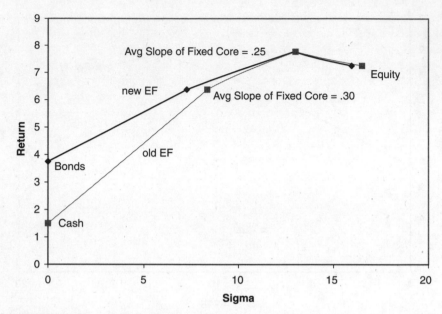

EXHIBIT 5.15 Bond-Relative and Cash-Relative Efficient Frontiers
Source: Morgan Stanley Research

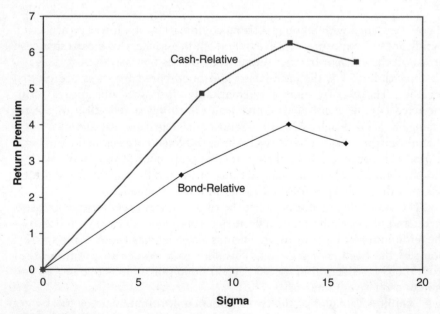

EXHIBIT 5.16 Risk Premium Frontiers
Source: Morgan Stanley Research

we have revised the diagram so that each frontier is now presented in terms of its return *premium* above its respective baseline. The downshift and flattening of the bond-relative case is now much more evident.

The difference between these two premium curves can best be explained on a segment-by-segment basis. In the first segment, the cash-based frontier rises rapidly as low-yielding cash is replaced with the higher-returning 60 percent core–40 percent bonds mixture. In contrast, the bond-relative frontier already has bonds as its starting point, resulting in a more moderate ascent to the 60 percent core–40 percent bond point. Once the fixed core segment is reached, the two frontiers are composed of exactly the same assets. In the bond-relative case, however, these assets are subject to the 2.25 percent drop in their return premiums. As a consequence, the second and third segment of the two frontiers are virtually parallel, with the bond-relative frontier falling well below the cash-based case. Since bonds serve as a much more appetizing minimum-risk alternative, the incentive for taking risk is generally lower across all risk levels.

While the return premium decline is roughly comparable across the second and third frontier segments, there are some interesting distinctions as one delves more deeply into the alpha and beta components. With the return premium for 100 percent equities dropping by the bond-cash gap, the beta return for all other assets declines accordingly. Naturally, as shown earlier, the higher-beta assets suffer the most in regard to their beta return. In contrast, the alpha returns take up the difference, so that the largest alpha declines occur with the low-beta assets.

THE ALPHA EFFECT

To isolate this effect, Exhibit 5.17 shows only the alpha returns for the two frontiers. The cash-based fixed core segment declines because bonds with a positive alpha are being replaced by equity with its solely beta-based return. By the same token, in the bond-relative fixed-core segment, the bond alpha has been removed so that this segment is now perfectly flat, with a constant alpha derived from the fixed 60 percent weight of the alpha core.

This result raises the further question as to whether an alpha core with higher betas would show better alpha returns. To explore this possibility, we consider an alternative alpha core with the same cash-based alpha but with a higher beta value of .80. The two frontiers—the higher-beta core and the original core—are then plotted together in Exhibit 5.18 in bond-relative terms. The higher-beta shifts the fixed core segment slightly to the right, but it also provides a significantly greater α^* uplift. While this higher-beta core portion is shifted into higher-risk territory, one could choose different swing asset mixtures to achieve a given level of total portfolio risk. Thus,

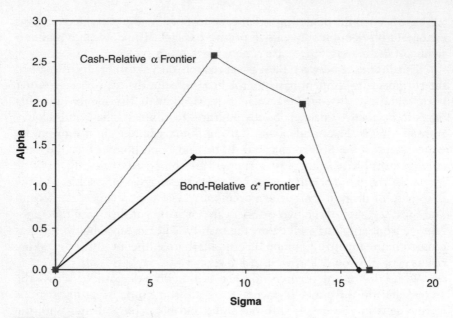

EXHIBIT 5.17 Alpha Frontiers
Source: Morgan Stanley Research

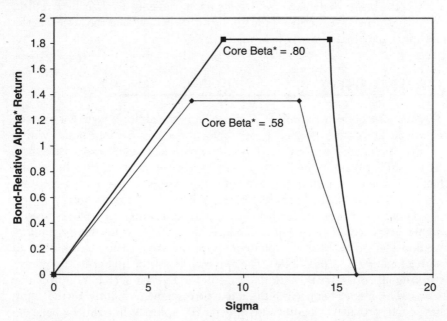

EXHIBIT 5.18 Bond-Relative Alpha* Frontiers with Different Core Beta*s
Source: Morgan Stanley Research

for example, to maintain the total risk at 10 percent, one could choose the higher-beta core together with a lower explicit equity weight within the swing assets.

Thus, as one moves to baseline assets such as bonds with higher expected returns, it would seem that better frontiers could be achieved by combining low explicit equity weights with higher-beta core ingredients. While this may follow as a strictly mathematical result, however, our earlier warning should be recalled that this analysis has not really changed any of the asset returns, but only recast how they are measured within a bond-relative framework. A more thorough economic analysis would have to address the underlying return dynamics that drive the fundamental interactions across all assets.

APPENDIX

Transformation to an Alpha*/Beta* Structure in Bond-Relative Space

When the cash return r_f forms the risk-free baseline, the return r_i of an asset can be decomposed into

$$\tilde{r}_i = (\alpha_i + r_f + \tilde{\varepsilon}_i) + \beta_i(\tilde{r}_e - r_f)$$

in which $\tilde{r}_e$ is the equity return and $\tilde{\varepsilon}_i$ is variable orthogonal to $\tilde{r}_e$ such that

$$E\{\tilde{\varepsilon}_i\} = 0$$
$$E\{\tilde{\varepsilon}_i\tilde{r}_e\} = 0$$

and we define

$$E\{\tilde{\varepsilon}_i^2\} = \sigma_{\alpha_i}$$

We make the assumption that the assets are correlated only through the equity factor,

$$E\{\tilde{\varepsilon}_i\tilde{\varepsilon}_j\} = 0 \qquad i \neq j$$

The regression coefficient β_i can then be determined from

$$\beta_i = \frac{Cov(\tilde{r}_i, \tilde{r}_e)}{Var(\tilde{r}_e)}$$
$$= \frac{Cov\{(\tilde{r}_i - r_f), (\tilde{r}_e - r_f)\}}{Var\{(\tilde{r}_e - r_f)\}}$$

By analogy, when $\tilde{r}_B$ becomes the baseline, we form the excess relative return, $\tilde{z}_i$,

$$
\begin{aligned}
\tilde{z}_i &= \tilde{r}_i - \tilde{r}_B \\
&= (\tilde{r}_i - r_f) - (\tilde{r}_B - r_f) \\
&= (\alpha_i + \tilde{\varepsilon}_i) - (\alpha_B + \tilde{\varepsilon}_B) + (\beta_i - \beta_B)(\tilde{r}_e - r_f) \\
&= (\alpha_i - \alpha_B) + (\beta_i - \beta_B)(\tilde{r}_e - r_f) + (\tilde{\varepsilon}_i - \tilde{\varepsilon}_B)
\end{aligned}
$$

and we can define $\beta_i{}^*$ as

$$
\begin{aligned}
\beta_i{}^* &= \frac{Cov\left\{(\tilde{r}_i - \tilde{r}_B),\, (\tilde{r}_e - \tilde{r}_B)\right\}}{Var\left\{(\tilde{r}_e - \tilde{r}_B)\right\}} \\
&= \frac{Cov\left\{(\tilde{z}_i,\, \tilde{z}_e\right\}}{Var\left\{(\tilde{z}_e\right\}}
\end{aligned}
$$

Proceeding with the new bond-relative returns, $\tilde{z}_i$ we have

$$
\bar{z}_i = (\alpha_i - \alpha_B) + (\beta_i - \beta_B)(\bar{r}_e - r_f)
$$

and

$$
\begin{aligned}
E\left\{\tilde{z}_i \tilde{z}_j\right\} &= (\alpha_i - \alpha_B)\left[(\alpha_i - \alpha_B) + (\beta_i - \beta_B)(\bar{r}_e - r_f)\right] \\
&\quad + (\beta_i - \beta_B)\left[(\alpha_j - \alpha_B)(\bar{r}_e - r_f) + (\beta_j - \beta_B)E\left\{(\tilde{r}_e - r_f)^2\right\}\right] \\
&\quad + E\left\{(\tilde{\varepsilon}_i - \tilde{\varepsilon}_B)(\tilde{\varepsilon}_j - \tilde{\varepsilon}_B)\right\} \\
&= (\alpha_i - \alpha_B)(\alpha_j - \alpha_B) + (\bar{r}_e - r_f)\left[(\alpha_i - \alpha_B)(\beta_j - \beta_B)\right. \\
&\quad \left. + (\alpha_j - \alpha_B)(\beta_i - \beta_B)\right] + E\left\{(\tilde{r}_e - r_f)^2\right\}\left[(\beta_i - \beta_B)(\beta_j - \beta_B)\right] \\
&\quad + E\left\{\tilde{\varepsilon}_i \tilde{\varepsilon}_j - \tilde{\varepsilon}_i \tilde{\varepsilon}_B - \tilde{\varepsilon}_j \tilde{\varepsilon}_B + \tilde{\varepsilon}_B^2\right\} \\
&= E\{\tilde{z}_i\}\, E\left\{\tilde{z}_j\right\} - (\beta_i - \beta_B)(\beta_j - \beta_B)(\bar{r}_e - r_f)^2 \\
&\quad + E\left\{(\tilde{r}_e - r_f)^2\right\}\left[(\beta_i - \beta_B)(\beta_j - \beta_B)\right] \\
&\quad + E\left\{\tilde{\varepsilon}_i \tilde{\varepsilon}_j - \tilde{\varepsilon}_i \tilde{\varepsilon}_B - \tilde{\varepsilon}_j \tilde{\varepsilon}_B + \tilde{\varepsilon}_B^2\right\}
\end{aligned}
$$

and

$$
\begin{aligned}
Cov(\tilde{z}_i,\, \tilde{z}_j) &= E\left\{\tilde{z}_i \tilde{z}_j\right\} - E\{\tilde{z}_i\}\, E\left\{\tilde{z}_j\right\} \\
&= (\beta_i - \beta_B)(\beta_j - \beta_B)\left[E\left\{(\tilde{r}_e - r_f)^2\right\} - (\bar{r}_e - r_f)^2\right] \\
&\quad + E\left\{\tilde{\varepsilon}_i \tilde{\varepsilon}_j - \tilde{\varepsilon}_i \tilde{\varepsilon}_B - \tilde{\varepsilon}_j \tilde{\varepsilon}_B + \tilde{\varepsilon}_B^2\right\} \\
&= (\beta_i - \beta_B)(\beta_j - \beta_B)\sigma_e^2 + E\left\{\tilde{\varepsilon}_i \tilde{\varepsilon}_j - \tilde{\varepsilon}_i \tilde{\varepsilon}_B - \tilde{\varepsilon}_j \tilde{\varepsilon}_B + \tilde{\varepsilon}_B^2\right\}
\end{aligned}
$$

At this point, we must be careful in assessing the last term for the different cases, in which $i \neq j$ versus $i = j$ and i or $j = B$ or e.

Since

$$E\left\{\tilde{\varepsilon}_i^2\right\} = \sigma_{\alpha_i}^2$$

$$E\left\{\tilde{\varepsilon}_i\right\} = 0$$

and by assumption

$$E\left\{\tilde{\varepsilon}_i \tilde{\varepsilon}_j\right\} = 0 \quad i \neq j$$

we obtain the following cases,

$$Cov(z_i, z_j) = (\beta_i - \beta_B)(\beta_j - \beta_B)\sigma_e^2 + \begin{cases} 0 & i \text{ or } j = B \\ \sigma_{\alpha_B}^2 & i \text{ or } j = e \\ \sigma_{\alpha_B}^2 & i \neq j, i \neq B, e, j \neq B, e \\ \sigma_{\alpha_i}^2 + \sigma_{\alpha_B}^2 & i = j, i \neq B, e \end{cases}$$

$$= \begin{cases} 0 & i \text{ or } j = B \\ (1 - \beta_B)(\beta_j - \beta_B)\sigma_e^2 + \sigma_{\alpha_B}^2 & i = e \\ (1 - \beta_B)(\beta_i - \beta_B)\sigma_e^2 + \sigma_{\alpha_B}^2 & j = e \\ (\beta_i - \beta_B)(\beta_j - \beta_B)\sigma_e^2 + \sigma_{\alpha_B}^2 & i \neq j, i \neq B, e, j \neq B, e \\ (\beta_i - \beta_B)^2 \sigma_e^2 + \sigma_{\alpha_i}^2 + \sigma_{\alpha_B}^2 & i = j, i \neq B, e \end{cases}$$

The presence of the $\sigma_{\alpha_B}^2$ term implies that, unlike the original cash-based assumptions, the residuals for the $\tilde{z}_i$ will generally have some level of correlation. (However, as before, for the typical portfolio that is overwhelmingly beta-dominated, this residual correlation will not have a material effect on its risk characteristics.)

Hence, for the regression coefficient β^* of $\tilde{z}_i$ on $\tilde{z}_e$

$$\beta^*(z_i, z_e) = \frac{Cov(\tilde{z}_i, \tilde{z}_e)}{Var(\tilde{z}_e)} = \frac{(1 - \beta_B)(\beta_i - \beta_B)\sigma_e^2 + \sigma_{\alpha_B}^2}{(1 - \beta_B)^2 \sigma_e^2 + \sigma_{\alpha_B}^2} \quad i \neq e, B$$

$$= \frac{(\beta_i - \beta_i\beta_B - \beta_B + \beta_B^2)\sigma_e^2 + \sigma_{\alpha_B}^2}{(1 - \beta_B)^2 \sigma_e^2 + \sigma_{\alpha_B}^2}$$

$$= \frac{(\beta_i - \beta_B - \beta_i\beta_B)\sigma_e^2 + \sigma_B^2}{(1 - 2\beta_B)\sigma_e^2 + \sigma_B^2}$$

in which

$$\sigma_B^2 = \beta_B^2 \sigma_e^2 + \sigma_{\alpha_B}^2$$

While we have been careful to distinguish the cases where $i \neq e$ or $i \neq B$, it turns out that this expression holds for any $i \neq B$, since

$$\beta^*(z_e, z_e) = \frac{(1 - \beta_B - 1 * \beta_B)\sigma_e^2 + \sigma_B^2}{(1 - 2\beta_B)\sigma_e^2 + \sigma_B^2}$$

$$= 1$$

For the case when $i = B$, we must go back to the preceding result,

$$Cov(z_B, z_j) = 0$$

so that

$$\beta^*(z_B, z_e) = 0$$

Approximating the Change in Alpha and Beta Returns

The beta-based return on an asset is defined as

$$\beta_{\text{return}} = \beta(\bar{r}_e - r_f)$$

or in bond-relative space,

$$\beta^*_{\text{return}} = \beta^*(\bar{r}_e - \bar{r}_B)$$

so that the difference becomes

$$(\beta^*_{\text{return}}) - (\beta_{\text{return}}) = \beta^*(\bar{r}_e - \bar{r}_B) - \beta(\bar{r}_e - r_f)$$

$$\cong \beta(r_f - \bar{r}_B),$$

in which we can treat $\beta^* \cong \beta$

Similarly, the α return can be expressed as

$$\alpha = (\bar{r} - r_f) - \beta(\bar{r}_e - r_f)$$

and by analogy

$$\alpha^* - \alpha = (\bar{r} - \bar{r}_B) - \beta^*(\bar{r}_e - \bar{r}_B) - \left\{ (\bar{r} - r_f) - \beta(\bar{r}_e - r_f) \right\}$$
$$\cong (r_f - \bar{r}_B) - \beta(r_f - \bar{r}_B)$$
$$\cong (1 - \beta)(r_f - \bar{r}_B)$$

and

$$(\alpha^* + \beta^*{}_{\text{return}}) - (\alpha + \beta_{\text{return}}) \cong [(1 - \beta) + \beta] \lfloor r_f - \bar{r}_B \rfloor$$
$$\cong \lfloor r_f - \bar{r}_B \rfloor$$

CHAPTER 6

Expanding the Alpha Core

*M*ost *institutional funds are beta-dominated in the sense that roughly 90 percent of their volatility risk derives from their exposure to U.S. equities. Incremental inclusion of alternative asset classes can act as allocation alphas, providing enhanced expected returns with relatively modest increases in total fund volatility.*

These allocation alphas arise from the covariance structure assumed for the policy portfolio, and as such are quite distinct from the more zero-sum incremental alphas associated with active management. Active alphas may either be portable or bound to their home-asset class. If a fund believes there are positive active alphas bound to a given asset class (even with the associated risks), then both active and allocation alphas should be incorporated into evaluating the asset class's potential role within the alpha core.

As long as the fund remains beta dominated, a moderately sized core based on bound-active alphas and allocation alphas, together with a potential overlay of portable alphas, should have a relatively minor impact on the fund's total volatility. Any positive return enhancement that results will therefore provide a very attractive risk-and-return ratio at the margin.

INHERENT CONSTRAINTS ON ALTERNATIVE ASSETS

Alternative asset classes appear to present a fund with the opportunity for return enhancement or risk diversification. However, in virtually all institutional portfolios of any size, there are a variety of explicit or, more often, implicit constraints placed upon the percentage that can be allocated to each asset class as well as to the general alternative category. These limitations have a major significance for alternatives' impact on the return and risk of the overall portfolio, especially when these returns are decomposed into alpha and beta components. Both alpha- and beta-based returns are additive and directly enhance the overall portfolio return (it should be pointed out that *enhancement* depends on the alphas having truly positive expected returns).

However, with respect to the risk dimension, the situation is somewhat more complex. A common perception is that alternatives diversify the portfolio's volatility risk. In fact, this is rarely the case to any significant degree. First of all, many alternatives have a significant level of correlation with the U.S. equity market, resulting in an implicit beta exposure. When this implicit beta is added to the explicit allocation to U.S. equities, it turns out that a wide spectrum of seemingly diversified portfolios all have roughly similar beta values, falling in the range of 0.50 to 0.65. Given the intrinsic volatility of U.S. equities, this common beta value helps explain the rather surprising result that the majority of U.S. pension funds, endowments, and foundations have volatilities falling into the same 10- to 11-percent range, with the beta value typically accounting for more than 90 percent of this total volatility.

Traditional portfolios with 50 to 65 percent weight in equities are overtly beta dominated. However, because of their implicit beta components, beta dominance also characterizes many highly diversified funds, even those with U.S. equity percentages as low as 20 percent. The net result is that the beta-dominated volatility of these funds overrides any alpha-based volatility derived from their alternative allocations. In other words, the alpha volatility is virtually totally submerged by the effective beta risk. The good news here is that these alpha sources can add to the fund's return, with their volatility having only a minuscule contribution to the overall fund volatility. The bad news is that moderate allocations of the alternatives provide little of the oft-cited diversification benefits—at least in regard to any expected reduction in volatility.

If alternative assets can then add to total portfolio return with only a minimal increase in total volatility, why shouldn't funds devote an increasing allocation to such golden assets? In addressing this issue, there are four important cautionary points that need to be emphasized:

1. Because of the many assumptions embedded in any risk-and-return model, a given fund may have legitimate concerns about being able to reliably extract positive alphas from any given alternative investment.
2. Even for those alternatives in which positive alphas are thought to be available to the fund, the allocations will virtually always be constrained by a variety of explicit or implicit constraints (for example, dragon risks).
3. The exposure to alternatives can expose the fund to other forms of risk beyond those captured in any estimated volatility measure.
4. To the extent that the total alternative exposure grows beyond a certain level, the alpha risks may increase to the point at which they challenge the initial beta dominance and begin to have a significant adverse impact on the overall volatility.

BUILDING AN ALPHA CORE

A fund's constraints on alternatives play a fundamental role in the ultimate outcome of any allocation study, even when the implicit limits are only discovered through a sequential process of tortured optimizations. We have used the term *alpha core* to describe the best possible alternative subportfolio. Moreover, we have suggested that funds should consider reversing the usual allocation process and focus their initial efforts on carefully (and realistically) designing this alpha core. Given the typical situation of beta dominance, the initial focus should be less on the volatility risks of alternatives (other than their beta contributions), and more on their potential returns as well as their other risks that fall outside the standard volatility estimates. Once this alpha core is structured, the implied beta risk can be estimated and the traditional swing assets (U.S. equity, bonds, and cash) can then be chosen to achieve the targeted level of overall portfolio volatility.

The alpha core formed in this fashion can act as a basic source of incremental expected return. When a fixed aggregate weight is assigned to the alpha core, its structure should generally be kept stable, even as the overall portfolio volatility is adjusted through varying mixes of the swing assets. This principle of conservation of the alpha core leads to a greatly simplified efficient frontier consisting of three segments:

1. A fixed-core segment, in which the core is maintained at its maximum percentage and an overall volatility range is determined by varying bond/ and equity mixtures
2. An equity extension segment, in which volatility is extended by increasingly substituting equity for decreasing percentages allocated to the alpha core
3. A cash-core line, in which volatility is decreased by substituting cash for the bonds and core mix at the front end of the fixed-core segment

However, this fixed-core situation tacitly assumes that the core has already been expanded to the maximum tolerable extent. The more general situation is when the current alpha core is still in the process of being built out, and there is further room for its potential expansion within the portfolio.

MAXIMUM-RETURN ALPHA CORES

In this analysis, the alpha core is characterized by an aggregate alpha return, alpha volatility, and implicit beta value. For the sake of simplicity, we limit the swing assets to cash and U.S. equity (that is, excluding bonds). With this simplification, the swing asset subportfolio can be completely defined in terms of its beta value. Thus, the portfolio beta is determined solely by the literal equity exposure together with the implicit beta embedded in the alpha core.

Exhibit 6.1 shows the resulting unconstrained frontier in the standard total return–volatility format. Exhibit 6.2 presents the allocation alphas and betas for each of the asset classes, and Exhibit 6.3 then shows an efficient frontier (unconstrained) in pure alpha space.

The problem with this unconstrained alpha frontier is that it does not address the inherent limitations placed on alternative assets. At the outset, we have set the maximum limit for the entire alpha core at 30 percent, with its internal composition also subject to the hypothetical set of individual asset constraints depicted in Exhibit 6.4.

Exhibit 6.5 displays the efficient frontiers for this 30 percent alpha core in the alpha risk-and-return space, both with and without the constraints listed earlier. In the unconstrained case, the highest alpha return (and the

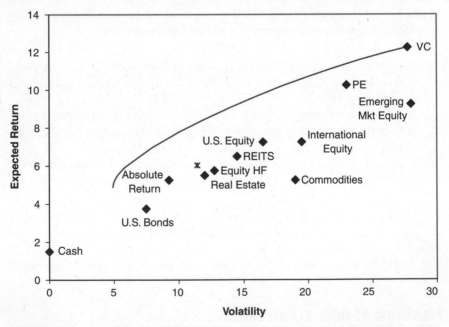

EXHIBIT 6.1   Unconstrained EF in Return-Volatility Space
Source: Morgan Stanley Research

EXHIBIT 6.2 Asset Class Characteristics

Asset Class	Expected Return	α	β	σ	$\beta\sigma$	σ_α
Alpha Core						
Venture Capital	12.25	7.37	0.59	27.75	9.71	25.99
Commodities	5.25	5.41	−0.29	19.00	−4.75	18.40
Real Estate	5.50	3.58	0.07	12.00	1.20	11.94
Emerging Mkt Equity	9.25	3.36	0.76	28.00	12.60	25.00
Private Equity	10.25	3.14	0.98	23.00	16.10	16.43
REITS	6.50	2.22	0.48	14.50	7.98	12.11
Absolute Return	5.25	2.14	0.28	9.25	4.63	8.01
International Equity	7.25	1.33	0.77	19.50	12.68	14.82
Equity Hedge Funds	5.75	0.47	0.66	12.75	10.84	6.72
Swing Assets						
U.S. Bonds	3.75	1.47	0.14	7.50	2.25	7.15
U.S. Equity	7.25	0.00	1.00	16.50	16.50	0.00
Cash	1.50	0.00	0.00	0.00	0.00	0.00

Source: Morgan Stanley Research

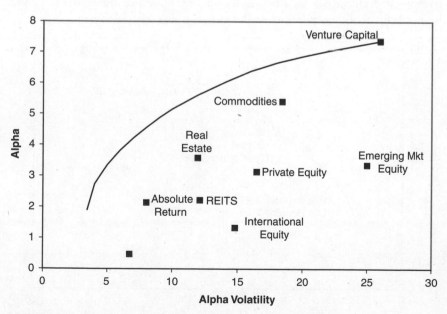

EXHIBIT 6.3 Unconstrained Efficient Frontier in Alpha Space
Source: Morgan Stanley Research

EXHIBIT 6.4 Asset Constraints

Asset Class	Constraint
Alpha Core	
Venture Capital (VC)	10%
Commodities (Com)	10%
Real Estate (RE)	20%
Emerging Mkt Equity (EM)	10%
Private Equity (PE)	10%
REITS	10%
Absolute Return (AR)	20%
International Equity (IE)	30%
Equity Hedge Funds (EH)	25%

Source: Morgan Stanley Research

greatest volatility) is obtained by deploying all 30 percent weight into VC. In contrast, in the constrained case, the highest return (and again, the highest volatility) requires allocation to the three highest alpha classes, subject to their respective constraints. Thus, as might be expected, the constrained frontier in Exhibit 6.5 falls below its unconstrained counterpart, with the higher return–higher volatility segment being severely curtailed.

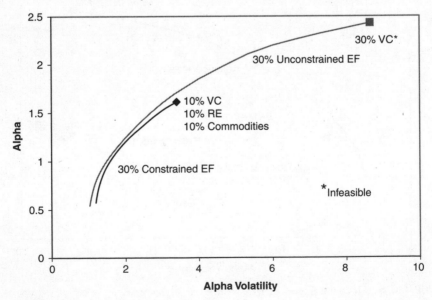

EXHIBIT 6.5 Alpha Core Frontiers
Source: Morgan Stanley Research

The highest alpha mixture point on the constrained frontier has a return of 1.64 percent and volatility of 3.40 percent, resulting in a Sharpe ratio of 0.48. There are lower volatilities and better Sharpe ratios at various points along this constrained frontier. However, within a highly beta-dominated overall portfolio, the larger alpha return becomes far more important than the submergible alpha volatility. Thus, in such situations, the maximum return mix will approximate the preferred alpha core.

Suppose 10 percent is the target volatility for the overall portfolio. With the alpha core percentage initially fixed at 30 percent, its return-and-risk contributions can be determined as shown in Exhibit 6.6. With the alpha core having a 3.40 percent volatility, we can then achieve this targeted 10 percent volatility by having an overall fund beta of

$$\beta_{total} = \frac{1}{16.5}\sqrt{(10)^2 - (3.40)^2}$$
$$= .57$$

Because of commodities' assumed negative beta, this 30 percent core has a very low *implicit* beta value of .04. Consequently, the swing asset mix will just consist of an explicit 53 percent weight in U.S. equities (= .57 − .04). The total portfolio then consists of the 30 percent core, the 53 percent literal equity weight, and 17 percent cash (recall that cash was assumed to act as a proxy for all fixed income to simplify the exposition). The resulting portfolio return is 6.43 percent and the overall volatility corresponds to the targeted level of 10 percent. The overall portfolio beta value of 0.57 accounts for 94 percent of the fund's total volatility, resulting in a highly beta-dominated situation.

THE FLOWER DIAGRAM

The nature of this beta domination and the core's return-enhancing role can be dramatically illustrated by transforming the standard risk-and-return diagram into the flower format shown in Exhibit 6.7.

The dashed line is the cash-equity line. The initial pure beta subportfolio is plotted at its return of 4.78 percent (that is, .57 × 5.75 percent equity risk premium + 1.50 percent risk-free rate) and its 9.41 percent volatility (that is, 0.57 × 16.5 percent equity volatility). The flower pattern sprouting from this point represents an increasing weight assigned to the alpha core. When this assigned core percentage reached 30 percent, we have the portfolio described earlier, with its 6.42 percent total return and its prescribed 10 percent volatility.

EXHIBIT 6.6 30 Percent Alpha Core Portfolio

Alpha Core Structure	30% Alpha Core
Venture Capital	10%
Commodities	10%
Real Estate	10%
Emerging Mkt Equity	
Private Equity	
REITS	
Absolute Return	
International Equity	
Equity Hedge Funds	
Total	30%
TOTAL FUND STRUCTURE	
% Cash Alpha Core	30%
% Leveraged Alpha Core	0%
Total Alpha Core Exposure	30%
% Equity	53%
% Swing Cash	17%
% Leveraged	0%
Total Swing Assets	70%
RISK-AND-RETURN CHARACTERISTICS	
30% Alpha Core Contribution	
Alpha Return	1.64
Alpha Volatility	3.40
Alpha Sharpe Ratio	0.48
Implied Beta	0.04
Beta Return	0.23
Beta Volatility	0.66
70% Swing Assets	
Explicit Beta	0.53
Beta Return	3.06
Beta Volatility	8.78
Sharpe Ratio	0.35
100% Cash Return	1.50
Total Portfolio	
Expected Return	6.43
Beta	0.57
Beta Volatility	9.44
Total Volatility	10.00
Beta % of Total Volatility	94.4%

Source: Morgan Stanley Research

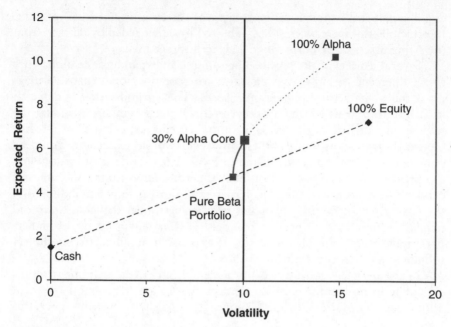

EXHIBIT 6.7 The Risk-and-Return Flower
Source: Morgan Stanley Research

This flower diagram also shows how the portfolio's return and risk would rise if additional weight could theoretically be added to the given core structure. Of course, such additions are not really possible since we have reached the maximum allowable limits on VC and commodities. The key point of the flower diagram, however, is to show how the addition of the core enhances the risk-and-return characteristics of the overall portfolio. In particular, with a low core percentage and a high level of beta domination, the flower sprouts up almost vertically, indicating significant return enhancement with minimal added volatility. At the same time, as we move beyond the 30 percent weight, the flower bends increasingly to the right, as the incremental volatility addition becomes more significant.

EXPANDING THE ALPHA CORE

With the alpha core being such an important source of incremental return, it is natural to consider enlarging the weight assigned to it. For the moment, let's assume that the asset class constraints were not binding, and that we could consider a hypothetical leveraging of the core weight to 60 percent. In principle, this increase could be achieved by either redeploying cash from the swing assets or by borrowing funds to leverage the core.

Several aspects of the problem are altered in expanding the alpha core to a 60 percent weight. Given the same core composition, expansion magnifies the alpha return and risk measures. This magnification is depicted in Exhibit 6.8 in which the 30 percent constrained frontier, including the maximum return point chosen as the initial core, is just enlarged by a factor of two. However, as noted earlier, any such twofold expansion would be constricted by the constraints listed in Exhibit 6.4. For example, doubling our previous alpha core would entail a 20 percent allocation to VC, an asset class whose exposure is limited to 10 percent. Thus, as shown in Exhibit 6.8, the properly constrained 60 percent frontier lies under the simple twofold magnification of the 30 percent frontier. This nested shrinkage of higher-percentage frontiers is characteristic of expansion of subportfolios subject to individual asset constraints.

In the properly constrained 60 percent frontier, the maximum return subportfolio now consists of 20 percent real estate (RE) and 10 percent allocations to EM, VC, PE, and Commodities. As shown in Exhibit 6.9, this

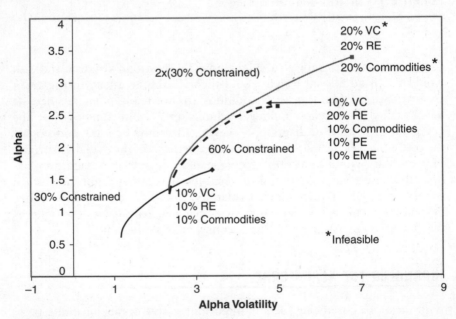

EXHIBIT 6.8 Constrained Alpha Frontiers
Source: Morgan Stanley Research

EXHIBIT 6.9 Leveraged Alpha Core Portfolios

Alpha Core Structure	30% Alpha Core	60% Alpha Core 30% Leveraged	90% Alpha Core 60% Leveraged
Venture Capital	10%	10%	7.89%
Commodities	10%	20%	10.00%
Real Estate	10%	10%	18.12%
Emerging Mkt Equity		10%	3.87%
Private Equity		10%	8.39%
REITS			10.00%
Absolute Return			20.00%
International Equity			4.34%
Equity Hedge Funds			7.39%
Total	30%	60%	90%
TOTAL FUND STRUCTURE			
% Cash Alpha Core	30%	30%	30%
% Leveraged Alpha Core	0%	30%	60%
Total Alpha Core Exposure	30%	30%	30%
% Equity	53%	31%	22%
% Swing Cash	17%	9%	0%
% Leveraged	0%	0%	−12%
Total Swing Assets	70%	40%	10%
RISK-AND-RETURN CHARACTERISTICS			
30% Alpha Core Contribution			
Alpha Return	1.64	2.64	2.91
Alpha Volatility	3.40	4.98	4.41
Alpha Sharpe Ratio	0.48	0.53	0.66
Implied Beta	0.04	0.21	0.32
Beta Return	0.23	1.22	1.85
Beta Volatility	0.66	3.51	5.31
70% Swing Assets			
Explicit Beta	0.53	0.31	0.22
Beta Return	3.06	1.78	1.27
Beta Volatility	8.78	5.13	3.63
Sharpe Ratio	0.35	0.35	0.35
100% Cash Return	1.50	1.50	1.50
Total Portfolio			
Expected Return	6.43	7.15	7.53
Beta	0.57	0.52	0.54
Beta Volatility	9.44	8.63	8.94
Total Volatility	10.00	10.00	10.00
Beta % of Total Volatility	94.4%	86.3%	89.5%

Source: Morgan Stanley Research

new alpha core contributes a significantly greater alpha return of 2.64 percent, an alpha volatility of 4.98 percent, and a considerably higher implicit beta contribution of 0.21. To achieve the targeted 10 percent volatility, the explicit equity weight must now be reduced to 31 percent. The portfolio now consists of the 60 percent core, 31 percent equity, and 9 percent cash. However, the combined 0.52 beta still leaves the overall portfolio highly beta dominated, with the U.S. equity exposure accounting for 86 percent of the total volatility.

The flower diagram (Exhibit 6.10) for this 60 percent core portfolio illustrates the impact of the leveraging:

- The pure beta portfolio has a somewhat lower position on the cash-equity line.
- The flower still sprouts up almost vertically because of the continued beta domination.
- The expected portfolio return rises to 7.15 percent as a result of the higher alpha return.

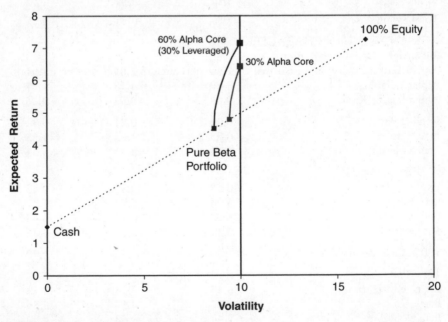

EXHIBIT 6.10   The Leveraged Flower
Source: Morgan Stanley Research

MOVING BEYOND BETA DOMINATION

In an ideal world, the portfolio with the highest risk-and-return ratio would have a more balanced combination of alpha and beta volatilities. In such a situation, we would not have beta domination, and we could no longer ignore the core's alpha volatility and just presume that the maximum-return core is approximately optimal. As we move toward this more global optimum, the interplay of the alpha and beta volatilities would lead us toward alpha cores with better Sharpe ratios, reflecting their more attractive risk-and-return tradeoff.

Our final leveraged portfolio represents an effort to move toward this global optimum, with a 90 percent weight being assigned to a more efficient alpha core. As shown in Exhibit 6.9, this new alpha core now includes some weight in each of the alternative assets. For certain assets such as emerging markets, the assigned weights are well below the limits encountered earlier in the preceding maximum-return core. With 90 percent weight now in the core, an equity weight of 22 percent is needed to reach the targeted fund volatility of 10 percent. Thus, at this point, the cash component must be −12 percent, that is, leverage must be employed.

Exhibit 6.11 shows the constrained 90 percent frontier as nestled below the 3 × (30 percent frontier) and the $1\frac{1}{2}$ × (60 percent frontier). We can see that the selected core falls below the maximum return point, moving to a position that reflects its better Sharpe ratio of .66.

Finally, Exhibit 6.12 shows this 90 percent core in a flower diagram format. With its higher alpha return and lower volatility, this 90 percent flower sprouts strongly upward, eventually achieving the higher 7.53 percent return at the 10 percent target volatility. All in all, this highly leveraged alpha portfolio could be viewed as theoretically superior, assuming that all the models and preconditions involved in the leveraging process were both credible and acceptable.

At the same time, it should be pointed out that the resulting portfolio is still subject to 89 percent beta domination. Given our covariance matrix and the assumed constraints, any sizable alpha core will tend to contribute a significant amount of implicit beta value (that is, unless one could allow higher percentages in low beta assets such as commodities and real estate). Thus, it generally becomes difficult to reduce the beta dominance and still obtain the 10 percent target volatility for the overall portfolio.

To obtain a more theoretical optimal structure, we would need a significant overlay of return and risk from active alphas, different covariance assumptions, an expanded range of asset classes, looser constraints on

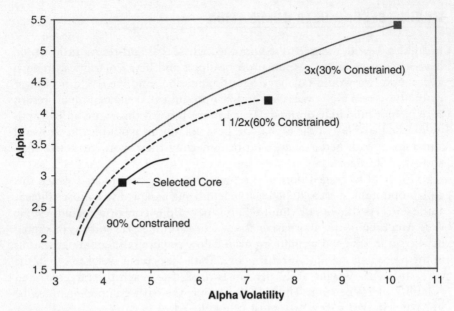

EXHIBIT 6.11 Sequence of Constrained Alpha Frontiers
Source: Morgan Stanley Research

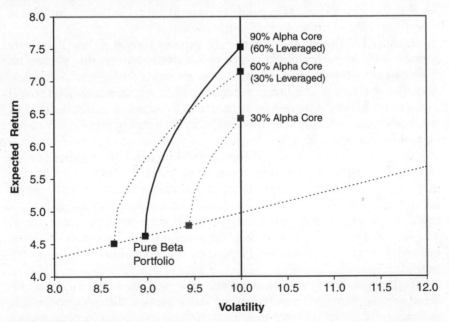

EXHIBIT 6.12 The 90 percent Leveraged Flower
Source: Morgan Stanley Research

the lower-beta alternatives, and more flexibility on the target volatility. In various ways, recent trends can be interpreted as moving toward making such enhanced degrees of freedom available to modern portfolio management.

DUAL ACTIVE-ALLOCATION ALPHAS

The high-embedded betas associated with alpha cores present a major obstacle to obtaining a productive balance of alpha and beta volatilities. As the alpha core is leveraged further, the implicit beta contribution is also leveraged. It therefore becomes very difficult to bring the pure alpha volatility up to a level at which it can challenge (and then help diversify) the dominant beta volatility. As we saw in Exhibit 6.9, even with a 90 percent alpha core weight, the beta value still accounted for 89 percent of the total portfolio volatility.

In all the preceding discussions, the focus has been restricted to structural allocation alphas, that is, the residual return after extracting an asset's implied beta component. These allocation alphas are derived solely from the general asset class characteristics embedded in the fund's return-covariance model. There is no assumed alpha benefit from active management or selection of better vehicles or better asset managers.

If we were to augment our allocation alpha with such (presumably positive) active alphas, the benefits accruing to leveraging an alpha core could be considerably greater. Such active alphas may be either portable from one asset class to another, or intrinsically bound to their home assets. In the latter case, the return (and risk) characteristics of the bound active alpha should theoretically be integrated into a combined alpha for the underlying asset class. This combined active and allocation alpha could naturally have a significant impact on the asset class's appeal, and thus affect the composition of the alpha core. Moreover, to the extent that these active alphas (whether portable or bound) are viewed as independent of U.S. equity movements, the risk contribution would add primarily to the alpha, rather than to the beta volatility. Thus, positive active alphas could certainly lead to an improved risk-and-return profile at the overall fund level.

The evident benefits of this dual-alpha approach would seem to suggest that the basic return and covariance should perhaps be extended to incorporate these potential active alpha effects. An important caveat, however, is that different levels of judgment and confidence are entailed. On the one hand, a fund's return-covariance matrix is primarily used to develop a strategic policy allocation. As such, it is intended to be an objective reflection of generic market characteristics. It is no coincidence that one finds considerable commonality in the return-covariance models used in practice. On the other hand, active alpha assumptions are intrinsically fund-specific, reflecting an individual fund's structural advantages and experience in extracting incremental returns from specific asset classes.

Consequently, one would have to exercise considerable caution in combining these very different inputs into a cohesive dual alpha model. At the same time, it is clear that both sources of alpha should theoretically enter into any comprehensive analysis of how the alpha core should be formulated, and how far it can be legitimately expanded or leveraged within a given portfolio context.

CONCLUSION

The typical set of capital market assumptions tends to imply positive allocation alphas for various asset classes. For funds that find themselves in the virtually universal situation of being beta-dominated, it is usually well worth exploring the potential for development or expansion of an alpha core. The benefits obtained will depend critically on the limits set for individual alpha-producing assets as well as on the aggregate weight allowed for the core itself.

In general, as the allocation to the core weight is expanded, the composition and associated risk-and-return benefits will progress through the following sequence of phases:

- Selection of the highest alpha return assets up to their respective maximums
- Movement toward inclusion of the next highest alpha-returning assets that remain open
- A more diversified subportfolio, with improving Sharpe ratios as the alpha volatility becomes more relevant, and finally reaching
- An alpha core that fully uses most of its maximum exposure limits

At some point during this expansion enlargement, the core will reach a point of diminishing returns, beyond which further enlargement will lead to decreasing total returns given a specified total fund volatility.

The focus here has been on total portfolio volatility as the sole gauge of risk. However, as pointed out earlier, annualized volatility is only one facet of risk. In particular, when dealing with the less-standard assets that comprise the alpha core, there are a multitude of other considerations that enter into the setting of allocation limits, for example, accessibility, liquidity, model risk, headline concerns, drawdown scheduling, vehicle selection, valuation complexity, dragon risks, and so on. Thus, each fund must use its own criteria and exercise its own judgment in assessing how far it should move in the direction of expanding its alpha core.

CHAPTER 7

Alpha-Driven Efficient Frontiers

Nonstandard assets are typically subject to both explicit and implicit constraints that place some limit on their role in strategic portfolios. These constraints tend to be particularly binding on those asset classes that are large sources of allocation alphas. We have used the term alpha core to reflect the best possible subportfolio of these alpha-producing asset classes.

We have suggested that funds should consider reversing the usual allocation process and focus their initial efforts on designing this alpha core. Given the typical situation of beta dominance, the focus should be less on the volatility risks of alternatives (other than their beta contributions), and more on their potential returns, as well as those other risks that fall outside the standard volatility estimates. Once this alpha core is structured, the implied beta risk can be estimated and the traditional swing assets (U.S. equity/bonds/cash) can then be chosen to achieve the targeted level of overall portfolio volatility. In this study, we show how an efficient frontier (EF) can be developed for the alpha core and how this alpha frontier can be integrated with the complementary beta factor to develop an optimal EF for the total fund.

This alpha core approach can be generalized to explore how the portfolio composition changes across a range of total volatilities. At low fund volatilities, when the constraints are not yet binding, the risk-and-return ratio is paramount. The optimal portfolio consists of a mixture of beta together with all available alpha assets. At the higher fund volatilities, however, the constraint on the alpha exposures become binding and the optimal portfolios are forced to become beta-dominated. In this region, the alpha volatility becomes virtually irrelevant, and a fixed core consisting of the highest alpha-returning assets turns out to provide a near-optimal portfolio. This fixed alpha core can be composed by simply filling up the highest alpha-return assets in sequential order of capacity until the maximum weight for the entire core is reached. Finally, at the very highest volatilities, the fund must buy more beta for it to extend volatility.

THE EFFICIENT FRONTIER IN ALPHA SPACE

The constraints placed on individual assets are a key input in any risk-and-return analysis, but another important constraint is the one placed on the entire weight allowed in the alpha core. At the outset, we set the maximum limit for the entire alpha core at 30 percent, with its internal composition also subject to the set of individual asset constraints depicted in Exhibit 7.1.

Exhibit 7.2 displays the EF for this 30 percent core in alpha risk-and-return space. The frontier can be roughly segmented into three parts. At low alpha volatilities, the EF takes the form of a straight line based on the mixture that generates the highest Sharpe ratio of alpha return to alpha risk. The best Sharpe ratio usually entails a wide distribution that includes all available asset classes, with no one class being dominant. The individual allocations therefore tend to be modest in size and generally well below the maximum individual constraints. Within a sufficiently low volatility range, the distribution of risky assets will remain constant and the lower-risk levels will be achieved by simply adding cash to the core.

As we move toward higher-risk levels, the constraints become more of a factor and the frontier begins to curve downward from its initial straight line. Finally, in the general case, the frontier may reach a globally maximum return, with declining returns associated with the very highest volatility levels. The highest-return point along the entire frontier will typically require allocation to the highest-return alpha classes, subject to their respective constraints, for example, for the 30 percent aggregate core weight, this

EXHIBIT 7.1 Asset Constraints

Asset Class	Constraint
Alpha Core	
Venture Capital (VC)	10%
Commodities (Com)	10%
Real Estate (RE)	20%
Emerging Mkt Equity (EM)	10%
Private Equity (PE)	10%
REITS	10%
Absolute Return (AR)	20%
International Equity (IE)	30%
Equity Hedge Funds (EH)	25%

Source: Morgan Stanley Research

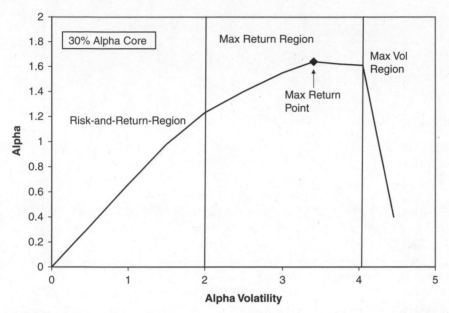

EXHIBIT 7.2 The Efficient Frontier in Alpha Space
Source: Morgan Stanley Research

would imply 10 percent each to venture capital (VC), commodities (Com), and real estate (RE).

To integrate the alpha frontier into a full frontier, we must combine these alpha and beta components to achieve each one's given volatility level for the overall fund. In Exhibit 7.3, the dotted line superimposes the beta risk-and-return line on the alpha frontier. At higher volatility levels, beta becomes more attractive versus alpha. Therefore, funds will add beta rather than alpha when seeking to increase overall portfolio volatility beyond a certain point.

For a given alpha volatility, there will always be one beta volatility that achieves the target fund volatility and provides the best return. Exhibit 7.4 displays the alpha and beta volatility combinations that yield total portfolio volatilities of 2 percent, 10 percent, and 15 percent. At the very low total volatility of 2 percent, a variety of alpha and beta mixtures can be selected to achieve the targeted 2 percent value. However, at the higher fund volatilities of 10 percent and 15 percent, the curves are relatively flat, implying that only a very limited range of high beta values can lead to the specified fund volatility. Moreover, these high beta levels force beta dominance, that is, the point at which the U.S. equity exposure accounts for at least 90 percent of the total volatility.

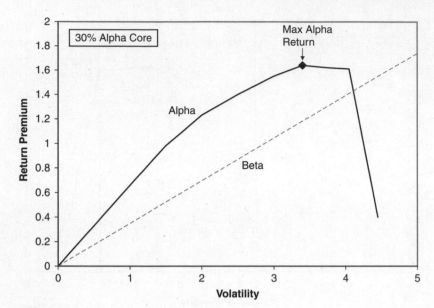

EXHIBIT 7.3   Alpha and Beta Frontiers
Source: Morgan Stanley Research

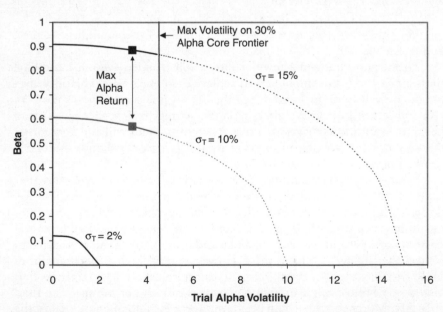

EXHIBIT 7.4   Required Beta versus Alpha Volatility to Generate Specified Total
Fund Volatility (σ_T)
Source: Morgan Stanley Research

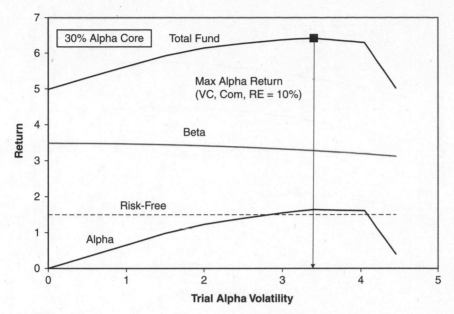

EXHIBIT 7.5 Return Components for Total Fund Volatility of 10 Percent
Source: Morgan Stanley Research

The alpha-space EF from Exhibit 7.2 can be combined with the required beta from Exhibit 7.4 to determine the total return for a given portfolio volatility. For each trial alpha volatility, the required beta from Exhibit 7.4 corresponds to a beta return that, together with the associated alpha return from Exhibit 7.4, adds to the total fund return. Exhibit 7.5 shows the resulting total return frontier of alpha and beta combinations as a function of the trial alpha volatilities. Since all points along this frontier achieve the specified 10 percent volatility, the trial alpha volatility that provides the maximum return corresponds to the optimal alpha and beta combination. In this case, the maximum return of 6.4 percent is achieved at an alpha volatility of 3.4 percent and a 30 percent alpha core that consists of the three highest-alpha assets: VC, Com, and RE, each at 10 percent.

We can perform the same analysis for any target portfolio volatility. Exhibit 7.6 displays the total fund return for fund volatilities of 2 percent, 5 percent, 10 percent, and 15 percent, with the maximum return portfolios represented by the dots on each line. For the higher fund volatilities ($\sigma_T =$ 5 percent, 10 percent, 15 percent), the maximum return occurs at or very near the same maximum return point on the alpha EF. In contrast, for $\sigma_T =$ 2 percent, the maximum return for the total portfolio is reached at a much lower point along the EF.

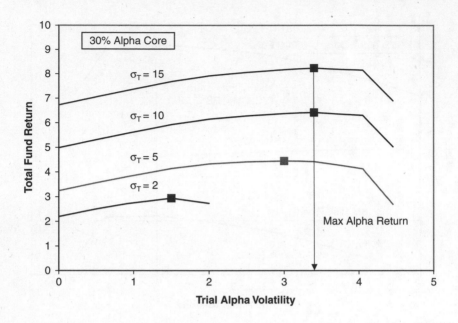

EXHIBIT 7.6   Total Fund Return versus Trial Alpha Volatility for Various Fund Volatilities
Source: Morgan Stanley Research

Exhibit 7.7 provides the allocation details of the EF portfolio for the specified total fund volatilities. For all portfolios with $\sigma_T \geq 5$ percent, the optimal portfolio has the 30 percent core with 10 percent weight allocated to each of the highest alpha return assets. For a total fund volatility of 5 percent, the returns between the optimal core and maximum return subportfolio are comparable even though their compositions are somewhat different. Only for the very low $\sigma_T = 2$ percent does one find a broader distribution of alpha sources with more balanced risk-and-return ratios. (It should be noted that, at the extreme volatilities of 2 percent and 15 percent, the negative equity and negative cash positions indicate an ability to use both short and long beta futures.)

For typical funds, the beta dominance is so great that the alpha volatilities become essentially so irrelevant that only the alpha returns matter. This point is further demonstrated in Exhibit 7.8, where the optimal EF for the total fund is plotted together with a simplified fixed core segment consisting of the maximum return alpha core together with varying cash and equity

EXHIBIT 7.7 Efficient Portfolios at Various Fund Volatilities: 30 Percent Core Constraint

Total Portfolio Volatility	2.00	5.00	8.00	10.00	15.00
Alpha Core					
Venture Capital	2.5%	8.2%	10.0%	10.0%	10.0%
Commodities	3.7%	9.7%	10.0%	10.0%	10.0%
Real Estate	5.8%	8.2%	10.0%	10.0%	10.0%
Emerging Mkt Equity	1.2%	1.5%	0.0%	0.0%	0.0%
Private Equity	2.7%	2.4%	0.0%	0.0%	0.0%
REITS	3.4%	0.0%	0.0%	0.0%	0.0%
Absolute Return	7.5%	0.0%	0.0%	0.0%	0.0%
International Equity	1.3%	0.0%	0.0%	0.0%	0.0%
Equity Hedge Funds	1.9%	0.0%	0.0%	0.0%	0.0%
Total	30.0%	30.0%	30.0%	30.0%	30.0%
Swing Assets					
U.S. Equity	−2.4%	18.1%	40.2%	53.3%	84.8%
Cash	72.4%	51.9%	29.8%	16.7%	−14.8%
Total	70.0%	70.0%	70.0%	70.0%	70.0%
Alpha	0.98	1.55	1.64	1.64	1.64
Alpha Volatility	1.50	3.00	3.40	3.40	3.40
Alpha Sharpe Ratio	0.65	0.52	0.48	0.48	0.48
Beta	0.08	0.24	0.44	0.57	0.89
Beta Volatility	1.32	4.00	7.24	9.40	14.61
Total Return	2.94	4.44	5.66	6.42	8.23
Total Volatility	2.00	5.00	8.00	10.00	15.00
Beta %	66.1%	80.0%	90.5%	94.0%	97.4%

Source: Morgan Stanley Research

mixtures. (We have excluded bonds as an asset class for the sake of simplicity.) The virtual coincidence of the two curves overall $\sigma_T \geq 5$ percent demonstrates the near-optimality of the fixed maximum core approach.

INCREASING THE ALPHA CORE PERCENTAGE

If we perform the same analysis for a 60 percent aggregate constraint on the core, there are some significant differences in the composition of the optimal portfolios. As shown in Exhibits 7.9 and 7.10, the initial linear Sharpe ratio

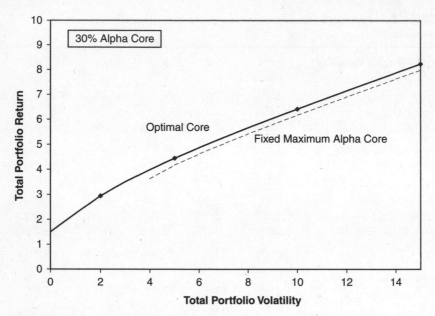

EXHIBIT 7.8 Total Fund Frontiers with Optimal and Fixed Alpha Cores
Source: Morgan Stanley Research

segment in the 60 percent case extends further than with the preceding 30 percent limit. Moreover, the allocations are somewhat more broadly distributed, with convergence to the fixed maximum-return core occurring at higher volatility levels.

However, as shown in Exhibit 7.10, this compositional difference leads to a virtually negligible difference in the EF for volatilities greater than 7 percent, that is, for all institutionally relevant portfolios. This suggests that the fixed core approach can also serve at this 60 percent core weight as a pragmatic and more transparent proxy for the standard black box optimization.

Finally, we have looked at two additional frontiers in Exhibit 7.11: one with a 100 percent constraint on the alpha core and one that allows for full leverage of the aggregate alpha core (subject to the same individual asset class constraints). At low-risk levels, there is virtually no difference between any of the frontiers. At the mid-level risk levels, the frontiers diverge as they begin to curve downward at different points. Finally, at the higher-risk levels, the frontiers converge to a set of parallel straight lines. In this region, higher portfolio volatility is obtained by buying beta and the resulting marginal risk-and-return gain just corresponds to the equity Sharpe ratio.

EXHIBIT 7.9 Efficient Portfolios at Various Fund Volatilities: 60 Percent Core Constraint

Total Portfolio Volatility	2.00	5.00	8.00	10.00	15.00
Alpha Core					
Venture Capital	2.5%	9.6%	10.0%	10.0%	10.0%
Commodities	3.7%	10.0%	10.0%	10.0%	10.0%
Real Estate	5.8%	15.8%	18.9%	20.0%	20.0%
Emerging Mkt Equity	1.2%	3.2%	3.8%	5.1%	9.3%
Private Equity	2.7%	6.5%	7.4%	9.9%	10.0%
REITS	3.5%	4.9%	3.6%	2.5%	0.7%
Absolute Return	7.6%	9.9%	6.3%	2.5%	0.0%
International Equity	1.4%	0.0%	0.0%	0.0%	0.0%
Equity Hedge Funds	2.4%	0.0%	0.0%	0.0%	0.0%
Total	30.7%	60.0%	60.0%	60.0%	60.0%
Swing Assets					
U.S. Equity	−3.8%	0.3%	23.1%	34.2%	64.3%
Cash	73.1%	39.7%	16.9%	5.8%	−24.3%
Total	69.3%	40.0%	40.0%	40.0%	40.0%
Alpha	1.04	2.45	2.53	2.58	2.64
Alpha Volatility	1.63	4.00	4.25	4.50	4.90
Alpha Sharpe Ratio	0.64	0.61	0.60	0.57	0.54
Beta	0.07	0.18	0.41	0.54	0.86
Beta Volatility	1.16	3.00	6.78	8.93	14.17
Total Return	2.94	5.00	6.39	7.19	9.08
Total Volatility	2.00	5.00	8.00	10.00	15.00
Beta %	57.8%	60.0%	84.7%	89.3%	94.5%

Source: Morgan Stanley Research

There are limited benefits from leveraging the alpha core since the unleveraged 100 percent case has already reached the individual constraint levels for the highest-alpha producing assets. Thus, as we increase the leverage in the alpha core, there are fewer sources of positive allocation alphas that have not already been pushed to their maximum limits.

We note that these leverage effects could change with different covariance assumptions, an expanded range of asset classes, looser constraints on the low-beta alternatives, and more flexibility on the target volatility. Also,

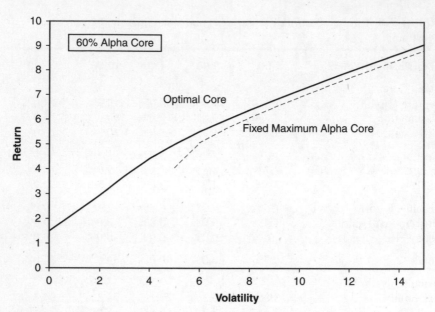

EXHIBIT 7.10 60 Percent Alpha Core Portfolio Frontier
Source: Morgan Stanley Research

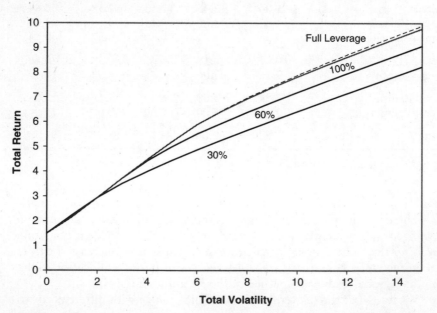

EXHIBIT 7.11 Total Fund Frontiers for Various Aggregate Core Constraints
Source: Morgan Stanley Research

if we were to augment our allocation alpha with active alphas, the benefits accruing to leveraging the alpha core could be considerably greater. Such active alphas may be either portable from one asset class to another, or intrinsically bound to their home assets. A combined active/allocation alpha could naturally have a significant impact on a given asset class's appeal, and thus affect the composition of the alpha core. Moreover, to the extent that these active alphas are viewed as independent of U.S. equity movements, the risk contribution would add primarily to the alpha volatility, rather than to the beta volatility. Thus, credibly positive active alphas could lead to significant further improvements in the risk-and-return profile at the overall fund level.

CONCLUSION

The composition of an optimal efficient frontier for a fund can be viewed as having three distinct phases. First, at low fund volatilities, when the constraints are not yet binding, the optimal portfolio consists of a Sharpe ratio mixture of cash and beta together with all available alpha assets. This risk-and-return ratio remains constant (in the form of straight line for the frontier) until the frontier enters a transition phase where individual asset class constraints become binding and the frontier begins to slope downward (leading to declining Sharpe ratios). In this transition phase, the alpha core moves toward the higher alpha return assets subject to their individual constraints. At higher volatilities, the constraint on the weight in the entire alpha core reaches its maximum and the frontier again approaches a straight line. In this region, further volatility is added by buying beta, with the slope of the frontier converging to the equity Sharpe ratio.

This more refined EF analysis validates the concept of a simplified EF based on a fixed alpha core. Moreover, it shows that a near optimal form of the fixed alpha core can be constructed by simply filling up the highest alpha-return assets in sequential order of capacity until the maximum core weight is reached. This result suggests that funds should consider reversing the traditional allocation process and focus their initial efforts on designing this alpha core. Once this alpha core is structured, the implied beta risk can be estimated and the traditional swing assets can then be chosen to achieve the targeted level of overall fund volatility.

CHAPTER 8

The Societal Efficient Frontier

*T*he standard characterization of an efficient frontier is a convex envelope. This frontier represents the highest-return portfolios for a range of
volatilities that can be constructed from a given universe of assets. When one
considers the actual constraints that are placed upon various institutional
investors, however, this simple form splinters into a multiplicity of frontiers
that depend on the particular institutional category.

Fixed income funds have the lowest baseline frontiers based on some
version of the yield curve. Fixed income funds rarely have the opportunity
to have significant equity investments and they are certainly proscribed from
alternative assets. Consequently, their frontier is determined by the shape
and position of the yield curve and generally represents the lowest baseline
frontier.

The next higher frontier would be for a swing asset portfolio that included U.S. equity. To the extent that equity can be incorporated freely
without position limits, this swing asset frontier would rise above the fixed
income frontier since it incorporates all fixed income assets as well.

A third level would be the constrained alpha frontier with some limited
allocation to alternatives. Because the swing assets could be included as a
subset, this constrained alpha frontier would lie between the swing asset
frontier and the totally unconstrained frontier.

In reality, all these smooth frontiers are artificial since institutional assets
are highly concentrated within quantum volatility states. These risk bands
form a nonconvex, discontinuous societal frontier *that reflects where asset
management activity actually takes place. This societal frontier may also
help identify certain investment opportunities for more flexible funds.

STANDARD EFFICIENT FRONTIERS

The standard efficient frontier presented in the textbooks consists of the
upper bound of all long-only portfolios of risky assets. Exhibit 8.1 depicts

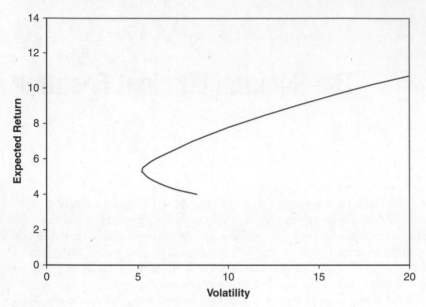

EXHIBIT 8.1 Unconstrained Efficient Frontier
Source: Morgan Stanley Research

one such frontier that includes all risky assets including alternatives, without any constraints on their respective weights (other than requiring that they should be nonnegative and add to 100 percent).

The front part of the frontier can then be completed by a straight line representing a mixture of the risk-less asset, cash, together with a tangency subportfolio of risky assets (Exhibit 8.2). In the hypothetical situation in which unlimited leverage is allowed at the cash rate, this straight line could be extended to comprise the entire optimal frontier (Sharpe 1964).

THE SWING ASSET FRONTIER

A more basic efficient frontier would consist of the swing assets—cash, fixed income, and U.S. equities (Exhibit 8.3). Such a swing asset frontier would reflect the best unconstrained portfolios for a long-only institutional fund locked into these three traditional asset classes.

In moving toward inclusion of alternative assets, virtually every institutional fund inevitably encounters a series of constraints. To a large extent, these constraints are critical in determining the optimal alpha core, that is, the best subportfolio of alternative assets. Even with these constraints, an

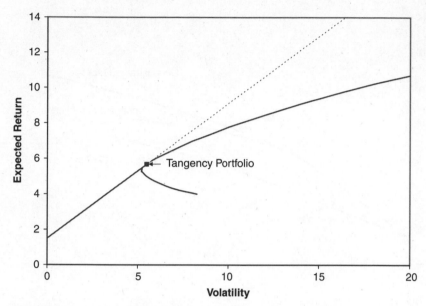

EXHIBIT 8.2   Unconstrained Efficient Frontier with Tangent Line
Source: Morgan Stanley Research

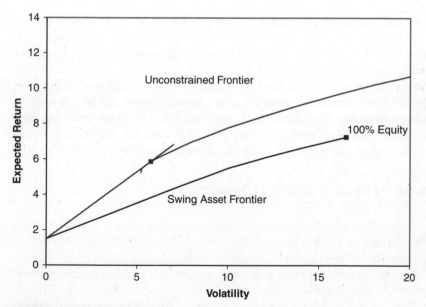

EXHIBIT 8.3   Swing Asset Frontier
Source: Morgan Stanley Research

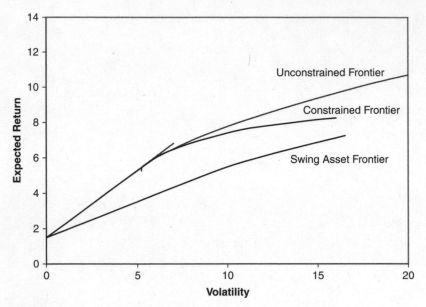

EXHIBIT 8.4   Constrained Frontier
Source: Morgan Stanley Research

alpha core can provide return enhancement beyond the basic return from the swing assets. The net result is that a constrained alpha-core frontier will have expected returns that are higher than the swing asset frontier, but lower than the unconstrained frontier.

In the early part of the cash-mixed region, the constraints will not yet be binding, and hence an optimal mixture of risky assets can be achieved. In this low-volatility region, the constrained and unconstrained alpha frontiers will therefore start off with the same straight line—up to the point at which the constrained frontier starts to bend downward, as shown in Exhibit 8.4.

THE CONCEPT OF A SOCIETAL FRONTIER

All of the aforementioned efficient frontiers are traditional representations of the optimal portfolios for a single investor that can theoretically choose freely across the entire range of volatilities. A radically different concept would be the highest-return portfolios available to funds that find themselves restricted to particular volatility regions.

This societal frontier would have to reflect the different constraints that typically apply to each category of funds (Markowitz 2005). For example,

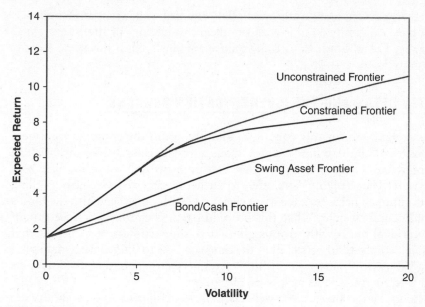

EXHIBIT 8.5   Bond-Cash Frontier
Source: Morgan Stanley Research

funds that are required to maintain very low volatilities are likely to be highly limited in their choice of asset classes. They will probably be invested primarily in fixed income securities, possibly with some modest weight in equities. It is pretty certain that they will have to avoid any significant allocation to alternatives. Consequently, the initial line of ascent from the risk-free rate will be based on a rather suboptimal mixture, and hence would have a much lower slope than any of the preceding frontiers (Exhibit 8.5).

As this frontier proceeds toward the intermediate volatilities, the relevant funds are likely to be able to accommodate increasing proportions of U.S. equity. At the outset, these portfolios may still be proscribed from any significant holdings in alternative assets. Continuing along the volatility dimension, the equity proportion increases until reaching the traditional portfolios holding 60- to 65-percent equities, with fund volatilities in the 10- to 11.50-percent range. There are few U.S. institutional funds that lie beyond this volatility barrier.

In recent years, more and more institutions have been granted the flexibility to incorporate significant holdings of alternatives. However, virtually all such funds are at the outer limit of the standard volatility measure, that is, they are concentrated near the 10- to 11.50-percent volatility barrier together with the more traditional 60/40 funds. It may seem at first curious that highly diversified funds with significant weightings in alternative assets and very low allocations to U.S. equities are clustered in this same narrow volatility band.

TOTAL BETAS AND THE DIVERSIFICATION PARADOX

The explanation for this common volatility lies in the common total beta exposure of all these funds. The various alternative assets have a statistical co-movement with U.S. equity that can be expressed as an implicit beta exposure. The term *total beta* refers to the net sensitivity derived from rolling up the implicit betas for each asset class and combining them with the fund's explicit equity weight. When this procedure is applied to a wide spectrum of institutional funds with various alternative subportfolios, it turns out that virtually all the total betas fall in the range of 0.55 to 0.65. These same total beta values are found even in funds with very large alternative allocations and U.S. equity weights as low as 15 percent.

Many of the alternative asset classes have significant alpha volatility derived from sources other than their co-movement with U.S. equities. However, because of the typically fragmented allocations across the alternative asset classes, these alpha volatilities do not exert a significant impact on the total fund volatility. Consequently, a fund's portfolio-level volatility is dominated by its total beta exposures. And since the total beta values fall into the tight 0.55–0.65 band described earlier, it is understandable that these alternative-rich funds have volatilities that cluster in the same 10- to 11.50-percent band as 60/40 funds.

Thus, contrary to an oft-cited view, the allocation to a wider distribution of alternatives does not lead to better diversification in the sense of reduced fund volatility. Rather, the benefit from such diversification lies in the enhanced expected return derived from those assets having positive allocation alphas, that is, that component of expected return that remains after extracting the return derived from the co-movement with U.S. equities. (It should be noted that these allocation alphas are *passive* in nature, and hence quite distinct from the *active* alphas derived from a fund manager having some special skills or structural advantages.)

DRAGON RISK CONSTRAINTS AND CLIMBING THE ALPHA WALL

Since positive alpha sources can provide an enhanced expected return without a significant impact on fund volatility, it would seem that these alpha sources should be pursued with great vigor. However, there are always various constraints that limit any fund's position in alternative assets. These constraints are reflections of a large set of concerns, many of which cannot be fully captured in any standard covariance models. These multiple risks, which we refer to as *dragon risks,* lead to setting constraints that limit the allocations in this area (eight).

Alternative-rich funds may garner incremental alpha returns without an increase in the standard volatility risk, but they do incur higher levels of dragon risks. The willingness to accept such risks is definitely correlated with the capacity to also take sizable risks in standard volatility terms. This observation has major implications for the shape of the societal efficient frontier.

As noted earlier, low-volatility portfolios (A, B, and C) are likely to be composed of only cash and bonds, thereby having returns that fall below the swing asset frontier.

In the middling range of volatilities, the portfolios would incorporate a greater exposure to U.S. equities, and their frontier would therefore move toward the swing asset frontier. However, there are actually relatively few institutional portfolios that fall in this middling range.

U.S. pension funds, endowments, and foundations have portfolio volatilities concentrated in the 10- to 11.50-percent band. Once this volatility band is reached, the main differentiation among funds is derived from their level of diversification into alternatives. Traditional 60/40 funds with little or no alternatives will lie on the swing asset frontier (D). There are some institutions that are willing and able to take on the various dragon risks associated with alternative investments. These funds can then be viewed as garnering enhanced expected returns with minimally greater volatility, thereby climbing the alpha wall from the swing asset frontier up toward a constrained alpha frontier (E).

A SOCIETAL FRONTIER OF QUANTUM RISK STATES

Putting this all together, the societal frontier takes the form of several discrete concentrations of risk states (Exhibit 8.6): fixed income funds (A, B, C), a convergence toward the 0.55 to 0.65 beta funds along the swing asset frontier (D), and then, a rather steep ascent toward some constrained alpha frontier for those funds that are able to climb the alpha wall (E).

The very curious societal frontier (Exhibit 8.7) is obviously highly conjectural in character, but it does raise a number of immediate questions. First, it is far from the convex shape associated with the standard frontier. Frontier convexity is achieved by the ability to mix a higher and lower volatility to

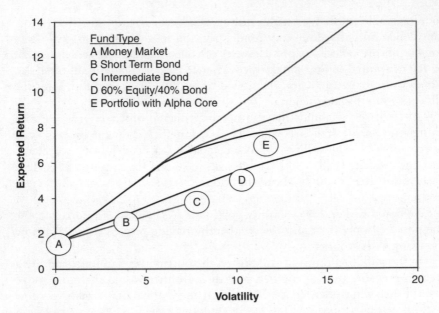

EXHIBIT 8.6   Efficient Frontiers for Various Institutional Concentrations
Source: Morgan Stanley Research

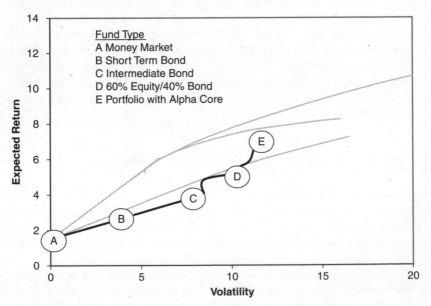

EXHIBIT 8.7   Societal Frontier
Source: Morgan Stanley Research

create a bridge with a higher return over the interim volatilities. This process fills in the intervening risk-and-return space. Such bridging is not possible in the societal situation, however, because middle-range investors are not able to accept even a small proportion of the dragon risks that accompany an alpha core's higher returns.

ACTIVE ALPHAS AND OTHER RISK-AND-RETURN TRADEOFFS

Up to this point, the discussion of alpha sources has focused on the nonzero-sum, passive alphas derived from a generic investment in alternative assets. Some funds, however, may wish to court the potentially higher active alphas that are derived from skill-based pursuits. Such active pursuits could be viewed as a form of climbing further up the alpha wall.

For another perspective on this alpha wall analogy, consider a fund that is positioned along the swing asset frontier. At this point, its allocation does not incorporate alternative assets. Now suppose that the committee reviews its allocation and reaches a conclusion that a certain allocation to alternative assets should become permissible. At this point, its effective efficient frontier has just moved upward to a constrained-alpha frontier that reflects the potential inclusion of these new assets with their presumed positive alpha returns. As the portfolio then invests in these newly available assets, it is moving from its current (now inefficient) position toward an allocation that is closer to its revised efficient frontier. Moreover, because of the minimal volatility impact, this movement is a near-vertical ascent toward the higher-returning new frontier. The fundamental point is that by accepting the dragon risks associated with expanded alpha constraints, the fund has achieved higher expected returns with only a modest change in total volatility.

A related question is whether there might even be circumstances when funds might consider trading off beta risk for dragon risk, that is, using higher alpha returns as an offset to lower beta risk and hence lower beta returns. This question would become even more poignant in a situation in which the risk premium for equities declined to the point at which it became less satisfactory in regard to the risk-and-return tradeoff.

Another question is why the alternative allocations are themselves diversified rather than being focused on the highest-returning single asset. The answer is that diversification across multiple alternative assets may not have much impact on the standard fund-level volatility, but it certainly does reduce the associated dragon risks. Thus, the act of diversification into multiple alternative assets enables a greater percentage allocation to alternative assets, thereby generating a larger alpha boost while keeping the aggregate dragon risk within acceptable bounds.

SOCIETAL GAPS AND OPPORTUNITIES

The frontier presented in Exhibit 8.7 is shown as a continuous curve. In reality, however, there are major gaps and discontinuities resulting from the regulatory restrictions and habitual behavior of institutional funds in the United States.

In the fixed income arena, the primary asset categories consist of money market funds, short term funds, and intermediate term funds. (In spite of the widespread discussion regarding long-duration funds, their aggregate size seems to be relatively modest at this point.) By and large, the different maturity groups remain sealed off from one another, with relatively little movement of dollars between them.

With respect to equity-based funds, the volatility concentration is even greater, with most such funds having volatilities of 10 to 11.50 percent, that is, comparable to that of the traditional 60 percent equity–40 percent bond allocation. While there are U.S. institutional funds that have only 20 percent equity allocations, these tend to also have lower bond allocations and a larger alpha core. As noted earlier, the net result is that their beta falls in the 0.55 to 0.65 band, which, in turn, drives their fund volatility into the common 10- to 11.50-percent region.

Thus, the equity-based realm is even more highly concentrated along the volatility dimension than in the bond world. The primary differentiating feature among equity-based funds is the level of ascent of the alpha wall (together with acceptance of the associated dragon risks that are not visible in a standard return/volatility space).

The basic concept of an efficient frontier serves to display the various allocation choices available to a fund in terms of risk-and-return trade-offs. Given the regulatory and behavioral restrictions that circumscribe the flexibility of U.S. institutional funds, a societal frontier along the lines of Exhibit 8.7 reflects the limited degree of freedom granted to various categories of funds.

These discontinuities also raise a question as to whether institutional funds really do pursue well-defined risk-and-return tradeoffs, either between or within the various quantum states of volatility risk.

The discontinuities in the societal frontier also highlight the potential opportunities for portfolio improvement available to those funds that can develop the requisite investment flexibility. In theory, growth in such flexibility, together with the process of equilibration, should ultimately move the societal frontier toward a more continuously convex shape. In reality, however, the questions raised and the opportunities presented by this societal frontier are likely to be with us for a very long time.

REFERENCES

Markowitz, H. M. 2005. "Market efficiency: A theoretical distinction and so what?" *Financial Analysts Journal* 61 (5): 17–30.

Sharpe, W. F. 1964. "Capital asset prices: A theory of market equilibrium under conditions of risk." *Journal of Finance* 19 (3): 425–442.

CHAPTER 9

Equilibration

*P*ositive alphas are particularly attractive to beta-dominated funds. For the typical U.S. pension fund, endowment fund, or foundation, the prospect of a truly positive alpha source should be highly attractive in terms of the standard risk-and-return measures, even though a variety of other considerations may limit the weight that can be assigned to such an asset class.

New dollar flows should create downward pressure on positive alphas. Funds that control a large pool of assets are becoming increasingly flexible in their allocation philosophy and will naturally deliver a significant dollar flow into positive alpha sources. This new demand will lead to upward pressure on pricing, and all else being equal, will have a negative effect on the expected (going forward) alpha premium.

Beta-dominated funds will focus pressure on the highest alphas. With the alpha-seeking beta-dominated funds, alpha erosion will be focused initially on those alternatives providing the highest expected alpha return. The associated alpha volatility will receive less attention, as it has only a minor impact on the total fund volatility.

Other funds may focus on the highest Sharpe ratio. Funds that are either less constrained or not beta-dominated may be more concerned with the associated alpha volatility and therefore seek those alternatives that have the higher Sharpe ratios. This would lead to a very different equilibration process, with the higher Sharpe ratios being brought down in a cascading fashion.

Equilibration suggests the need for a more fluid policy portfolio. A dynamic equilibration process and the resulting ebb and flow of realized returns and going-forward alphas should sound a cautionary note against an overly rigid policy portfolio.

BETA DOMINATION AND CONSTRAINED ALTERNATIVES

Any feasible allocation to alternatives, after an appropriate portfolio-level beta adjustment, will contribute a virtually negligible increment to over-all fund volatility. Consequently, if such passive investments can offer the prospect of a positive alpha without a material increase in fund volatility, they should naturally be highly appealing to institutional funds. Although allocations to such alpha sources are generally limited by a host of other con-siderations, the trend toward diversification into various alternative assets provides some evidence of this attraction.

At the same time, the growing acceptance (and even fashionability) of these asset classes engenders new dollar flows that could lead to a reduction in its going-forward alpha return. When the source of an alpha is limited, return erosion would be the natural evolution as a market moves toward a rational equilibrium under the pressure of new demand. Thus, as an al-pha source becomes ever more integrated into the standard institutional framework, its going-forward alpha should continue to decline as long as it still provides a positive incremental return. If there were no other sources of demand, these flow-vulnerable alphas would decline to zero over time. However, there will always be other markets for a given asset that are not beta-dominated, and the return erosion should therefore ultimately reach some positive value representing a balanced equilibrium across all sources of demand.

ALPHA DECAY UNDER BETA DOMINATION

This combination of beta domination and alternative constraints has a num-ber of dramatic implications. First of all, it suggests that the traditional Sharpe and Treynor ratios should play a lesser role in the selection of the preferred alpha sources. As an alternative asset's alpha volatility becomes less relevant, it is the alpha return that becomes the key variable. Thus, the fund should fill up on the highest alpha source to the extent that it can be comfortably accommodated, then proceed to the next highest alpha source, and so forth.

The resulting alpha core subportfolio will contribute some implicit beta value to the fund's overall beta. The fund can then achieve the desired total beta value by adjusting the weights in its equity and fixed income compo-nents. Given a strict focus on standard measures of total fund volatility, it will be the alpha returns—and not the alpha volatilities—that play the central role in constructing the optimal alpha core. Basically, in this narrowly defined context, it is only the alpha returns and the associated constraints that matter. Of course, there remain the other beyond-model dragon risks, such as liquidity limits, headline risks, and so forth. The associated Sharpe and Treynor ratios will play a minimal role other than as information ratios that can help to statistically validate the reliability of realized excess returns.

REALIZED RETURNS VERSUS GOING-FORWARD ALPHAS

It should be emphasized at the same time that just because an alpha deteriorates over the course of time does not mean that the return to the early investors also deteriorates. In fact, quite the contrary: As the alpha declines, there may be a significant increase in the realized return, depending on the specific duration characteristics of the individual asset class relative to its going-forward risk premium. Indeed, in some cases, these superior realized returns might attract even greater dollar flows from those addicted to past performance.

It is worth taking a closer look at how this equilibration process might unfold. Suppose we have two alpha sources, H and L, with initial alphas H1 and L1 (Exhibit 9.1). H's higher alpha should be the greater magnet for beta-dominated funds, and these flows would exert an upward pressure on H's price, driving down H's going-forward alpha. At some point, H's alpha will fall to the point H2, where it coincides with L's alpha, L1 (Exhibit 9.2). From this point forward, their alpha returns would decline in concert (Exhibit 9.3). Any other alpha sources with initially lower returns would then be sequentially captured by these collapsing ceilings of return.

SHARPE RATIO DECAY

Up to this point, the discussion has focused on beta-dominated funds. There are situations, however, in which a different balance prevails between alpha and beta risks. Thus, in a long-only portfolio with high volatility sensitivity but without alpha constraints, it can be shown that the optimal mixture would include each asset class with a weight proportional to its Sharpe ratio (Treynor and Black 1973; Sharpe 1994). In particular, this mixture might also occur at low volatilities, in which a high cash level keeps the optimal alpha weights below their constraint limits. In such low-volatility situations,

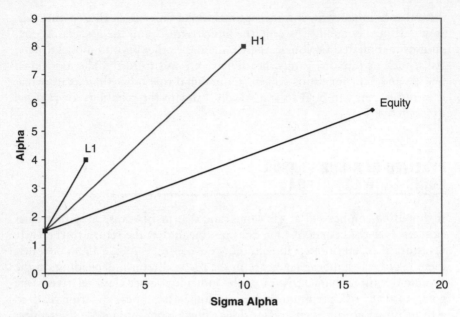

EXHIBIT 9.1   Initial Alpha Returns and Volatilities
Source: Morgan Stanley Research

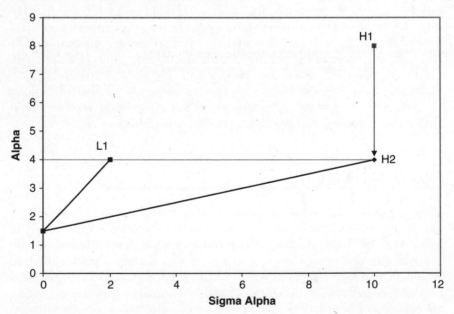

EXHIBIT 9.2   H's Alpha Declines to Match L's Alpha
Source: Morgan Stanley Research

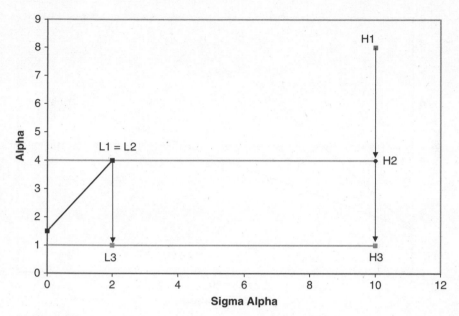

EXHIBIT 9.3 H's and L's Alpha Returns Decline Together
Source: Morgan Stanley Research

the optimal frontier would just consist of a straight line with a slope determined by all the Sharpe ratios for the relevant assets.

The market pressures in such an environment could lead to a very different equilibration process, with the assets having the higher Sharpe ratios becoming the preferred target for new flows. For example, suppose that H has a higher alpha than L, but with a much greater volatility, so that H's Sharpe ratio of alpha return over volatility is lower than L's (that is, as depicted in Exhibit 9.4). In this context, with free access to all asset classes, L would become the preferential target for the incremental flows that would exert downward pressure on the going-forward alpha.

The preceding discussion has simplistically focused only on changes in the alpha return. In reality, there would be many variables in motion as the equilibration process unfolds. The market value of the asset class might grow, new supply might be forthcoming, volatility might be changing, and a whole host of other pricing factors might also be brought into play. For the moment, however, assume that L's higher Sharpe ratio was the main attractor. L's alpha return would then decline under the incremental flows, dragging down its Sharpe ratio until it coincides with H's Sharpe ratio (Exhibit 9.4). Once the ratios converge, the two alpha returns will be quite

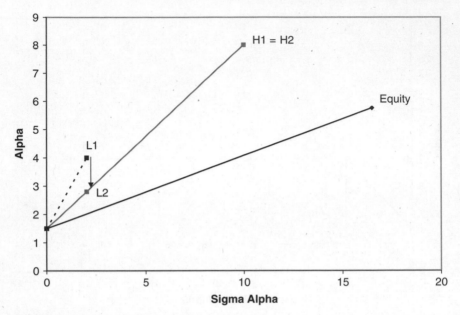

EXHIBIT 9.4   H and L Sharpe Ratios Coincide
Source: Morgan Stanley Research

different, with H's alpha now exceeding L's by an even wider margin. From this point forward, the two coincidental Sharpe ratios should decline at the same pace, but H's higher volatility would lead to a much faster decline in its alpha return.

Theoretically, after sufficient market pressure, the common Sharpe ratio for L and H might drop to the level of the Sharpe ratio of equities (Exhibit 9.5). The question then arises as to the behavior of the alpha Sharpe ratios from that point forward. The basic principle is that any statistically independent asset with a positive Sharpe ratio should be included in forming an optimal unconstrained portfolio. Thus, assuming that the equity market risk premium remains unchanged, the two Sharpe ratios for the alpha sources H and L would theoretically continue to decline in concert right down to the point at which they reach zero (Exhibit 9.6). Under our assumptions, the only way this can happen is for the alpha returns themselves to be driven down to zero.

Of course, in reality there are always multiple sources of demand for a given asset class. As the alphas are pushed down by one new source of demand, they will at the same time be driving away other pre-existing sources of support. At some point, the net effect of attracted new demand

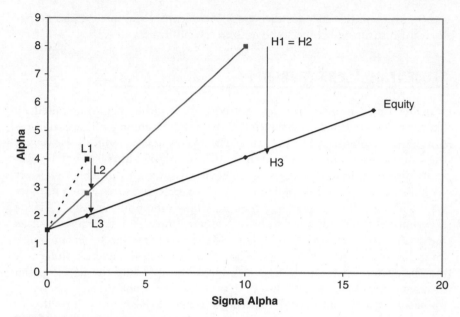

EXHIBIT 9.5 H and L Drop to Equity Sharpe Ratio
Source: Morgan Stanley Research

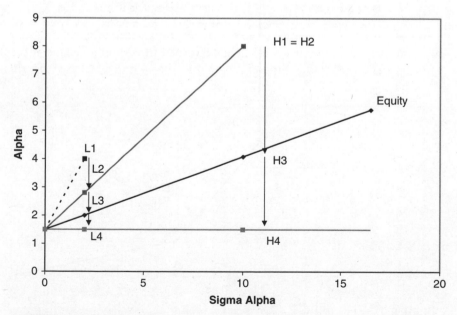

EXHIBIT 9.6 H and L Decline to a Zero Sharpe Ratio
Source: Morgan Stanley Research

(or supply) will just balance the egress of the earlier supporters, and going-forward returns will reach some nonzero equilibrium value.

SEQUENTIAL ALPHA EROSION

Whether one assumes that the environment is either beta-dominated or Sharpe ratio–maximizing, the ultimate theoretical outcome of the equilibration process will always be the same: The alphas will be reduced. However, the sequence of events and the alpha paths for this equilibration will be radically different. Indeed, one can even envision situations in which we start with a pure beta-dominated context, with market pressures acting initially on the alpha returns alone, and then moving to the point at which Sharpe ratio–motivated funds start to have a greater interest and begin to act as the price setters (Exhibit 9.7). To the extent that some funds become more intent on overcoming beta domination and bringing the overall alpha risk into balance with the total beta risk (possibly involving the use of alpha leverage), the efficient portfolios may well develop alpha preferences based upon some combination of the Sharpe ratio and the alpha return itself.

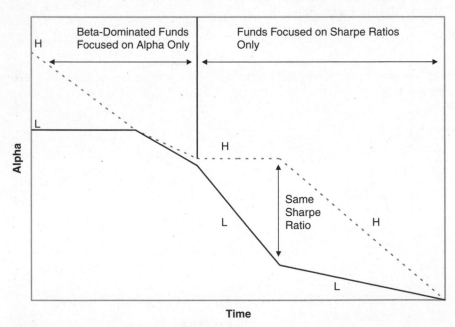

EXHIBIT 9.7   Alpha Returns over Time
Source: Morgan Stanley Research

EQUILIBRATION ACROSS THE SOCIETAL FRONTIER

Of course, the marginal price setters would always be those funds that are most energetic in pursuit of a given alpha source. In the current institutional market, the price setters are likely to be the beta-dominated funds. By their very nature, these funds are already the greater risk takers, and they are likely to be willing to incur even further risk by climbing up the alpha wall.

One can envision an efficient frontier that reflects not an individual fund's set of choices but rather the behavioral characteristics of investors as a group. This frontier would have some strange characteristics. For example, in the lower volatilities, most alternative assets would be either ruled out or subject to very tight constraints. Indeed, even the equity weight would be quite constrained. In a low-volatility region, this societal frontier would be heavily fixed income oriented, and would have a slope that was far lower than that of the unconstrained optimal frontier.

At the higher volatility levels associated with traditional long term funds having greater risk appetites, the frontier would begin to incorporate greater equity weight, eventually reaching the traditional 60/40 allocation with a volatility of roughly 10 percent. Beyond that, there may not be much increase in incremental volatility, as few funds seem willing to venture beyond the volatility barrier of 11.50 percent. Rather, any further risk seeking would take the form of climbing the alpha wall, that is, moving into more alpha sources. Thus, the frontier at this extreme right-hand point would retain the same 10- to 11.50-percent volatility, but would move vertically into higher expected returns. The greater risks incurred would then fall more into the category of the dragon risks, which would not be visible in standard return-and-volatility space.

This societal frontier would be vastly different from the traditional convex efficient frontier. It would appear to have terraced effects at both the point at which it transitions into the equity-accepting funds and then subsequently when it moves into the more alpha-accepting funds.

This frontier may help shed light on the respective habits of various types of investors and on the forces that affect the pricing of asset classes over time. In terms of the equilibration process, the societal frontier would rise in volatility regions in which funds were able to expand their alpha cores, and then subside in those regions encountering alpha erosion from excessive new flows.

This dynamic environment has some major implications for the development of policy portfolios. A stable policy portfolio serves many valuable organizational needs. However, with a seemingly inevitable ebb and flow in alpha returns (as well as in equity and bond risk premiums), perhaps more thought should be given to the appropriate balance between the benefits of policy stability versus the adaptability of a more fluid policy portfolio.

REFERENCES

Sharpe, W. F. 1994. "The Sharpe ratio." *Journal of Portfolio Management* 21 (1): 45–58.

Treynor, J., and F. Black. 1973. "How to use security analysis to improve portfolio selection." *Journal of Business* 46 (1): 66–86.

CHAPTER 10

Shortfall Risks and Efficient Frontiers

*S*hortfall risk provides a simple way of integrating portfolio risk and return. The shortfall risk is the probability of falling below some specified minimum return or asset level. By combining a shortfall probability with an efficient frontier, one can determine the range of portfolios that satisfy any given minimum threshold condition.

A tight shortfall constraint over short horizons can lead to very low-risk portfolios. Typical institutional portfolios have a 25 percent probability of negative returns over one-year periods. To have a high assurance of earning positive returns over short horizons, one would have to settle for portfolios having an unacceptably high cash percentage and far too low a return.

Longer time horizons reduce shortfall probability. Over longer time horizons, high-return–higher-risk portfolios become more acceptable under various shortfall constraints. For example, in moving from a one-year to a four-year time horizon, a typical institutional portfolio would have the probability of negative returns declining from 25 percent to 9 percent. Thus, the shortfall approach helps to demonstrate that the combination of a long time horizon and a reliably positive expected return can serve as a powerful antidote to volatility risk.

IMPORTANCE OF SHORTFALL RISK IN PORTFOLIOS

One of the key considerations for institutional funds in forming their policy portfolios is to set sector and overall risk limits that fall within comfortable ranges. One technique for addressing certain facets of this risk envelope is the shortfall risk—the probability of falling below some specified minimum return or asset level.

Shortfall risk provides a particularly simple way of integrating portfolio volatility and return. Institutions often have some explicit (or at least implicit) minimum return or asset level that they would be loathe to fall below. This critical threshold may be articulated as an annualized return over a specific benchmark such as cash, bonds, inflation, and so forth. By combining a shortfall probability with an efficient frontier, one can determine the range of portfolios that satisfy a given threshold condition. Shortfall risk can also be particularly helpful in showing how longer horizons affect the allocation decision.

Most institutional portfolios seem to be clustered within a rather narrow range of risk, with one-year volatilities of 10 to 11 percent. Portfolios with such volatility levels have a 25 percent probability of generating negative returns over a one-year period. To have a high assurance of earning positive returns over the one-year horizon, one would have to settle for portfolios having an unacceptably high cash percentage and far too low a return.

Most efficient frontiers are developed within the standard framework of a one-year horizon. However, under some further assumptions, the frontiers can be extended to longer investment periods. As we lengthen the time horizon, the *annualized* expected returns remain essentially the same as for the one-year case. Assuming a pure independent random walk, however, the annualized volatility declines by $1/\sqrt{n}$, in which n is the number of years. Thus, the efficient frontier becomes steeper as the horizon lengthens.

The shortfall approach helps to demonstrate that a combination of a long time horizon and a reliably positive expected return can serve as a powerful antidote to volatility risk. Over these longer time horizons, high-return–higher-risk portfolios become more acceptable under various shortfall constraints. For example, in moving from a one-year to a four-year time horizon, a typical institutional portfolio could see its probability of negative returns decline from 25 percent to 9 percent (see the appendix for calculations).

Indeed, one might speculate whether a broadly held desire to avoid negative results over the long term might be one of the factors behind the rather surprising herding of institutional portfolios into the same 10- to 11-percent volatility range.

EFFICIENT FRONTIERS USING FIXED ALPHA CORES

Exhibit 10.1 is a graphical display of a three-part efficient frontier over a one-year horizon with cash as the risk-free base. The middle fixed core segment is composed of a 60 percent alpha core of alternative assets. The remaining 40 percent weight is deployed into varying mixtures of U.S. bonds

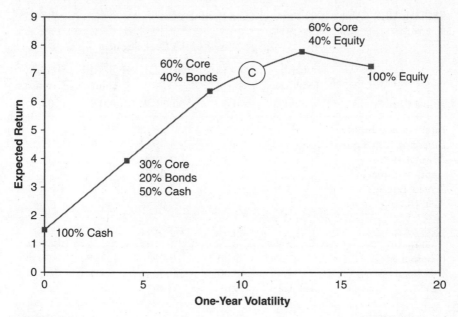

EXHIBIT 10.1 The Efficient Frontier Using a Fixed 60 Percent Alpha Core
Source: Morgan Stanley Research

and equities. In practice, most allocations will fall within the middle segment, that is, the fixed alpha core segment, in which the 60 percent core is mixed with bonds and equity.

Exhibit 10.2 provides more detail on how the asset structure in Portfolio C can be used to develop an alpha core. To achieve portfolio risk levels that lie higher or lower than the fixed core segment, the endpoint portfolios are mixed with greater concentrations of cash or equity. At the higher-risk end of the core segment, the portfolio has 60 percent core and 40 percent equity. To attain even higher risk levels, the frontier moves into an equity extension whereby the equity replaces the alpha core until reaching 100 percent equity. For lower risk levels, cash is mixed with the fixed core segment's lower risk point (60 percent core and 40 percent bonds).

SHORTFALL PROBABILITIES

There can be no absolute guarantee that any portfolio will achieve a given minimum return. Assuming returns are normally distributed, however, there are combinations of portfolio return and volatility that will provide a

EXHIBIT 10.2 Alpha Core Frontier from Portfolio C

		Fixed Alpha Core Segment			
	Cash Extension	Low Risk Point	Portfolio C	High Risk Point	Equity Extension
Alpha Core %	0.0%	60.0%	60.0%	60.0%	0.0%
International Equity			15.00		
Emerging Mkt Equity			5.00		
Absolute Return			10.00		
Venture Capital			10.00		
Private Equity			10.00		
Real Estate			10.00		
Swing Assets %		40.0%	40.0%	40.0%	
U.S. Equity		0.00	20.00	40.00	100.00
U.S. Bonds		40.00	20.00	0.00	
Cash	100.00	0.00	0.00	0.00	
Overall Portfolio					
Expected Return	1.50	6.38	7.08	7.78	7.25
β	0.00	0.40	0.57	0.75	1.00
β-Return	0.00	2.30	3.29	4.28	5.75
α	0.00	2.58	2.28	1.99	0.00
r_f	1.50	1.50	1.50	1.50	1.50
σ_α	0.00	5.12	4.48	4.25	0.00
σ	0.00	8.35	10.45	13.01	16.50

Source: Morgan Stanley Research

prescribed probability of not falling below a specified threshold. For example, one possible shortfall condition is that positive returns be achieved with a probability of 90 percent; in other words, that the shortfall probability of negative returns be less than 10 percent. As shown in the appendix, this shortfall constraint will be satisfied by any portfolio having expected returns that are greater than 1.28 times its volatility (Leibowitz et al., 1991, 1996).

Exhibit 10.3 shows a normal distribution graph of Portfolio C with its expected return of 7.08 percent and volatility of 10.45 percent. For this expected return and volatility, there is 25 percent probability that returns

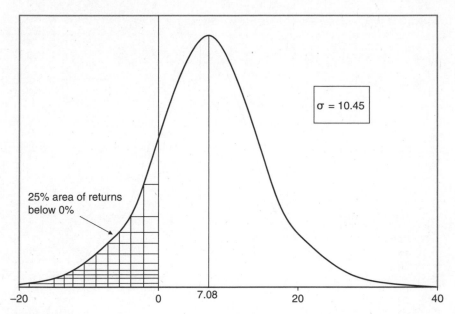

EXHIBIT 10.3 Portfolio C's 25 percent Probability of Negative Returns over a One-Year Horizon
Source: Morgan Stanley Research

will fall below zero percent over a one-year period. In other words, the area of C's shortfall region below zero percent amounts to 25 percent of all possible returns.

By increasing the expected return, we can reduce Portfolio C's shortfall region to the point at which only 10 percent of returns fall below zero percent. The key is to shift the distribution sufficiently to the right so that the left-hand tail contains only 10 percent of the area.

To obtain this shift, we can hypothetically increase the expected return to 13.40 percent while holding the volatility constant at 10.45 percent. This results in a rightward shift of the distribution as shown in Exhibit 10.4. This artificially greater expected return of 13.40 percent then equates to 1.28 times the volatility of 10.45 percent. The net result is that negative returns now account for only 10 percent of the probability.

The other possibility is to lower the volatility of Portfolio C while holding its expected return constant at 7.08 percent. A lower volatility of 5.52 percent leads to the more narrow distribution shown in Exhibit 10.5. Once again, the shortfall constraint is met since the expected return of 7.08 percent now equals 1.28 times the reduced volatility of 5.52 percent.

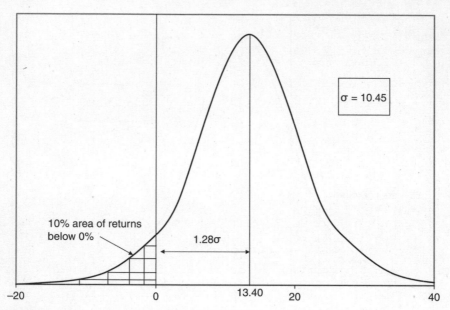

10% area of returns below 0%

1.28σ

σ = 10.45

−20   0   13.40   20   40

EXHIBIT 10.4 Satisfying the Shortfall Condition through an Increase in Expected Return
Source: Morgan Stanley Research

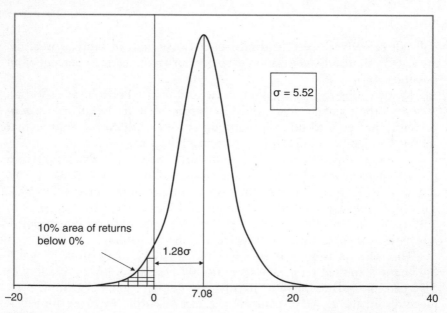

10% area of returns below 0%

1.28σ

σ = 5.52

−20   0   7.08   20   40

EXHIBIT 10.5 Satisfying the Shortfall Condition through a Reduced Volatility
Source: Morgan Stanley Research

The shortfall concept has considerable appeal, given its computational simplicity and highly intuitive nature. Nevertheless, it should be pointed out that it is an incomplete measure of risk. For example, the shortfall probability does not gauge the magnitude of potential shortfalls. Moreover, there are arguments (from utility theory) that give preference to the variance, rather than the standard deviation, as a measure of portfolio risk.

SHORTFALL REGIONS IN A RISK-AND-RETURN SPACE

From the preceding, we see that satisfying the shortfall condition requires that a portfolio's expected return must exceed 1.28 times its associated volatility. In the risk-and-return space, a line drawn from the origin with a slope of 1.28 will then define a region at which this shortfall condition is satisfied.

Exhibit 10.6 displays the risk-and-return region that satisfies the 10 percent shortfall constraint over a one-year period. Portfolios on or above the shortfall line will meet or exceed this shortfall condition, while portfolios below the line will not. We can see that over the one-year horizon, Portfolio C would not satisfy this shortfall condition.

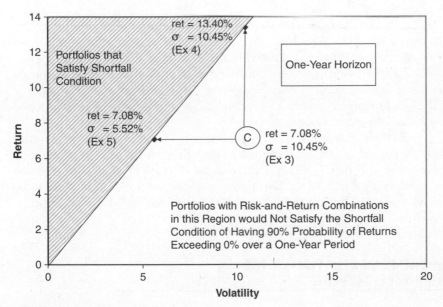

EXHIBIT 10.6 The Shortfall Line
Source: Morgan Stanley Research

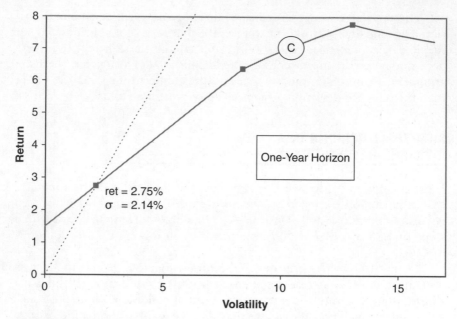

EXHIBIT 10.7   The Efficient Frontier with the Shortfall Line
Source: Morgan Stanley Research

Exhibit 10.7 combines the efficient frontier from Exhibit 10.1 with the 10 percent shortfall probability line. All of the points on the efficient frontier that lie above the shortfall line will satisfy the shortfall condition. We can see that in the 10 percent case, the intersection point of the efficient frontier and shortfall line occurs along the lowest risk (and lowest return) segment of the efficient frontier, where 75 percent cash is mixed with 15 percent alpha core and 10 percent bonds.

In Exhibit 10.8, we reverse the process to determine the minimum return that Portfolio C would be expected to provide with 90 percent probability over a one-year period. (This line is parallel to the 10 percent shortfall line in Exhibits 10.6 and 10.7.) This minimum return threshold turns out to be −6.30 percent. Thus, over the one-year time frame, the downside risk for Portfolio C is quite substantial.

SHORTFALLS RELATIVE TO THE RISK-FREE BASELINE

Another interesting feature of the shortfall approach is that the slope of the efficient frontier can be used to calculate the probability of a shortfall

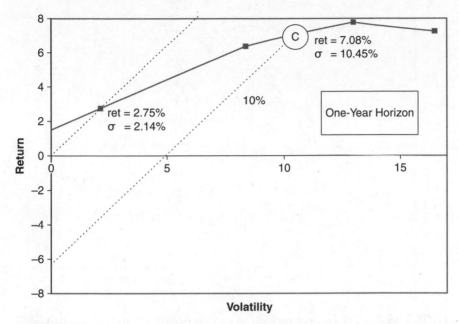

EXHIBIT 10.8 Minimum Return Threshold for Portfolio C over One Year
Source: Morgan Stanley Research

below the return of the minimum risk asset, that is, the 1.50 percent return of cash. Given the slope of our frontier's first segment, there is a 28 percent probability of a shortfall below 1.50 percent for all portfolios along this initial segment (Exhibit 10.9). In other words, all portfolios along this segment have a 72 percent probability of providing a one-year return above 1.50 percent.

As we move toward the fixed core segment, the slope declines and the shortfall probability rises, as shown in Exhibit 10.9. At the right-most point of the frontier, the portfolio consisting of 100 percent equity has a 36 percent probability of returns falling below 1.50 percent.

Shortfall levels anchored at the risk-free rate can also be interpreted in terms of Sharpe ratios—the slope of the return premium to the volatility risk (see the appendix). Thus, a higher Sharpe ratio corresponds to an increased probability of returns that exceed the risk-free rate. Exhibit 10.10 demonstrates this relationship in a graph that is basically a plot of the standardized normal distribution. We see that for Portfolio C's Sharpe ratio of 0.53, we have a 30 percent shortfall probability relative to the 1.50 percent cash rate. (This shortfall probability contrasts with our earlier reference to Portfolio C's 25 percent probability relative to the lower threshold of just providing a positive return.)

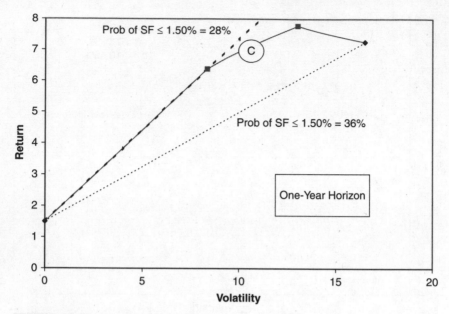

EXHIBIT 10.9   The Efficient Frontier as its Own Shortfall Line
Source: Morgan Stanley Research

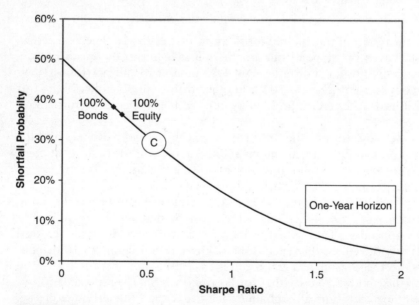

EXHIBIT 10.10   Sharpe Ratio as a Measure of Shortfall Probability Relative to the Risk-Free Rate
Source: Morgan Stanley Research

SHORTFALL PROBABILITIES ALONG
THE EFFICIENT FRONTIER

In Exhibit 10.11, we go back to looking at shortfalls relative to the critical threshold of zero percent, that is, achieving positive returns. The graph then displays the shortfall probability associated with each position along the efficient frontier. We see that most of the efficient frontier has shortfall probabilities well in excess of the 10 percent level. In particular, as we saw earlier, Portfolio C has a shortfall probability of 25 percent, placing it well outside the bounds of acceptability given a 10 percent criterion for positive returns over a one-year period.

MULTIPLE HORIZON COMPARISONS

We now consider longer investment horizons and explore how this affects the relationship between the efficient frontier and the shortfall condition. Assuming the most basic process for how returns evolve over a time period of n years, expected returns accumulate by a factor of n while the cumulative

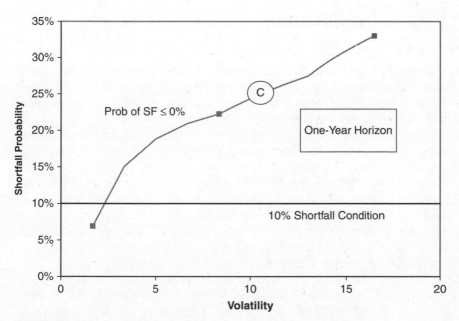

EXHIBIT 10.11 Shortfall Probability along the Efficient Frontier
Source: Morgan Stanley Research

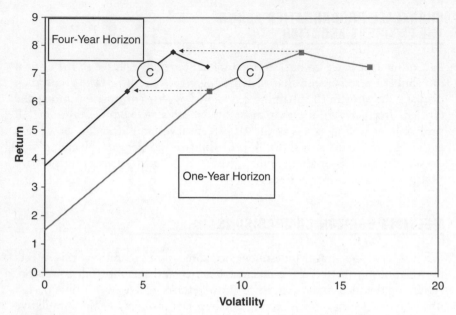

EXHIBIT 10.12 Annualized Efficient Frontiers over One-Year and Four-Year Horizons
Source: Morgan Stanley Research

volatility only increases by a multiple of $\sqrt{n}$. When transformed into annualized values (again, in the simplest possible fashion), the expected return remains roughly the same as the one-year rate while the volatility declines to $(1/\sqrt{n})$th of the one-year volatility.

By plotting all returns and volatilities in annualized terms, we can see how the risk-and-return characteristics change across multiple time horizons. Exhibit 10.12 compares the frontiers for a one-year and a four-year horizon. Note that over the longer horizon, a four-year duration bond becomes the more appropriate risk-free asset. Also, while we have stayed with the standard normal distribution, a more theoretically correct analysis would be to move to a lognormal characterization. (The appendix presents the assumptions used to develop this graph and also points out some of the considerations required for a more comprehensive analysis.)

The shortfall threshold can also be interpreted as an annualized return over each of the respective horizons. Within this framework, the shortfall line will remain unchanged as we move from one horizon to another. In particular, for the threshold requirement of positive returns, the 10 percent shortfall line will always originate from the origin and have a slope of 1.28.

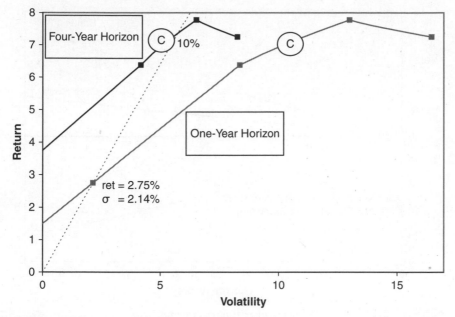

EXHIBIT 10.13 Shortfalls over Different Horizons
Source: Morgan Stanley Research

Thus, as shown in Exhibit 10.13, we can compare the maximum return portfolios that satisfy this shortfall condition, given different horizons. For the one-year horizon, as we saw earlier, we had to revert to a very low-risk portfolio to have a high confidence of positive returns. When we move to a four-year period, however, most portfolios along the first and middle segment (including Portfolio C) now meet the 10 percent shortfall criterion for positive returns.

Exhibit 10.14 presents a different view of the shortfall returns for Portfolio C. The solid lines show the growth of $100 invested and compounded at –5 percent, zero percent, the 1.50 percent cash rate, and the 3.75 percent bond rate. The dotted line then displays the minimum asset line that Portfolio C would achieve with 10 percent probability over the indicated time period. As time progresses, this shortfall level for Portfolio C rises, passing the zero percent mark just before the fourth year and rising above the cash level before the sixth year.

Exhibit 10.15 compares the shortfall probability along the efficient frontier for the one-year versus the four-year horizon. The longer time horizon has a significant impact on lowering the shortfall probability. In particular, we once again see that Portfolio C has quite a high probability (25 percent)

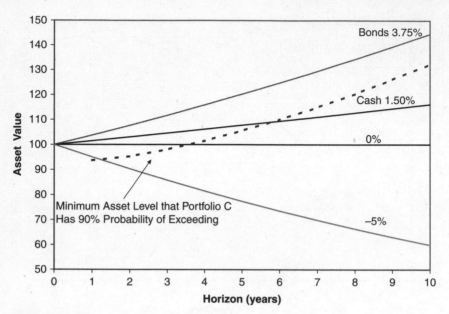

EXHIBIT 10.14   Asset Value Comparisons over Time
Source: Morgan Stanley Research

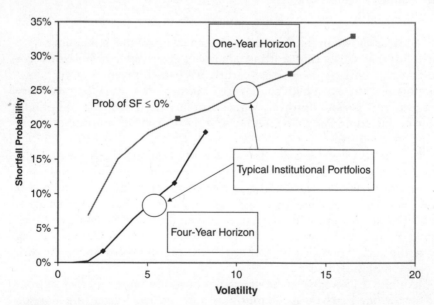

EXHIBIT 10.15   Horizon Effect on Shortfall Probability along the
Efficient Frontier
Source: Morgan Stanley Research

of negative returns over the one-year horizon. To satisfy the shortfall requirement over one year, a portfolio would have an unacceptably high cash percentage with far too low a return for a long term oriented portfolio. Once the horizon is extended to four years, however, a large portion of the fixed core segment becomes acceptable.

Thus, while Portfolio C does not satisfy the 10 percent requirement for a positive return over a one-year period, the longer four-year period brings Portfolio C right into acceptability. Given that most institutional portfolios have risk characteristics comparable to Portfolio C, it is tempting to wonder whether institutions implicitly set risk levels with some such longer horizon in mind.

APPENDIX

The Shortfall Constraint

With a normal distribution of returns $\tilde{r}$ having a mean $\bar{r}$ and standard deviation σ, let

$$P(\tilde{r} \leq r_o | \bar{r}, \sigma) = p$$

in which p is the probability of returns falling below some minimum threshold r_o. Regarding a variable $\tilde{x}$ from the standardized normal N (0,1), this probability can be expressed as

$$P(\tilde{x} \leq \frac{(r_o - \bar{r})}{\sigma} | 0,1) = p$$

If we let $-k_p$ be the cutoff for the left tail of N (0,1), having area $p\%$, then

$$P(\tilde{x} \leq -k_p | 0,1) = p$$

and

$$-k_p = \frac{(r_o - \bar{r})}{\sigma}$$

or

$$k_p = \frac{(\bar{r} - r_o)}{\sigma}$$

Thus, any portfolio having a combination of an expected return $\bar{r}$ and a volatility σ will have a shortfall probability p of falling below r_o as long as

$$\bar{r} - k_p\sigma = r_o$$

More generally, this minimum shortfall condition will be satisfied by any portfolio having a $(\bar{r}, \sigma)$ combination that exceeds this cutoff value, that is,

$$\bar{r} - k_p\sigma \geq r_o$$

or

$$\bar{r} \geq r_o + k_p\sigma.$$

The Relationship

$$\bar{r} = r_o + k_p\sigma$$

defines a line with slope k_p in risk-and-return space that intersects the $\sigma = 0$ axis at r_o. All the $(\bar{r}, \sigma)$ portfolios on—or above—this line will satisfy the shortfall constraint of providing a probability of at most p of penetrating the threshold r_o. For example, a 10 percent shortfall probability for the standard normal $N(0,1)$ corresponds to $k_p = 1.28$. Thus, with a positive return as the threshold, we have $r_o = 0$, and the shortfall line is just given by $\bar{r} = 1.28\sigma$.

The shortfall concept is one basic approach to integrating a portfolio's expected return with its volatility risk. It has the virtues of being both highly intuitive and extremely simple to display in a risk-and-return space. Indeed, it corresponds to the primitive notion of a downside risk as a failure to achieve or surpass some defined objective. It also has the benefit of clearly demonstrating how a combination of longer horizons and positive expected returns can counteract volatility risk.

However, the shortfall risk also suffers from being too simplistic in a number of ways. First of all, it fails to address the expected magnitude of any penetration through the shortfall threshold. Second, while a normal distribution may be the simplest characterization of asset returns, it is not necessarily the best, even over a short horizon. Indeed, over any span of years, a random walk based on one-year returns generally migrates toward a lognormal distribution. While the shortfall idea can be extended to a larger class of probability distributions, the distributions in this paper have been assumed to be normal over all time horizons.

A more general discussion on the subject of asymmetric measures for portfolio risk can be found in the referenced papers (Bawa and Lindenberg 1977; Harlow and Rao 1989).

Multiple Horizon Returns

Over longer periods, we have assumed that our normal-based returns progress in a simple random walk, with the expected returns accumulating linearly over n years and the volatility rising by a factor of $\sqrt{n}$. When annualized by dividing by n, the annualized expected return has the desirable quality of remaining constant. At the same time, the annualized volatility declines by a factor of $\frac{1}{\sqrt{n}}$.

When combined with the shortfall condition, a portfolio with one-year $(\bar{r}, \sigma)$ will meet the n-year shortfall constraint when

$$\bar{r} \geq r_o + k_p \frac{\sigma}{\sqrt{n}}$$

Under these assumptions, lengthening the time horizon will always expand the set of acceptable portfolios.

As with our shortfall model, however, this view of how returns evolve over time represents a highly limited treatment of this topic. First, as mentioned earlier, asset returns tend to migrate over time toward having lognormal distributions. Second, the arithmetic mean return is not the best measure of centrality over longer periods. Moreover, volatility itself can erode the growth of expected returns over sufficiently long horizons. And finally, the very model of a pure random walk fails to account for mean or volatility reversions and other compression effects that arguably come into play over longer periods (Campbell and Viceria 2002, 2005).

In keeping with the simplifying assumptions that led to our three-segment efficient frontier, however, our belief is that the selected models, while limited, are sufficient to convey the pragmatic implications of the key issues discussed in this chapter.

The Shortfall Probability for a Given Portfolio

We showed in the preceding section how a given threshold and shortfall probability can be used to designate a region of acceptable portfolios in a risk-and-return space. This methodology can easily be reverse engineered, however, to find the shortfall probability for a given portfolio and a specified threshold.

The basic procedure is to solve the preceding equation for k_p,

$$k_p = \frac{(\bar{r} - r_o)}{\sigma/\sqrt{n}}$$

For a portfolio with a risk-and-return combination $(\bar{r}, \sigma)$, a specified threshold r_o, and a time horizon n, we can then compute the value k_p. This value represents a cutoff as the number of standard deviations to the left of the mean of a standardized normal distribution $N(0,1)$. The area below this cutoff value corresponds to the shortfall probability that the portfolio $(\bar{r}, \sigma)$ will provide n-period returns falling below the threshold r_o.

As an example, consider Portfolio C with its expected return of 7.08 percent and its volatility of 10.45 percent. If we set $r_o = 0$ as the threshold for positive returns, then over a one-year horizon,

$$k_p = \frac{(7.08 - 0)}{10.45/\sqrt{1}}$$

$$= .68$$

The left-hand tail of $N(0,1)$ lying below $-.68$ corresponds to a probability of 25 percent. Thus, Portfolio C has a high 25 percent probability of generating negative returns over one year.

In contrast, over four years,

$$k_p = \frac{(7.08 - 0)}{10.45/\sqrt{4}}$$

$$= 1.35$$

The left-hand tail below -1.35 in $N(0,1)$ implies only a 9 percent probability of negative returns. Thus, the move from a one-year to a four-year horizon brings the probability of negative returns from a high 25 percent level to a more palatable 9 percent. (However, in fairness, it should be noted that a zero percent return over four years would represent a considerably more adverse outcome than zero percent over one year!)

The Sharpe Ratio as a Shortfall Probability

If we set the risk-free rate as a return threshold, that is, $r_o = r_f$, the preceding equation becomes

$$k_p = \frac{(\bar{r} - r_f)}{\sigma/\sqrt{n}}$$

In particular, for $n = 1$, the cutoff value k_p then just equals the Sharpe ratio for the portfolio $(\bar{r}, \sigma)$,

$$k_p = \frac{(\bar{r} - r_f)}{\sigma}$$

Thus, the Sharpe ratio directly determines the shortfall probability in relation to the risk-free rate.

REFERENCES

Bawa, V., and E. B. Lindenberg. 1977. "Capital market equilibrium in a mean, lower partial moment framework." *Journal of Financial Economics* 5 (2): 189–200.

Campbell, John Y., and Luis M. Viceira. 2002. *Strategic asset allocation*. New York: Oxford University Press.

———. 2005. "The term structure of the risk-return trade-off." *Financial Analysts Journal* 61: 34–44.

Harlow, W. V., and R. Rao. 1989. "Asset pricing in a generalized mean-lower partial moment framework: Theory and evidence." *Journal of Financial and Quantitative Analysis* 24 (3): 285–311.

Leibowitz, M. L., L. N. Bader, and S. Kogelman. 1991. "Asset allocation under shortfall constraints." *Journal of Portfolio Management* 17: 18–23.

———. 1996. *Return targets and shortfall risks*. New York: Irwin Professional Publishing.

CHAPTER 11

Convergence of Risks

*O*ne of the main drawbacks to the shortfall risk concept is that it only addresses the probability of an event occurring at the end of a time period. It is important to realize that the probability of an event occurring at any point during the time period will be greater than the probability of the same event happening only at the end of the period.

Using Monte Carlo simulation, we explore the within-period outcomes from two additional shortfall measures: the probability of penetrating a prescribed asset level threshold, and the probability of a given percentage decline from a high watermark asset value.

For the same threshold, these latter two risk measures are more stringent than the simple end-of-period shortfall. Therefore, to achieve some degree of comparability, we set the threshold asset values at 100 percent for the end-of-period measure, at 90 percent for the within-period shortfall, and at −15 percent for the high watermark case.

These risk measures are all quite sensitive to the investment horizon, but in different ways. The end-of-period probability declines with longer horizons, as the expected return provides an ever-growing lift to the return distribution. In contrast, the shortfall probability for the two within-period measures rises with longer investment horizons due to the increased number of opportunities for seriously adverse outcomes. However, for an investment horizon of four years or so, there appears to be a convergence of fulfillment in which these three (admittedly arbitrary but not unreasonable) risk thresholds are simultaneously satisfied. One can speculate whether one or more of such risk thresholds forms a common basis that leads to so many institutional funds having roughly the same 10- to 11-percent volatility.

END-OF-PERIOD SHORTFALL PROBABILITIES

The probability of falling below a specific threshold can be determined analytically from the properties of the normal distribution. Using the example of Portfolio C with its expected return of 7.08 percent and a volatility of 10.45 percent, there is a 25 percent probability that Portfolio C will fall below its initial value (that is, generate negative returns) over a one-year period. Moreover, as we increase the time horizon to four years, this probability of falling below its initial value decreases to 9 percent.

The shortfall probability has the virtue of being a very intuitive measure of risk but it does not begin to emphasize the full set of statistics that can characterize shortfall events (Bawa and Lindenberg 1977; Harlow and Rao 1989). For example, the average magnitude of shortfall penetration can be an important item of information in certain situations. Our narrow focus on the shortfall probability, however, is motivated by the need for simplicity (in an already sufficiently complex analysis), as well as by a recognition of the intrinsic limitations in the probabilistic asset return models themselves.

We have used Monte Carlo simulations to create return paths over time, based on random draws from the normal distribution. (To be consistent within common usage over relatively short horizons, the normal distribution was used rather than the more theoretically correct lognormal.) We then superimpose shortfall conditions on this set of return paths and develop the various outcome statistics. For the basic case of the end-of-period shortfall probability of negative returns, these empirical simulation results are consistent with the analytical calculations (Exhibits 11.1 and 11.2).

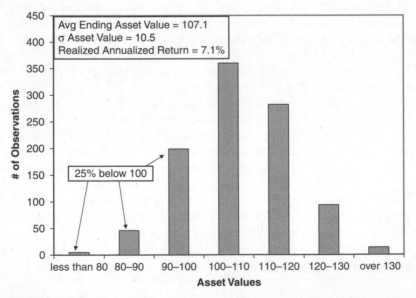

EXHIBIT 11.1 Twenty-five percent Frequency of Falling Below 100 at the End of a One-Year Horizon
Source: Morgan Stanley Research

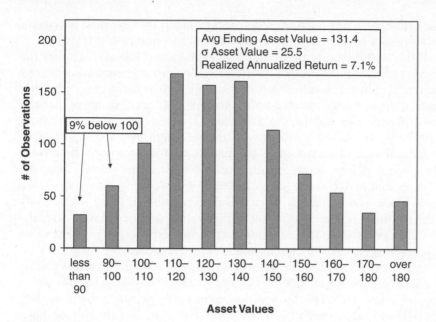

EXHIBIT 11.2 Nine percent Frequency of Falling Below 100 at the End of a Four-Year Horizon
Source: Morgan Stanley Research

We see that as we move from a one-year to a four-year horizon, the greater lift from the expected return reduces the frequency of the shortfall to only 9 percent. The simulation results also illustrate how the distribution moves from a normal to a more lognormal distribution. This is due to the effects caused by the compounding of annual returns.

WITHIN-PERIOD STOP-LOSS PROBABILITIES

We know that the probability of falling below 100 is 25 percent at the end of one year and 9 percent at the end of four years, but what is the probability of falling below 100 at the end of *any* year within a four-year horizon? As Mark Kritzman has pointed out, it is certainly reasonable for an institutional portfolio to be concerned with the probability of falling a certain percentage below the initial value at any point during the investment horizon (Kritzman 2000; Kritzman and Rich 2002). Such a within-period event could lead the fund to adopt a lower risk allocation, a shift that is comparable to a stop-loss condition. Therefore, we shall adopt this terminology. Since most funds would be highly resistant to such a departure from their initial policy allocation, one might expect that they might even set their initial risk characteristics so as to reduce this probability to a minimal level.

If this within-period threshold is set at the same 100-asset level as the end-of-period case, the probability rises to 32 percent of penetration for any year-end within the four-year period. As this high penetration probability suggests, the 100 stop-loss threshold is considerably more stringent than the same 100 end-of-period threshold. We have lowered the stop-loss threshold to a more reasonable 90 in order to attain some rough level of comparability.

Exhibit 11.3 illustrates three hypothetical paths for a portfolio's value over a 4-year period. In the middle path the value drops below 100 at the end of years 1 and 2, then rises to 103 after year 3, before finally dropping to 100 at the end of year 4. Since this path is assumed to be subject only to the end-of-period condition, the earlier values do not interfere with the portfolio's progression through time. At the end of the fourth year, the value drops to (or through 100) and a shortfall event is recorded.

In contrast, if a within-period stop-loss at 100 were in place, this middle path would have terminated at the end of the first year when the value dropped below 100. This termination event is illustrated by the top path, at which the value rises to 105 after the first year, but then drops back to 100 and triggers the stop-loss at the second year-end. The bottom path encounters a stop-loss condition at 90 at the end of the third year. In our

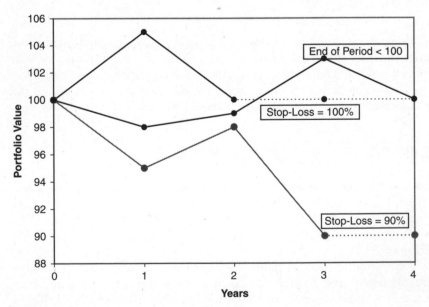

EXHIBIT 11.3   Three Illustrative Portfolio Value Paths
Source: Morgan Stanley Research

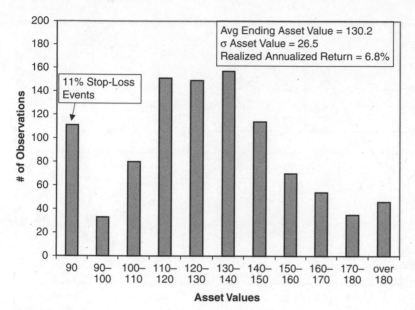

EXHIBIT 11.4 Eleven percent Frequency of Falling below 90 Any Year within a Four-Year Horizon
Source: Morgan Stanley Research

simulation, any within-period triggering event fixes the final asset value, for example, a penetration of the 90 stop-loss level generates a terminal asset value of 90.

Exhibit 11.4 displays the simulation results for a stop-loss of 90 over a four-year time frame. The stop-loss is triggered in 11 percent of the iterations. Even though the triggering probabilities are nearly the same, it is worth noting that this within-period stop-loss results in an average realized return of 6.8 percent, significantly lower than the 7.1 percent realized in the end-of-period case (Exhibit 11.2).

Our analysis has assumed that the portfolio is valued only at each year-end. If the portfolio had been valued continuously over the horizon, we would find considerably higher probabilities of stop-loss. For example, to achieve the same 11 percent probability with a continuous stop-loss condition, we would have to lower the stop loss threshold to 85.

HIGH WATERMARK SHORTFALLS

The high watermark refers to the highest value that a fund has achieved up to the current time. The compensation of many fund managers depends on

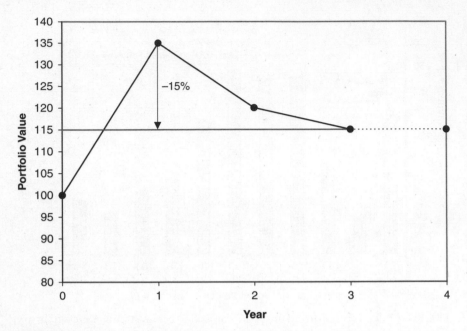

EXHIBIT 11.5   A –15 Percent High Watermark Violation
Source: Morgan Stanley Research

their performance relative to such high watermarks. If a fund experiences losses after reaching a high watermark, the fund must rise above the mark before generating any further performance awards. More generally, funds such as endowments embed some form of high watermarks into their spending plans. A subsequent decline of significant magnitude could therefore engender major organizational stress. In such cases, these high watermark conditions can obviously become a major contributor to overall fund risk.

Exhibit 11.5 shows a hypothetical return path that violates the condition of falling 15 percent below the portfolio's high watermark. In this case, the portfolio reaches a high watermark of 135 in year 1, drops to 120 in year 2, and falls to 114.75 in year 3. Since this value is 15 percent below the high watermark of 135, a violation occurs, and the terminal value is frozen at 114.75. In a sense, this treats the high watermark case as a sort of trailing stop-loss condition.

Exhibit 11.6 displays the distribution of results over a four-year period from our simulation. It turns out that the high watermark events occur with a 10 percent frequency. The percentage of trigger events cannot be read from the histogram alone, however, since these events can now cross a wide range of asset levels. We have used the solid portion of the bars to indicate

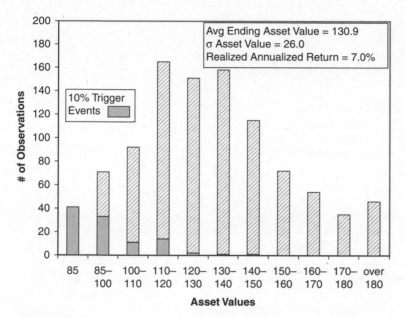

EXHIBIT 11.6 A –15 Percent High Watermark Simulation Results
Source: Morgan Stanley Research

the asset value location at which the penetration events have occurred. It is interesting to see that by allowing the stop to take place at higher asset levels, this high watermark case provides a somewhat higher return than at the fixed 90 stop-loss (Exhibit 11.4).

CHANGING THE THRESHOLDS AND HORIZONS

Each of the three shortfall probability measures depend critically on the specified threshold that defines an adverse triggering event. From Exhibit 11.7, we see that all three shortfall probabilities experience significant declines as we relax these threshold levels. As the threshold drops to very low levels, the probability of any triggering event approaches zero and all three return distributions converge on the unconstrained case. Exhibit 11.7 again shows how our choice of the three threshold limits results in approximately the same 10 percent shortfall probability.

Exhibit 11.8 illustrates how the shortfall probability measures change as the horizon increases. The probability of falling below 100 at the end of period starts at high levels in the early years, when the volatility dominates

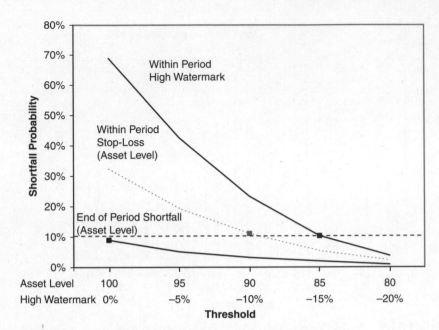

EXHIBIT 11.7 Shortfall Probabilities at Different Thresholds
Source: Morgan Stanley Research

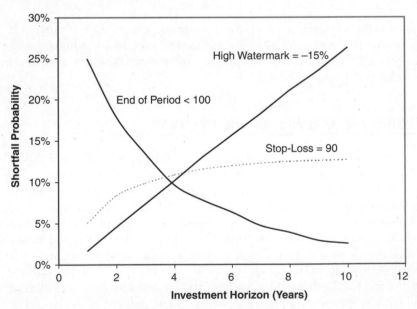

EXHIBIT 11.8 Shortfall Probabilities versus Time
Source: Morgan Stanley Research

the accumulated expected return. It then decreases rather sharply with time as the expected return accumulates. In contrast, the within-period events have a low probability for short horizons, which limit the spread of adverse outcomes. For the stop-loss at 90, the prospect of triggering events is concentrated in the early years. Consequently, the probability flattens out at about 13 percent after the eighth year. For the high watermark case, however, the number of opportunities for triggering continues to increase as time passes, resulting in ever higher shortfall probabilities.

It is interesting to note how all three measures again converge at roughly 10 percent probability for time horizons between three and five years. For shorter horizons, the end-of-period measure has worse outcomes, while for longer horizons, the within-period measures fail more often.

SHORTFALL PROBABILITIES ALONG THE EFFICIENT FRONTIER

The middle fixed core segment of the efficient frontier in Exhibit 11.9 is composed of a 60 percent alpha core of alternative assets abstracted from

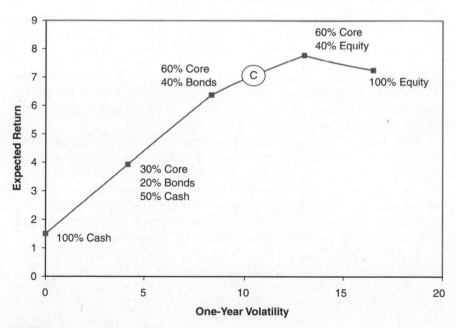

EXHIBIT 11.9   Efficient Frontier for a One-Year Horizon
Source: Morgan Stanley Research

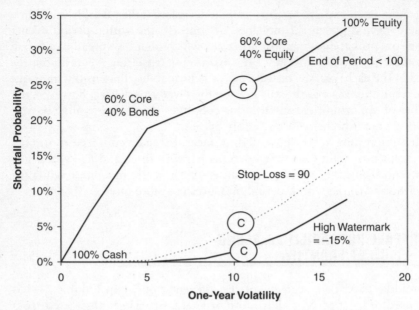

EXHIBIT 11.10 Shortfall Probabilities along the Efficient Frontier over a One-Year Horizon
Source: Morgan Stanley Research

the Portfolio C. The remaining 40 percent weight is deployed into varying mixtures of U.S. bonds and equities. In practice, most allocations will fall within the middle segment, that is, the fixed alpha core segment, where the 60 percent core is mixed with bonds and equity.

In Exhibit 11.10, we have displayed the three shortfall probabilities associated with each volatility position along the efficient frontier for a one-year horizon. We see that although the shortfall probabilities rise quickly as the volatility increases in the stop-loss and high watermark case, most of the efficient frontier points have shortfall probabilities below 10 percent. The points along the fixed core segment in the end-of-period case have shortfall probabilities in the totally unacceptable 20- to 30-percent range.

Exhibit 11.11 compares the more meaningful shortfall probabilities along the efficient frontier for the four-year case. In this graph, we have kept the one-year volatility as the horizontal axis to more clearly mark the position along the efficient frontier. With this longer horizon, the shortfall probability increases in the within-period stop-loss and high watermark cases but decreases in the end-of-period case. We see that Portfolio C falls at a volatility position in which all three risk measures are close, with each having a roughly 10 percent shortfall probability.

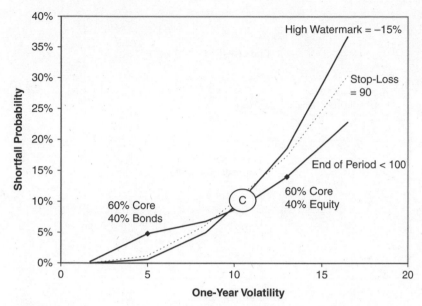

EXHIBIT 11.11 Shortfall Probabilities along the Efficient Frontier over a Four-Year Horizon
Source: Morgan Stanley Research

ACCEPTABLE RISK-AND-RETURN REGIONS

For each of the three shortfall conditions, the combination of expected return and volatility risk determines the probability of triggering. If we fix the shortfall probability at some specific level, such as 10 percent, then this requirement will define *shortfall curves* in a risk-and-return space consisting of portfolios that just meet the given conditions. Portfolios having risk-and-return combinations above this curve will satisfy the shortfall constraint, while portfolios below the curve will not. For the constraint that the value fall above 10 percent at the end of a four-year horizon, the shortfall curve is displayed in Exhibit 11.12. It turns out to be straight line radiating from the origin (Harlow and Rao 1989).

In Exhibit 11.12, even though these results are based on the four-year horizon, we have used the one-year volatility as a marker along the horizontal axis. This choice enables us to superimpose the efficient frontier in its standard one-year form. The point at which the shortfall line intersects the frontier indicates the maximum volatility that satisfies the shortfall condition. In Exhibit 11.12, we see this maximum volatility falls between 11 and 12 percent, which just brings Portfolio C into the region of acceptability.

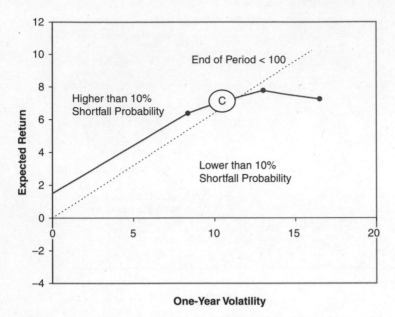

EXHIBIT 11.12   Risk-and-Return Space: Shortfall Line for End-of-Period Asset Value Less than 100
Source: Morgan Stanley Research

For the two within-period measures, volatility tends to become more critical than the expected return, leading to the upward bending shortfall curves shown in Exhibit 11.13. We get roughly similar results, in that Portfolio C lies in the proximity of both shortfall curves. As we move up the efficient frontier past Portfolio C (toward increasing volatility), the higher-risk portfolios fail to meet either of these shortfall criteria.

CONCLUSION

The standard risk measure is the volatility of return realized at the end of some investment period. Most institutional allocations are formed by choosing portfolios that provide the maximum return within some acceptable level of risk. However, it seems likely that these risk limits are based on investment horizons longer than one year—probably in the range of three to five years. These longer horizons bring into play a number of additional within-period risk measures with characteristics that are quite different from the standard end-of-period volatility. We have examined two such within-period risk measures—the fixed stop-loss and the high watermark constraint. In contrast to the end-of-period volatility, these within-period shortfalls tend to grow in significance as the horizon lengthens.

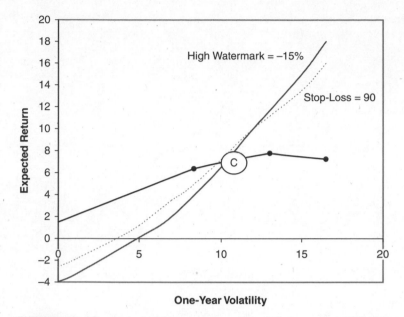

EXHIBIT 11.13   Risk-and-Return Space: Shortfall Curves for Within-Period Constraints
Source: Morgan Stanley Research

In this chapter, we have set admittedly arbitrary thresholds for these three measures, but at levels that are not unreasonable from the viewpoint of comparability. With these illustrative values, there is a striking convergence in the shortfall probabilities—and their time paths—for portfolios in the 10- to 11-percent volatility range, which happens to be where most institutional portfolios seem to be located.

REFERENCES

Bawa, V., and E. B. Lindenberg. 1977. "Capital market equilibrium in a mean, lower partial moment framework." *Journal of Financial Economics* 5 (2): 189–200.

Harlow, W. V., and R. Rao. 1989. "Asset pricing in a generalized mean-lower partial moment framework: Theory and evidence." *Journal of Financial and Quantitative Analysis* 24 (3): 285–311.

Kritzman, M. P. 2000. *Puzzles of Finance.* New York: John Wiley & Sons, Inc.

Kritzman, M. P., and D. Rich. 2002. "The mismeasurement of risk." *Financial Analysts Journal* 58 (3): 91–99.

CHAPTER 12

Active Alphas: Bound, Portable, and Integrated

*A*llocation *alphas and active alphas are fundamentally different. Allocation alphas arise from passive investments, given the same market assumptions that formed the basis for the development of a fund's policy portfolio. In contrast, active alphas are derived from skill-based initiatives or structural advantages and are (at best) zero-sum in nature.*

Active alphas come in two distinct forms: portable and bound. With portable alphas, the active return component can be readily extracted and layered onto the policy portfolio. However, for bound alphas, some continuing investment in the asset class is required to pursue the active increment. A bound alpha will typically relate to asset classes in which the fund does not have access to efficient hedging vehicles.

Bound-active alphas and allocation alphas can be judiciously integrated. While recognizing the differences in assumptions and risks entailed, bound-active alphas can enhance the potential returns for the reference asset classes. Consequently, the allocation alphas and the bound alphas associated with an asset class should both be considered in developing an alpha core for the fund as a whole.

ALLOCATION ALPHAS

With U.S. equities determining over 90 percent of the volatility in U.S. institutional portfolios, the volatility risk associated with these alpha sources will almost always be submerged and become a relatively unimportant component of the total portfolio risk. One might therefore expect that the alpha core—the subportfolios of alpha-sourced asset classes—should be assigned a high percentage weight in every policy portfolio. Assets with positive

EXHIBIT 12.1 Alpha and Beta Characteristics

Asset Class	Expected Return	Total σ	Return Decomposition		Volatility Decomposition	
			α	β	$\beta\sigma$	σ_α
Alpha Core						
Venture Capital (VC)	12.25	27.75	7.37	0.59	9.71	25.99
Commodities (Com)	5.25	19.00	5.41	−0.29	−4.75	18.40
Real Estate (RE)	5.50	12.00	3.58	0.07	1.20	11.94
Emerging Mkt Equity (EM)	9.25	28.00	3.36	0.76	12.60	25.00
Private Equity (PE)	10.25	23.00	3.14	0.98	16.10	16.43
REITS	6.50	14.50	2.22	0.48	7.98	12.11
Absolute Return (AR)	5.25	9.25	2.14	0.28	4.63	8.01
International Equity (IE)	7.25	19.50	1.33	0.77	12.68	14.82
Equity Hedge Funds (EH)	5.75	12.75	0.47	0.66	10.84	6.72
U.S. Bonds Govt			1.15	0.15		
U.S. TIPS			0.96	0.14		
Swing Assets						
U.S. Equity	7.25	16.50	0.00	1.00	16.50	0.00
U.S. Bonds	3.75	7.50	1.47	0.14	2.25	7.15
Cash	1.50	0.00	0.00	0.00	0.00	0.00

Source: Morgan Stanley Research

allocation alphas, however, tend to fall into a nonstandard or alternative category, in which their strategic role is limited by explicit or implicit constraints on their allocated weights.

Exhibit 12.1 presents the assumed expected returns and volatilities for various asset classes, and their decomposition into alpha and beta components. Exhibit 12.2 then provides an illustrative set of exposure constraints on these alpha-producing assets. Together with a 50 percent limit on the aggregate alpha exposure, these characteristics determine the efficient frontier in alpha space that is shown in Exhibit 12.3. The point S in Exhibit 12.3 represents the alpha core of a strategic portfolio that we will use as a starting point for our discussion. The allocation details for S are given in Exhibit 12.4.

EXHIBIT 12.2 Asset Constraints

Asset Class	Maximum Constraint
Alpha Core	
Venture Capital (VC)	10%
Commodities (Com)	10%
Real Estate (RE)	20%
Emerging Mkt Equity (EM)	10%
Private Equity (PE)	10%
REITS	10%
Absolute Return (AR)	20%
International Equity (IE)	30%
Equity Hedge Funds (EH)	25%
U.S. Bonds Govt	5%
U.S. TIPS	5%
Aggregate Core Limit	50%
Swing Assets	
U.S. Equity	—
U.S. Bonds	—
Cash	—

Source: Morgan Stanley Research

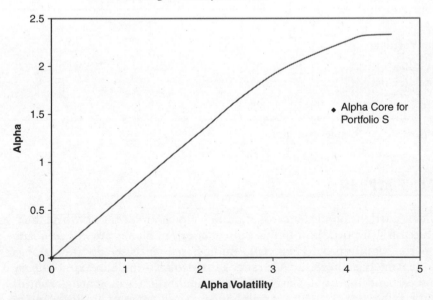

EXHIBIT 12.3 Efficient Frontier in Alpha Space
Source: Morgan Stanley Research

EXHIBIT 12.4 S Allocation Details

	S Basic Allocation	Alpha	Beta	Alpha Volatility
Alpha Core				
Venture Capital	5.0%	0.37	0.03	1.30
Commodities	—	—	—	—
Real Estate	5.0%	0.18	0.00	0.60
Emerging Mkt Equity	—	—	—	—
Private Equity	—	—	—	—
REITS	5.0%	0.11	0.02	0.61
Absolute Return	15.0%	0.32	0.04	1.20
International Equity	20.0%	0.27	0.15	2.96
Equity Hedge Funds	—	—	—	—
Total	50.0%	1.25	0.25	3.56
Swing Assets				
U.S. Equity	30.0%	0.00	0.30	0.00
U.S. Bonds	20.0%	0.29	0.03	1.43
Cash	—	—	—	—
Total	50.0%	0.29	0.33	1.43
Alpha	1.54			
Alpha Volatility	3.83			
Beta	0.58			
Beta Volatility	9.57			
Total Return	6.38			
Total Volatility	10.31			
Beta %	92.8%			

Source: Morgan Stanley Research

ACTIVE ALPHAS

In large part, the opportunity for allocation alphas arises from the beta dominance of U.S. portfolios. In this sense, allocation alphas are *not* zero-sum opportunities. Improved expected returns based on these allocation alphas can remain available to a wide range of portfolios—until an extraordinary (and perhaps impossible) level of market equilibrium is ultimately reached! Consequently, such *allocation* alphas are very different from the more commonly discussed *active* alphas that depend on the ability to extract returns beyond what is passively available in the respective asset classes. These active alphas result from judicious selection of managers, choice of better vehicles, successful timing decisions, more insightful active management of individual securities, more effective rebalancing techniques, or better weighting of subsectors within the general asset class. As such, they are generally viewed to be zero-sum at best (and possibly somewhat less than zero-sum for the investor universe as a whole, given the role of transaction costs acting as a wedge).

Active alphas are similar to allocation alphas in that they provide a certain expected return, bear a certain riskiness associated with the pursuit of that expected return, and are constrained in the magnitude that can be pursued within a given portfolio. However, it should be pointed out that assumptions regarding active alphas are much more heroic than the typically consensual, long-term assumptions that form the basis for the policy portfolio. It clearly takes a deeper assessment of a given fund's management skills and structural advantages to assess what active alphas it may find to indeed be reliably and credibly available. Because of this intrinsic difference in the nature of these risks, many funds maintain separate risk categories for active alphas versus the risks associated with the policy portfolio and any revised strategic portfolio.

PORTABLE ALPHAS

The predominant focus of most discussions of active alphas has been on so-called portable alphas, in which various derivatives can be used to port the incremental active return back to some component of the policy portfolio. One key to achieving such portability is the ability to short an entire asset class, thereby skimming off the incremental active return (and risk). We maintain the simplifying assumptions that all active alphas are independent from one another and from the allocation alphas, that they are (or can be rendered) beta free, and that they can become fully portable without the need for a cash reserve. These are obviously very strong assumptions that might have to be modified in any practical situation.

These portable alphas are also subject to various constraints that limit their role within a given portfolio. With their portability, the active alpha subportfolio is essentially independent of the portfolio's allocation structure, and the returns and the risks associated with these alphas can essentially be layered on top of the strategic allocation. Consequently, there is no integrating relationship between the policy or strategic allocations and these portable active alphas.

BOUND-ACTIVE ALPHAS

Not all active alphas are freely portable, however, and as such must be more tightly integrated with the relevant strategic allocation (Asness 2004; Dalio 2004, 2005; Dopfel 2005; Gupta and Straatman 2005; Siegel 2003; Waring and Siegel 2003, 2005; Waring et al., 2000). There are various asset classes that are not fully hedgeable and the pursuit of the active incremental return is intimately bound to having some allocation weight assigned to the underlying asset class. One example of such a bound-alpha might be a university endowment that believes it has the network to better access and evaluate high-tech venture capital opportunities, thereby garnering an excess active return of about 2 percent (even though that incremental return would carry with it a high 10 percent level of added volatility risk). However, if there is no way to short the venture capital as an asset class, this active alpha could not be pursued without having a direct exposure in the venture capital. Such active alphas can be viewed as bound to the underlying asset class, and their availability may theoretically be limited by both how much opportunity exists as well as by the portfolio weight assigned to that asset class. For the purpose of simplicity, we assume that the effective constraint on the bound-alpha is set by the actual asset allocation of the underlying portfolio.

In Exhibit 12.5, we present a hypothetical set of returns, risks, and constraints associated with these two broad categories of active alphas: portable active alphas and bound active alphas. In one particular instance, emerging markets, we have assumed that there can be both portable and bound active alphas. This circumstance could only arise when certain sub-sectors of the asset class have derivatives available that would allow porta-bility. Thus, one might have portable alphas in some areas, but also have other bound opportunities that require a cash investment in the less liquid subsectors.

INTEGRATED ALPHAS

There are a variety of ways that the allocation alphas and active alphas can be combined in a comprehensive portfolio analysis. As a first step, we will treat the allocation alphas and bound-active alphas as essentially being bolted together at the asset class level, obtaining the integrated alphas' measures shown in Exhibit 12.6. By definition, the portable alphas can be accessed up to their individual constraints, regardless of the underlying allocation of the actual portfolio. Thus, the 58 basis points (bp) will be available for any allocation (as long as there are no violations of other constraints, such as tracking error). The bound-active alphas, however, can be obtained only

EXHIBIT 12.5 Active Alpha Characteristics

Alpha Core	Portable			Bound		
	Return	Sigma	Constraint	Return	Sigma	Constraint
Venture Capital (VC)	—	—	—	2.00	10.00	↑
Commodities (Com)	—	—	—	2.00	8.00	
Real Estate (RE)	—	—	—	2.00	6.00	
Emerging Mkt Equity (EM)	2.00	10.00	5%	1.50	6.00	Set by Underlying Fund Allocation
Private Equity (PE)	—	—	—	—	—	
REITS	1.00	5.00	10%	—	—	
Absolute Return (AR)	—	—	—	—	—	↓
International Equity (IE)	1.50	6.00	15%	—	—	
Equity Hedge Funds (EH)	—	—	—	1.00	3.00	
Swing Assets						
U.S. Equity	—	—	—	—	—	—
U.S. Bonds	0.75	4.00	20%	—	—	—
Cash	—	—	—	—	—	—
Total	0.58	1.40	None	Set by Allocation		

Source: Morgan Stanley Research

through an allocation in the underlying portfolio. If the expected return estimates for the allocation alphas and the bound-alphas have the same standing as far as credibility, then they should be combined at the asset class level. For example, in real estate, the allocation alpha of 3.58 percent and the bound-alpha of 2.00 percent provide an integrated alpha of 5.58 percent. This higher integrated alpha can thus act as a guideline for an improved deployment of the aggregate weight available for the alpha core.

The integrated alphas in Exhibit 12.6 are then applied to the underlying allocation S, leading to the risk-and-return results shown in the first panel of Exhibit 12.7. The basic (nonactive) portfolio S has a total return of 6.38 percent, composed of 1.50 percent risk-free rate, 3.34 percent derived from the beta of 0.58 (= 0.58 × 5.75 percent), and an allocation alpha of 1.54 percent. The active alphas then contribute an additional 0.78 percent,

EXHIBIT 12.6 Integrated Alpha Characteristics

	Allocation Alpha	Bound Alpha	Integrated Alpha	Allocation Sigma	Bound Sigma	Integrated Sigma
Venture Capital	7.37	2.00	9.37	25.99	10.00	27.85
Commodities	5.41	2.00	7.41	18.40	8.00	20.06
Real Estate	3.58	2.00	5.58	11.94	6.00	13.36
Emerging Mkt Equity	3.36	1.50	4.86	25.00	6.00	25.71
Private Equity	3.14	—	3.14	16.43	—	16.43
REITS	2.22	—	2.22	12.11	—	12.11
Absolute Return	2.14	—	2.14	8.01	—	8.01
International Equity	1.33	—	1.33	14.82	—	14.82
Equity Hedge Funds	0.47	1.00	1.47	6.72	3.00	7.36

Source: Morgan Stanley Research

consisting of 0.20 percent bound and 0.58 percent portable returns, resulting in a combined total return expectation of 7.16 percent.

Portfolio S has a 50 percent allocation to the various alpha-source assets. It is worth raising the question as to whether this same 50 percent aggregate exposure could be put to better use. In the second panel of Exhibit 12.7, we have used these integrated alphas as a guide to redistribute the 50 percent alpha weight to a revised portfolio R. In moving from S to R, the allocation of international equity has been reduced to 10 percent, together with a 5 percent reduction in both absolute return and REITS. The freed-up 20 percent weight is then redistributed to obtain higher integrated alphas, with 5 percent assigned each to emerging markets and venture capital, and 10 percent to real estate. This reallocation has the collateral effect of lowering the implicit beta contributed by the alpha core, necessitating a 5 percent shift from bonds to equity so as to maintain a constant fund beta of 0.58.

The net result of this move from S to R is an *increased* total return of 84 bp, with 47 bp derived from higher allocation alphas and another 37 bp from the higher bound-alphas available with the new allocation.

RISK BUDGETS

In beta-dominated portfolios, the overwhelming source of volatility is the implicit and explicit exposure to U.S. equities. By design, we have kept this beta exposure constant (at $\beta = 0.58$) as we moved from S to R. There is

EXHIBIT 12.7 R and S Portfolio Summaries

	Portfolio S	+ Bound Actives	+ Portables	Portfolio R	+ Bound Actives	+ Portables
Alpha Core						
Venture Capital	5.0%	5.0%	—	10.0%	10.0%	—
Commodities	0.0%	—	—	0.0%	—	—
Real Estate	5.0%	5.0%	—	15.0%	15.0%	—
Emerging Mkt Equity	0.0%	—	5.0%	5.0%	5.0%	5.0%
Private Equity	0.0%	—	—	0.0%	—	—
REITS	5.0%	—	10.0%	0.0%	—	10.0%
Absolute Return	15.0%	—	—	10.0%	—	—
International Equity	20.0%	—	15.0%	10.0%	—	15.0%
Equity Hedge Funds	0.0%	—	—	0.0%	—	—
Total	50.0%	10.0%	30.0%	50.0%	30.0%	30.0%
Swing Assets						
U.S. Equity	30.0%	—	—	35.0%	—	—
U.S. Bonds	20.0%	—	20.0%	15.0%	—	20.0%
Cash	0.0%	—	0.0%	0.0%	—	0.0%
Total	50.0%	0.0%	20.0%	50.0%	0.0%	20.0%
Alpha	1.54	1.74	2.32	2.01	2.58	3.16
Alpha Volatility	3.83	3.88	4.12	3.94	4.17	4.40
Beta	0.58	0.58	0.58	0.58	0.58	0.58
Beta Volatility	9.57	9.57	9.57	9.57	9.57	9.57
Total Return	6.38	6.58	7.16	6.85	7.42	8.00
Total Volatility	10.31	10.33	10.42	10.35	10.44	10.53
Beta %	92.8%	92.7%	91.8%	92.5%	91.7%	90.9%
Relative Return (RR)	vs S	0.20	0.78	vs R	0.57	1.15
TEV	vs S	0.58	1.51	vs R	1.37	1.96
RR/TEV	vs S	0.34	0.52	vs R	0.42	0.59

Source: Morgan Stanley Research

consequently only a negligible increase in basic (nonactive) fund volatility, that is, from 10.31 percent to 10.35 percent. As noted earlier, however, the assumptions regarding active opportunities—bound or portable—are fundamentally different from those forming the basic allocation decisions. As such, active risks, both portable and bound, may be assessed in terms of their tracking errors relative to the underlying portfolio. As shown in Exhibit 12.7, the bound-alphas have tracking error volatility (TEV) of 0.58 percent relative to S, while the portable alpha adds a further (independent) TEV of 1.40 percent. The combined TEV for both active sources then becomes a rather reasonable 1.51 percent. In terms of the active alpha and TEV ratios, one obtains $0.20/0.58 = 0.34$ for the bound-actives, $0.58/1.40 = 0.41$ for the portables alone, and $0.78/1.51 = 0.52$ for the combined active sources. In moving to the revised portfolio R, the corresponding ratios are improved significantly: $0.57/1.37 = 0.42$ for the bound-actives, the same $0.58/1.40 = 0.41$ for the portables, and $1.15/1.96 = 0.59$ for the combined actives. Note that these improvements do not even take account of the 0.47 percent increment from R's better allocation alphas. When combined with the active alphas overall, R's portfolio total return comes in at 8.00 percent versus S's 7.16 percent, with a total volatility that only increases from 10.42 percent to 10.53 percent.

EXPANDING THE ACTIVE UNIVERSE

We have assumed up to this point that the sources of active alpha only come from the universe of asset classes that could be potentially incorporated into the strategic portfolio. However, one can reach very far afield for sources of active alpha. For example, currency overlays may not be considered a potential asset class for the policy portfolio. Suppose a fund is well situated, however, to pursue viable opportunities for active alphas in various currency markets, even though they cannot accept a net currency exposure in their underlying portfolio. Moreover, because of the extraordinary availability of currency derivatives, there may well be various forms of active currency alphas that could be made fully portable and thus accessible to the fund.

For funds with sufficiently broad access to multiple sources of such portable alphas, there could be a significant expansion in the range of independent active alpha sources. In addition to boosting the level of active returns, this breadth of active alpha sources could provide diversification advantages that result in highly efficient levels of tracking error. Even though the TEV may seem quite modest in the context of overall fund volatility, diversification of alpha sources could provide the more stable alpha returns over the short run. Such stability may be a greatly valued tradeoff in highly uncertain markets in which the basic alpha risk-and-return models are themselves subject to some doubt as well as to intense scrutiny.

However, a broad expansion of the active alphas would perhaps raise the issue (discussed briefly earlier) of the need for some reserve cash or collateral to back up the derivative positions used to achieve portability. Moving toward such reserve requirements is, in a sense, tantamount to requiring that a portion of these active alpha positions be viewed as being bound to some level of allocated cash or liquid collateral.

SHIFTING POLICY PORTFOLIOS

In the preceding discussion, active alphas, both bound and portable, were presumed to be the basis of a separate set of decisions, and as such, might be subject to a separate risk budget. One could easily envision situations in which fund management would want to relate both the active as well as the strategic departures to the original policy portfolio. Given our example, the move from a basic, nonactive policy portfolio S to the portfolio R with the two active sources included, takes the total volatility from 10.31 percent to 10.53 percent, and incurs a total TEV of 2.17 percent relative to S.

The revised allocation R was determined and evaluated using the same basic return covariance matrix that was presumed to underlie the choice of the original portfolio S. The allocation R uses the same constraints as well as the same market assumptions that formed the basis for choosing S in the first place. One might therefore ask the question why the original policy portfolio S should be viewed as enshrined within a pre-Galilean universe as being absolute and unmoving as the center for risk measurements. In other words, should the reference portfolio mantle perhaps be passed on to the new strategic portfolio R since it is very consistent with the underlying criteria that established the original policy portfolio S. If that were the case, then it would be appropriate to evaluate the active tracking errors relative to the revised allocation R.

It is interesting to note that if we looked at the movement to the passive portfolio R as an active departure from the original portfolio S, then that tracking error would itself be on the order of 0.91 percent (quite apart from any of the active initiatives). With the resulting incremental return of 47 basis points, this would provide an information ratio of 0.52. On the other hand, if the move from S to R is viewed as the incremental risk entailed in moving to a new but acceptable policy portfolio, then the increase in total volatility from 10.31 percent to 10.53 percent is only 0.22 percent and the resulting risk-and-return ratio of $1.15/.22 = 5.23$ becomes irresistible!

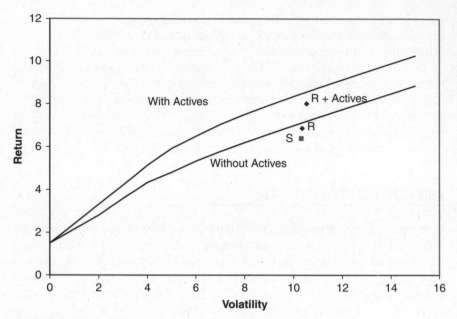

EXHIBIT 12.8   Moving from S to the Fully Active R
Source: Morgan Stanley Research

These relationships are portrayed graphically in Exhibit 12.8, which shows the move from the initial portfolio S to the basic allocation R and then to the inclusion of the bound and active alphas. The two efficient frontiers represent the optimal portfolios apart from any active alphas and the optimal portfolio that also fully incorporates all active alphas into both the risk-and-return dimensions. It is worth noting that the simply chosen portfolio R is near optimal as a policy portfolio and that the addition of the active alphas raises the return near to the fully integrated frontier. Moreover, the diagram makes the point that the move from the initial policy S to the fully active R, even though it incurs a 2.17 percent volatility tracking error, actually corresponds to a very modest increase in total fund volatility.

CONCLUSION

We thus see that pursuing allocation alphas can be interpreted as either one form of a tactical allocation decision, a revision in the fundamental policy portfolio, or some combination of the two. The initiatives involving active alphas however, require a different and more personalized assessment of skill-based zero-sum opportunities. Consequently, there are good reasons to distinguish the portfolio decisions on the basis of these two different types of incremental return. At the same time, there is an important feedback between the choice of the revised strategic portfolio and the opportunity to garner the active returns that are intrinsically bound to those allocations. It would appear that a comprehensive approach to choosing a strategic allocation should incorporate some consideration of the return increments from bound active alphas. While this would entail mixing different levels of assumptions, it could be argued that, when there is a high level of confidence regarding the bound alphas, they should indeed become an integral part of the allocation decision.

In summary, we see that the judicious integration of allocation alphas and bound active alphas can help achieve step-wise improvements in the policy portfolio together with enhanced active returns.

REFERENCES

Asness, C. 2004. "An alternative future." *Journal of Portfolio Management* 31 (1): 8–23.

Dalio, R. 2004. "Radical shift." *Pensions & Investments*, June 14.

———. 2005. "Engineering targeted returns and risks." *Alpha Manager*, January/February.

Dopfel, F. 2005. "Waiter! What's this hedge fund doing in my soup? How hedge funds fit into the institutional investor's portfolio." *Investment Insights* 8 (4). The investment research journal from Barclays Global Investors, March.

Gupta, P., and J. Straatman. 2005. "Skill-based investment management." SSRN Working Paper 737103.

Siegel, L. B. 2003. *Benchmarks and investment management*. Charlottesville, VA: CFA Institute.

Waring, M. B., and L. B. Siegel. 2003. "The dimensions of active management." *Journal of Portfolio Management* 29 (3): 35–51.

———. 2005. "The myth of the absolute return investor." *Investment Insights* 8 (4). The investment research journal from Barclays Global Investors, March.

Waring, M. B., D. Whitney, J. Pirone, and C. Castille. 2000. "Optimizing manager structure and budgeting manager risk." *Journal of Portfolio Management* 26 (3): 90–104.

CHAPTER 13

Beta-Based Performance Analysis

*T*he alpha/beta framework can act as a prism for deconstructing relative
performance on either a prospective or historical basis. This decomposition can provide both novel insights into the fundamental sources of
incremental return as well as suggestions for improved risk control.

The policy benchmark typically serves as a starting point for a two-step
portfolio construction process leading toward the fund's active portfolio.
First, the fund manager must decide whether to overweight or underweight
each asset class relative to its weight in the fund's benchmark, possibly including decisions relating to the need to fund some entirely new asset classes.
These active weighting decisions may add incremental alpha return to the
portfolio but may also create a beta difference between the original benchmark and final portfolio. If desired, any such beta gap could be adjusted
by altering the equity weight or by applying a beta overlay (through equity
futures). The second decision is whether to invest passively or take an active
position in each asset class.

A key measure of performance then becomes the actual portfolio's return
difference relative to the policy benchmark. By extracting any remaining beta
gap, the fund's relative performance can be subjected to a more insightful
analysis in terms of the respective contributions from active alphas versus
the basic weighting decisions.

ACTIVE VERSUS PASSIVE ALPHAS

Allocation alphas are the expected returns that remain after extracting the
beta effects from their co-movement with U.S. equities. These alpha returns
can thus be viewed as the asset's return that is passively available to a specific
fund with a given access and oversight capability in that asset class. Active

alphas result from judicious selection of managers, choice of better vehicles, successful timing decisions, more insightful active management of individual securities, more effective rebalancing techniques, or better weighting of subsectors within the generic asset class.

Active alphas themselves come in two distinct forms: portable and bound. With portable alphas, derivatives can be used to port the incremental active return back to some component of the policy portfolio. One key to achieving such portability is the ability to short the entire asset class, thereby retrieving only the incremental active return and risk. For the bound alphas, some continuing investment in the asset class is required to pursue the active increment.

In practice, many institutions will choose to pursue potentially portable active alphas through investments in the underlying asset class. This may be due to the fund's limitations on the use of derivatives. For simplicity in our examples, all active alphas will be treated as if they were essentially bound in nature. (Any ported alphas could then be viewed as a subsequent overlay at the overall portfolio level.)

DECOMPOSITION OF BENCHMARK RETURN

Exhibit 13.1 displays a schematic time graph of a benchmark's total return along with its beta-based return. The difference between these two lines represents the benchmark's passive alpha return.

The benchmark policy portfolio can be interpreted as the passive autopilot allocation that would be pursued by the sponsors in the absence of any active management. This policy allocation is generally based on long-term return prospects for the spectrum of potentially available asset classes. The allocation is often derived, in part, from an optimization process that makes use of a return-covariance model of market behaviors. The policy portfolio can then act as a center of neutrality for any subsequent active decisions. Exhibit 13.2 details the characteristics of the illustrative policy portfolio.

RELATIVE RETURN ANALYSIS

This chapter focuses on a prospective analysis of relative returns based on the alpha and beta values derived from the fund's own market assumptions. This same general approach, however, can also be applied to the historical performance of a portfolio versus its benchmark over time (Exhibit 13.3).

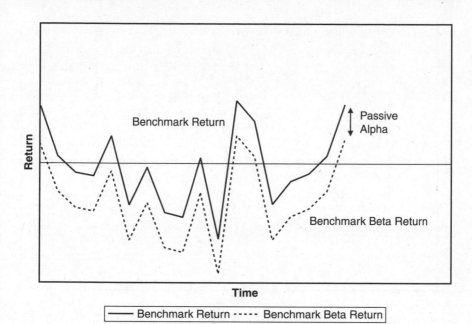

EXHIBIT 13.1 The Passive Alpha in Benchmark Returns
Source: Morgan Stanley Research

EXHIBIT 13.2 Benchmark Policy Portfolio

	% Weight	Benchmark Beta	Benchmark Passive Alpha
Alpha Core			
Real Estate	10.0%	0.07	3.58
Emerging Mkt Equity	10.0%	0.76	3.36
Absolute Return	10.0%	0.28	2.14
International Equity	20.0%	0.77	1.33
Weighted Core	50.0%	0.27	1.17
Swing Assets			
U.S. Bonds	20.0%	0.14	1.47
U.S. Equity	30.0%	1.00	0.00
Weighted Swing	50.0%	0.33	0.29
Total Portfolio	100.0%	0.59	1.47
Total Return	6.38	3.41	1.47
Associated Volatility	10.71	9.78	4.38

Source: Morgan Stanley Research

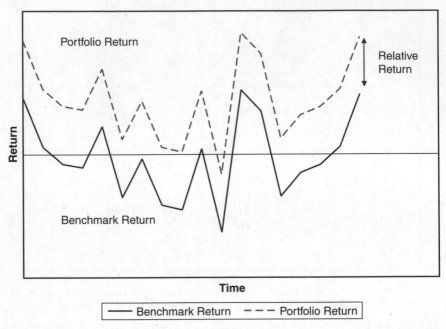

EXHIBIT 13.3 Historical Relative Return
Source: Morgan Stanley Research

The relative return over a benchmark does not in itself provide sufficient information as to the fundamental sources of value. As depicted in Exhibit 13.4, the alpha-beta framework can be used to identify three components of relative return. Passive alpha and beta returns are already embedded in the policy benchmark. All forms of active decisions that lead to an aggregate relative return can be analyzed as positive or negative returns on top of these benchmark components.

The first component of relative return is what we have termed the *active weightings effect*. It can be thought of as the incremental embedded alpha gained or lost by overweighting or underweighting an asset class versus its weight in the benchmark. As defined here, the active weightings effect has both active and passive aspects. An active decision is made to hold more or less of the asset class versus the benchmark. This resulting incremental return is viewed as being due to the passive embedded alpha.

If no leverage is used, an overweight position in an asset must obviously be offset by an underweight position somewhere else. If the fund manager

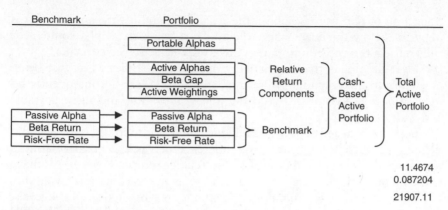

EXHIBIT 13.4 Relative Return Analysis
Source: Morgan Stanley Research

chooses to underweight an asset that is part of the alpha core, it will lose some of the passive alpha associated with that asset. (An underweight position in a nonalpha asset such as equity will affect the beta return but not result in any alpha loss.)

The second component of relative return is the beta gap. This is the difference in the beta (and beta return) between the benchmark and the final portfolio. This beta gap, or some part of it, may or may not be intentional. An intentional beta gap would suggest that the fund manager is taking an active position on the direction of the U.S. equity market. An unintentional beta gap may result if a fund manager thinks that he or she has fully matched the portfolio's beta exposure vis-à-vis the benchmark but has failed to take account of the implicit beta values from all the assets. In theory, such unintentional beta gaps could be neutralized by adjusting the final portfolio's equity percentage or by an overlay using equity futures. Even a small beta gap can loom quite large and swamp any positive relative return decisions. An effort should thus be made to avoid unintentional beta gaps in the final portfolio.

For simplicity, we have assumed that no inherent beta exists in the active alphas. Thus, a beta gap will only result from a reweighting of asset classes with different beta values. In actual practice, there could also be a difference between the beta from the actual investment in an asset class and the beta implied within the policy portfolio.

The third component of relative returns is the active alphas representing returns that are above and beyond the passive alphas in the benchmark. In our classification framework, the return contribution from active alphas is a function of the entire weight in the asset class, not just the amount that is above or below the benchmark weight. Thus, the active alpha component fully reflects the decision to pursue any available active investments.

Portable alphas that are actually ported can be viewed as just being layered onto the portfolio's allocation structure. There is consequently no integrating relationship between the policy allocation and these portable active alphas.

Both the final active portfolio and the policy portfolio will have a certain volatility in their total return. The difference between the two volatilities represents the incremental total risk. The relative return, however, will have its own volatility measure, often referred to as the tracking error volatility (TEV). Even if the active and policy portfolios are close in overall risk levels, their relative returns can be quite different in any specific scenario. The TEV will therefore generally be much larger than the difference in total risk, which raises a number of issues regarding the appropriate measures of incremental risk. In any case, both the TEV and the total risk can be deconstructed using the alpha/beta framework.

ACTIVE ALPHAS WITHOUT REWEIGHTING

Exhibit 13.5 illustrates a case in which the benchmark weights are maintained but active positions are taken in four asset classes. Also, although bonds serve as a swing asset, an active position can be taken in them so as to pursue an active alpha. A total of 100 bp of relative return (RR) is gained from the sum of these transactions. There are no beta gaps or reweighting effects in this case. The total volatility differs by only 11 bp, but the TEV of the final portfolio is 1.7 percent, resulting in a RR/TEV ratio of 0.58.

OVERWEIGHTING ACTIVE ALPHAS

We now consider an example in Exhibit 13.6 in which additional 5 percent positions in real estate and emerging market equity are funded by a 10 percent reduction in the U.S. equity position. In this case, all three relative return effects occur. The active weighting effect of 35 bp results from the 5 percent weight newly allocated to real estate and emerging market equity, with their higher passive alphas of 3.58 percent and 3.36 percent, respectively. A negative beta return gap of 33 bp is derived from the need to reduce the weight in the higher-beta U.S. equity. The active alpha component increases

	% Weight Benchmark	% Weight Portfolio	Δ Difference	Benchmark Beta	Benchmark Passive Alpha	Active Alpha	RR Contribution Active Alphas
Alpha Core							
Real Estate	10.0%	10.0%	0.0%	0.07	3.58	2.00	0.20
Emerging Mkt Equity	10.0%	10.0%	0.0%	0.76	3.36	1.50	0.15
Absolute Return	10.0%	10.0%	0.0%	0.28	2.14	2.00	0.20
International Equity	20.0%	20.0%	0.0%	0.77	1.33	1.50	0.30
Weighted Core	50.0%	50.0%	0.0%	0.27	1.17		0.85
Swing Assets							
U.S. Bonds	20.0%	20.0%	0.0%	0.14	1.47	0.75	0.15
U.S. Equity	30.0%	30.0%	0.0%	1.00	0.00	—	0.00
Weighted Swing	50.0%	50.0%	0.0%	0.33	0.29		0.15
Total	100.0%	100.0%	—	0.59	1.47		1.00

	Benchmark	Portfolio	Δ
Total Alpha Return	1.47	2.47	1.00
Total Beta Return	3.41	3.41	0.00
Risk-Free Return	1.50	1.50	0.00
Total Return	6.38	7.38	**1.00**
Beta	0.59	0.59	0.00
Alpha Volatility	4.38	4.63	0.26
Total Volatility	10.71	10.82	0.11
TEV		1.72	
RR/TEV		0.58	

EXHIBIT 13.5 Adding Higher Alphas to a Policy Portfolio
Source: Morgan Stanley Research

from 100 bp in the first example to 118 bp because of the greater weight in the actively invested assets. The net result is a 119 bp improvement in total return. The three relative return components contribute a total TEV of 2.6 percent, with the active alpha portion contributing the most.

ADDING A NEW ASSET CLASS

In the example shown in Exhibit 13.7, a new asset class is introduced that is not part of the policy benchmark. We have kept the same active positions as in Exhibit 13.5 except that the 10 percent U.S. equity is used to fund a new 10 percent position in venture capital (VC). However, for illustrative purposes, we have assumed that a –2 percent active alpha comes with this new allocation. This decrement reflects a situation in which a fund wishes to establish a presence in VC as an asset class but recognizes that it lacks a

	% Weight Benchmark	% Weight Portfolio	Δ Difference	Benchmark Beta	Benchmark Passive Alpha	Active Alpha	Relative Return Contributions		
							Active Weightings	Beta-gap	Active Alphas
Alpha Core									
Real Estate	10.0%	15.0%	5.0%	0.07	3.58	2.00	0.18	0.02	0.30
Emerging Mkt Equity	10.0%	15.0%	5.0%	0.76	3.36	1.50	0.17	0.22	0.23
Absolute Return	10.0%	10.0%	0.0%	0.28	2.14	2.00	0.00	0.00	0.20
International Equity	20.0%	20.0%	0.0%	0.77	1.33	1.50	0.00	0.00	0.30
Weighted Core	50.0%	60.0%	10.0%	0.27	1.17		0.35	0.24	1.03
Swing Assets									
U.S. Bonds	20.0%	20.0%	0.0%	0.14	1.47	0.75	0.00	0.00	0.15
U.S. Equity	30.0%	20.0%	−10.0%	1.00	0.00	—	0.00	−0.58	0.00
Weighted Swing	50.0%	40.0%	−10.0%	0.33	0.29		0.00	−0.58	0.15
Total	100.0%	100.0%	—	0.59	1.47		0.35	−0.33	1.18

1.19

	Benchmark	Portfolio	Δ
Total Alpha Return	1.47	2.99	1.52
Total Beta Return	3.41	3.07	−0.33
Risk-Free Return	1.50	1.50	0.00
Total Return	6.38	7.56	**1.19**
Beta	0.59	0.53	−0.06
Alpha Volatility	4.38	5.65	1.28
Total Volatility	10.71	10.47	−0.24
TEV			2.59
RR/TEV			0.46

	Active Weightings	Beta-gap	Active Alphas
TEV	1.39	0.96	1.96
RR/TEV	0.25	−0.35	0.60

EXHIBIT 13.6   Overweighting Higher Alphas
Source: Morgan Stanley Research

competitive advantage in VC. This −2 percent active alpha takes 20 bp away from the 100 bp of relative return derived from the other active sources. The total relative return becomes 130 bp. A total TEV of 3.3 percent results, with the reweighting effect now being the largest component of TEV.

BETA NEUTRALIZATION

In Exhibit 13.7, the final portfolio has a negative beta gap return of 24 bp, since it is 0.04 beta short versus the benchmark. If the fund manager wished to keep the beta constant with the benchmark, the percentages in the swing assets (U.S. bonds and U.S. equity) could be shifted as shown in Exhibit 13.8, yielding a relative return of 143 bp after the net positive effect of neutralization. The cost of this constant beta is an increase in overall portfolio volatility from 10.7 percent to 11.1 percent.

It should be pointed out that we have treated the implicit betas as having well-defined deterministic values. Of course, any covariance assumption will itself be subject to variability, and there will consequently always be some

	% Weight Benchmark	% Weight Portfolio	Δ Difference	Benchmark Beta	Benchmark Passive Alpha	Active Alpha	Active Weightings	Beta-gap	Active Alphas
							Relative Return Contributions		
Alpha Core									
Venture Capital	—	10.0%	10.0%	0.59	7.37	−2.00	0.74	0.34	−0.20
Real Estate	10.0%	10.0%	0.0%	0.07	3.58	2.00	0.00	0.00	0.20
Emerging Mkt Equity	10.0%	10.0%	0.0%	0.76	3.36	1.50	0.00	0.00	0.15
Absolute Return	10.0%	10.0%	0.0%	0.28	2.14	2.00	0.00	0.00	0.20
International Equity	20.0%	20.0%	0.0%	0.77	1.33	1.50	0.00	0.00	0.30
Weighted Core	50.0%	60.0%	10.0%	0.27	1.17		0.74	0.34	0.65
Swing Assets									
U.S. Bonds	20.0%	20.0%	0.0%	0.14	1.47	0.75	0.00	0.00	0.15
U.S. Equity	30.0%	20.0%	−10.0%	1.00	0.00	—	0.00	−0.58	0.00
Weighted Swing	50.0%	40.0%	−10.0%	0.33	0.29		0.00	−0.58	0.15
Total Return	100.0%	100.0%	—	0.59	1.47		0.74	−0.24	0.80

1.30

	Benchmark	Portfolio	Δ
Total Alpha Return	1.47	3.01	1.54
Total Beta Return	3.41	3.17	−0.24
Risk-Free Return	1.50	1.50	0.00
Total Return	6.38	7.68	**1.30**
Beta	0.59	0.55	−0.04
Alpha Volatility	4.38	5.41	1.03
Total Volatility	10.71	10.58	−0.13
TEV			3.34
RR/TEV			0.39

TEV	2.60	0.68	1.99
RR/TEV	0.28	−0.35	0.40

EXHIBIT 13.7   Adding a New Asset Class
Source: Morgan Stanley Research

uncertainty associated with any correlation-based beta estimate. Thus, the beta neutralization process should be viewed as a directional improvement rather than an absolute result.

ANALYZING HISTORICAL PERFORMANCE

Our development has looked at relative returns on a prospective level based on the alpha and beta values derived from a set of market assumptions. This analysis can also be applied to historical performance, however. The following information would be needed to perform such an analysis:

- A well-defined benchmark with specified asset class weights
- The generic asset class returns that are usually based on historical market indexes, a combination of indexes, or some compilation of peer group performance
- The weights invested in the fund's actual portfolio over the course of the measurement period. By comparing the fund's weights versus the policy weights, the impact of active weighting decisions can be determined.

	% Weight Benchmark	% Weight Portfolio	Δ Difference	Benchmark Beta	Benchmark Passive Alpha	Active Alpha	Relative Return Contributions		
							Active Weightings	Beta-gap	Active Alphas
Alpha Core									
Venture Capital	—	10.0%	10.0%	0.59	7.37	−2.00	0.74	0.34	−0.20
Real Estate	10.0%	10.0%	0.0%	0.07	3.58	2.00	0.00	0.00	0.20
Emerging Mkt Equity	10.0%	10.0%	0.0%	0.76	3.36	1.50	0.00	0.00	0.15
Absolute Return	10.0%	10.0%	0.0%	0.28	2.14	2.00	0.00	0.00	0.20
International Equity	20.0%	20.0%	0.0%	0.77	1.33	1.50	0.00	0.00	0.30
Weighted Core	50.0%	60.0%	10.0%	0.27	1.17		0.74	0.34	0.65
Swing Assets									
U.S. Bonds	20.0%	15.2%	−4.8%	0.14	1.47	0.75	−0.07	−0.04	0.11
U.S. Equity	30.0%	24.8%	−5.2%	1.00	0.00	—	0.00	−0.30	0.00
Weighted Swing	50.0%	40.0%	−10.0%	0.33	0.29		−0.07	−0.34	0.11
Total	100.0%	100.0%	—	0.59	1.47		0.67	0.00	0.76

1.43

	TEV	2.62	0.01	1.92
	RR/TEV	0.25	0.35	0.40

	Benchmark	Portfolio	Δ
Total Alpha Return	1.47	2.90	1.43
Total Beta Return	3.41	3.41	0.00
Risk-Free Return	1.50	1.50	0.00
Total Return	6.38	7.81	**1.43**
Beta	0.59	0.59	0.00
Alpha Volatility	4.38	5.33	0.95
Total Volatility	10.71	11.14	0.43
TEV			3.25
RR/TEV			0.44

EXHIBIT 13.8 Beta Neutralization
Source: Morgan Stanley Research

After accounting for the beta returns, these incremental returns can be viewed as solely a function of the passive alphas embedded in the benchmark returns

- The realized returns within each asset class

Once the benchmark and portfolio individual asset class returns are known, the betas for both can be estimated. This will determine whether a beta gap exists in the portfolio. Finally, by removing all beta exposures, the active alphas can be calculated by comparing the total alpha generated versus the corresponding passive alpha for each asset class.

Even without this level of detail regarding individual asset class returns and their weights, one can still get an improved insight into the relative returns between the total portfolio and the benchmark. By estimating the beta values for the portfolio and benchmark, the aggregate beta gap can be found. Any return difference remaining after accounting for this beta gap would represent the combined effect from the active weighting decisions and the active alphas.

CONCLUSION

This form of analysis can be applied to the alpha and beta values derived from either market assumptions or historical performance. By separating a portfolio's relative return versus its benchmark into three components, a fund manager can gain more insight into the specific sources of incremental value. The key step is to remove any beta gap in order to clarify the benefits of active alpha seeking or the fund's reweighting positions.

CHAPTER 14

Real Return Tents and Equity Durations

*P*rice and earnings (P/E) ratios are often shown as declining steadily under higher interest rates, suggesting a well-defined relationship between equity values and interest rates (sometimes referred to as the equity duration). When empirical data are subjected to the more stringent test of P/E changes versus interest rate changes, however, this pattern deteriorates.

The theoretical equity duration clearly depends on how a firm's future earnings can adapt to inflation shocks. Higher inflation-adjusted earnings could act as a numerator effect to offset to higher nominal discount rates, thereby reducing equity's effective duration.

One theoretical model replaces the standard fixed return on investment (ROI) with a corporate spread over the cost of capital. Higher nominal rates then lead to higher ROIs and larger earnings streams, providing a numerator effect that offsets the denominator effect of higher rates.

When the empirical P/E analysis is recast using real interest rates, the behavior of P/E levels changes dramatically. Rather than the monotonic decline witnessed with nominal rates, the P/Es now form a tent diagram with the highest P/Es lying in the 2- to 4-percent range of real rates, and then declining in both directions as real rates either rise—or fall!

This tentlike behavior could derive from the economic and monetary scenarios associated with extreme levels of real rates. Low real rates are likely to correspond to adverse growth environments, while high real rates generally imply tightening monetary conditions.

P/E RATIOS AND NOMINAL INTEREST RATES

One presentation commonly seen today is a histogram of price and earnings (P/E) ratios versus the level of interest rates. This chart generally shows that

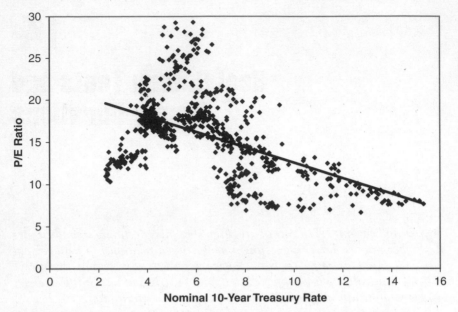

EXHIBIT 14.1   Price/Earnings Ratios versus Nominal 10-Year Treasury Rate
Levels (1954–2008)
Source: Morgan Stanley Research, BARRA, Thomson Financial, Standard &
Poor's, Federal Reserve, IBES, First Call

P/E ratios decline with high interest rates, and is sometimes used to justify
the current level of P/Es on the basis of today's low level of interest rates.

There can be some fairly major differences in how the P/Es are calculated. In some cases, the denominator consists of 10-year trailing earnings.
In other cases, they are based on prospective earnings. It is quite striking,
however, that no matter what the basis for calculation, the rough trend
seems to be that higher P/Es have historically occurred in lower interest rate
environments. Exhibit 14.1 is a scattergram of one such data series based
on a monthly series of S&P prices divided by 12-month trailing earnings
plotted against 10-year Treasury rates over the period from 1954 to 2008.
Exhibit 14.2 is a histogram of the same data.

In fixed income analysis, a bond's sensitivity to interest rate movements
can be gauged by the average duration to each of its cash flows, in which
the average is calculated on a present-value weighted basis. By analogy, the
concept of *equity duration* has been proposed as a characterization of a
stock price's sensitivity to changing interest rates.

This chapter examines the P/E- to interest-rate relationship from a
number of both theoretical and empirical considerations. We explore, in

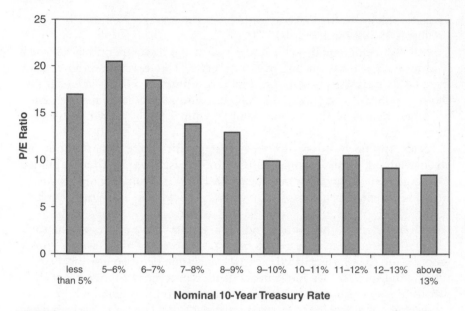

EXHIBIT 14.2 Histogram of Price/Earnings Ratios versus Nominal Interest Rate
Levels (1954–2008)
Source: Morgan Stanley Research, BARRA, Thomson Financial, Standard &
Poor's, Federal Reserve, IBES, First Call

particular, the implications that a steadily declining relationship between
P/Es and interest rates would have on the concept of equity duration, a
connection that appears to have been insufficiently studied to this point.

P/E RATIOS AND EQUITY DURATION

If the P/E ratio was as reliably related to interest rate levels as the histogram
in Exhibit 14.2 seems to suggest, then changes in interest rates would induce
corresponding changes in the P/Es. Moreover, since P/E changes are a major
source of volatility in short term stock returns, one might expect stock
returns to be closely tied to the changes in interest rates. In other words, if
this relationship held in the form of sequential movements over time, then
we should expect to see a reasonably large and persistent equity duration.

The early studies of equity duration were performed within the framework of the standard dividend discount model (DDM). A theoretical duration value was obtained by taking the derivative of the DDM with respect to
the discount rate. This procedure typically led to an extremely high duration

value, typically well in excess of 25, and in many cases, much greater (Williams 1938; Vanderhoof 1972).

All else being equal, a 1 percent rise in the discount rate would then lead to a 25 percent decline in equity price. This extreme result follows from DDM's growth assumptions that thrust much of a firm's value far into the future. Small changes in the discount rate would consequently generate large changes in the present value of equity, thereby creating the high duration values.

This approach led to the view that equities were long-duration instruments and, as such, could be used to defease long-duration liabilities. This argument is sometimes used as a basis to justify high equity exposure in defined benefit pension plans with very long-tailed liabilities (Dechow et al., 2004).

Over the years, this author and his associates have addressed the topic of equity duration in a series of papers. The first of these was a simple empirical analysis, which cited the low correlation between historical equity returns and interest rate movements. It then proceeded to argue that these empirical results suggested that the equity duration was quite low, possibly on the order of anywhere from two to five, depending on the time period, and was extremely unstable (Leibowitz 1986). Subsequent studies confirmed this latter point, especially with the correlation between stocks and bonds having shifted from positive to negative in subsequent time periods. The general conclusion from this study was that the concept of equity duration was not particularly useful as an investment planning tool. Several articles from a number of sources have come to basically the same conclusion (Nissim and Penman 2003; Litterman 2005; Viceiria 2007).

INFLATION VERSUS REAL RATE EFFECTS

However, the puzzle still remained: Why is there such a weak relationship between interest rate changes and equity returns when most valuation models incorporate interest rates as a critical ingredient? We returned to this subject in 1987 in a paper called "Total Differential Approach to Equity Duration" (Leibowitz et al., 1989). This paper was built upon a concept introduced by one of the co-authors that inflation effects flowed through into a stock's earnings stream (Estep and Hanson 1980). By making a series of seemingly reasonable assumptions about the magnitude of this flow-through, it could be shown that inflation-induced higher earnings in the numerator could compensate for an increased discount rate in the denominator, resulting in a much more muted inflation response. One could then obtain theoretical equity duration values that were more in line with what had been empirically observed. This paper also raised some interesting questions about the effect of changes in real rates, and concluded that such movements could lead to very high real-rate durations.

In a later work, the value of equity was divided into two components: a tangible value, reflecting the continuation of the current stream of earnings, and a franchise value, reflecting the net payoff from future investments (Leibowitz 2004). This separation turned out to be very useful in thinking about a number of issues, including the questions of equity duration and inflation flow-through. In a 1993 paper (Leibowitz and Kogelman 1993), it was argued that inflation should have a more deleterious effect on the tangible value because the current revenues and the costs would be relatively sticky, that is, less able to pass on inflationary pressures. In contrast, the franchise value component, based on future investments, could be more readily structured and priced so as to adapt to inflation effects. This flexibility would enable the franchise value to enjoy a high flow-through factor for sufficiently distant investments. While these polarized views were probably too extreme, it did provide a basis for developing theoretical equity durations that were even more in line with the lower values observed empirically.

SPREAD-DRIVEN DDMs

Another step in this direction was to view the return on investment (ROI) in the form of a corporate franchise spread over the cost of capital. In the basic DDM, future growth is described as one or more phases each having fixed growth rates for earnings or dividends. In a 2000 paper we explored the implications of expressing the opportunities for future corporate investments in terms of a franchise *spread* rather than a fixed ROI (Leibowitz 2000).

This simple and seemingly reasonable restatement enables us to look at the returns that fuel future earnings in a different way. The standard DDM treats the return on investment (ROI) as a fixed value. With such fixed ROIs, lower interest rates reduce the discounting effect while future earnings remain unchanged—a rather unlikely combination! In large part, it is this combination of constant earnings in the numerator with a lower discount rate in the denominator that leads to the exceedingly large equity durations obtained with the standard DDM.

In contrast, if the franchise spread is viewed as having greater stability than the ROI, then returns on new investments would be more closely tied to future interest rates, that is, lower rates would lead to lower ROIs. Since ROIs play a fundamental role in determining the firm's future earnings stream, the numerator and denominator effects would both be reduced under lower rates. This approach tends to dampen the effect of changing interest rates, thereby leading to much lower duration values. This paper also showed that further moderation in the duration values results when the franchise spread itself is assumed to be some monotonic function of the level of the discount rate.

Another study addressed the duration effects for various types of real estate equity and showed how they could be modeled by analogy to floating rate debt (Hartzell et al., 1988).

We draw in the current paper upon much of this earlier work to examine the implications of Exhibit 14.2's P/E-versus-interest-rate histogram. Our goal is to at least enrich the discussion, given that we have very little hope of achieving a complete resolution of this complex issue.

P/E RATIOS VERSUS INFLATION

As a next step toward a deeper empirical analysis, we decompose the interest rate into an inflation rate and a real rate. In Exhibit 14.3, we look at the historical P/E ratio versus the CPI rate. We have here a fairly clear-cut

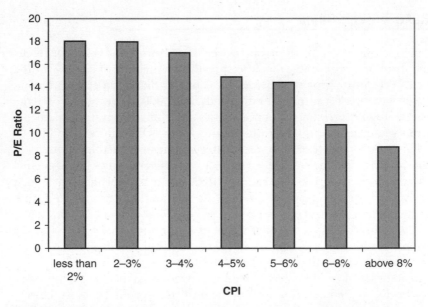

EXHIBIT 14.3   Histogram of Price/Earnings Ratios versus CPI Levels (1954 to 2008)
Source: Morgan Stanley Research, BARRA, Thomson Financial, Standard & Poor's, Federal Reserve, IBES, First Call

monotonic response, although it seems to bottom out with a very low P/E at very high CPI rates. Such a result would be roughly in accord with the franchise value theory in that the initial tangible value component would have relatively less defense against higher inflation levels. Various explanations for this behavior have been set forth, a number of which are based on the market's underestimation of the flowthrough effect (Modigliani and Cohn 1979). However, when we shift to the more relevant regression of one-year percentage P/E *changes* versus the corresponding *changes* in CPI rates, the correlation again deteriorates significantly, just as in the earlier case for nominal interest rates.

P/E RATIOS VERSUS REAL RATES

Exhibit 14.4 plots P/E *levels* against real rate *levels*. The resulting tentlike histogram is quite striking, seeming to suggest that both very high and very low real rates are associated with low P/Es. For real rates above 4.0 percent, the decline in the P/E ratio roughly parallels that of nominal interest rates.

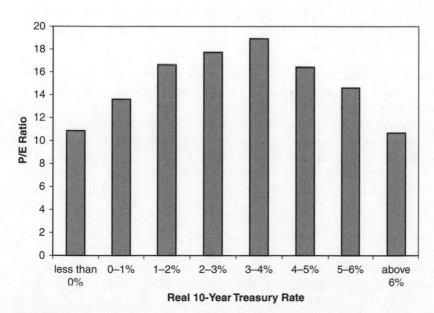

EXHIBIT 14.4 Histogram of Price/Earnings Ratios versus Real Interest Rate Levels (1954 to 2008)
Source: Morgan Stanley Research, BARRA, Thomson Financial, Standard & Poor's, Federal Reserve, IBES, First Call

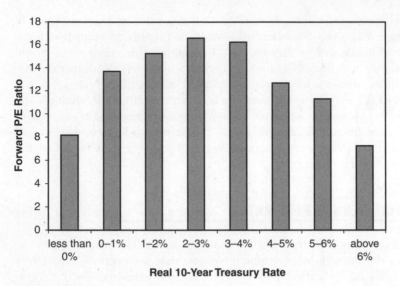

EXHIBIT 14.5   Histogram of Forward Price/Earnings Ratios versus Real Interest Rate Levels (1978 to 2008)
Source: Morgan Stanley Research, BARRA, Thomson Financial, Standard & Poor's, Federal Reserve, IBES, First Call

Below 1.0 percent, however, lower real rates seem to lead to lower P/E ratios, quite a departure from the one-way decline that we saw with nominal interest rates.

As a point of comparison, Exhibit 14.5 plots P/Es based on 12-month forward expected earnings versus real interest rates from 1978 to 2008. The same tent pattern exists as in Exhibit 14.4.

One tempting explanation for this curious result is that the real rate is formed as a balance point between the supply of funds and the economic conditions that create the demand for funds. In this sense, higher real rates beyond a certain point could imply a more deleterious effect from tighter monetary conditions than the benefits derived from the improved economic conditions that called for such money. In contrast, at very low real interest rates, one might have ample funds available, but with insufficient risk-adjusted opportunities to productively use them (Zeng et al., 2003). Somewhere in the middle range of real rates, there might be a sweet spot at which these two effects were well balanced.

The exhibits in this chapter do seem to argue for a fairly consistent relationship between the P/E and various interest rate measures. Moreover, we could build some wonderfully intricate theories to explain the divergent effects with real yields and inflation. However, when the P/E *changes* are regressed against *changes* in real rates, we again experience the same radical fall-off in the goodness of fit. Unfortunately, with these tougher tests based on *changes,* the correlations become too weak to form any reasonable empirical foundation.

Of course, we should not necessarily expect things to be simple. It can be argued that equity valuation should depend upon a large number of factors beyond the interest rate–related factors cited earlier, including the risk premium, current and anticipated monetary responses, anticipated economic conditions, and growth prospects, as well as the interactions among all these variables. One area that we have not addressed, which certainly deserves more attention, is the risk premium itself.

There are various ways of measuring the risk premium. Nevertheless, one would generally expect the risk premium to be a very critical determinant of the P/E ratio. In principle, one might expect the risk premium to be fairly stable in the sweet spot, and to become larger when economic circumstances become cloudier.

One controversy that has raged for quite some time is the relative roles of nominal rates versus real rates in equity valuation. Indeed, one of the criticisms of the so-called Fed model, in which the earnings yield is compared to the nominal interest rate as a gauge of fair valuation, is that the earnings yield should really be treated as a real variable (Campbell and Vuolteenaho 2004; Asness 2000, 2003). However, the earnings yield is of course just an inversion of the P/E ratio. From the preceding discussion, one can argue that the P/E ratio should really be viewed as a combination of a tangible value having an inflation-sensitive current earnings stream, and a franchise value that can more readily adapt to inflationary pressures. This would seem to suggest that the earnings yield should really be viewed as some spread off the real yield together with a second term that reflects some partial sensitivity to inflation.

CONCLUSION

The preceding discussion admittedly leaves us in a state of limbo. There is certainly a temptation to draw upon the level data and the various theoretical models to help explain the prospective response of the equity market to rate movements. On the one hand, virtually any theoretical analysis must incorporate all three discount rate components—the real rate, the inflation rate, and the risk premium. Also, the statistical analysis of *level* data does appear to support important relationships between the P/E ratio and these discount rate components. On the other hand, these statistical relationships do *not* survive unscathed when one moves to more stringent tests based on *changes* in P/Es and *changes* in rates. These negative empirical results should sound a cautionary note against any simplistic characterizations of the relationship between interest rates and equity returns.

This study certainly does not resolve these issues, nor did it have the heroic ambition of setting out to do so, but it has hopefully provided some basis for a richer discussion of this fascinating and important topic.

REFERENCES

Asness, C. S. 2000. "Stocks vs. bonds: Explaining the equity risk premium." *Financial Analysts Journal* 56: 96–113.

———. 2003. "Fight the Fed model: The relationship between stock market yields, bond market yields, and future returns." *Journal of Portfolio Management* 30: 11–24.

Campbell, J. Y., and T. Vuolteenaho. 2004. "Inflation illusion and stock prices." *American Economic Review* 94 (2): 19–23.

Dechow, P. M., R. G. Sloan, and M. T. Soliman. 2004. "Implied equity duration: A new measure of equity risk." *Review of Accounting Studies* 9 (2-3): 197–228.

Estep, T., and N. Hanson. 1980. *The valuation of financial assets in inflation.* New York: Salomon Brothers.

Hartzell, D. J., D. G. Shulman, T. C. Langetieg, and M. L. Leibowitz. 1988. "A look at real estate duration." *Journal of Portfolio Management* 15 (1): 16–24. Also reprinted in *Investing* (Chicago: Probus Publishing, 1992), 461–479.

Leibowitz, M. L. 1986. "Total portfolio duration." *Financial Analysts Journal* 43 (2): 83–84. Also reprinted in *Investing* (Chicago: Probus Publishing, 1992), 35–57.

———. 2000. "Spread-driven dividend discount models." *Financial Analysts Journal* 56 (6): 64–81. Also reprinted in *Franchise Value* (Hoboken, NJ: John Wiley & Sons, Finance Series, 2004), 372–402.

———. 2004. *Franchise value.* Hoboken, NJ: John Wiley & Sons, Finance Series.

Leibowitz, M. L., and S. Kogelman. 1993. "Resolving the equity duration paradox." *Financial Analysts Journal* 49 (1): 51–64. Also reprinted in Martin L. Liebowitz, *Franchise Value* (Hoboken, NJ: John Wiley & Sons, Finance Series, 2004), 219–242.

Leibowitz, M. L., E. H. Sorensen, R. D. Arnott, and H. N. Hanson. 1989. "A total differential approach to equity duration." *Financial Analysts Journal* 45 (5): 30–37. Also reprinted in *Investing* (Chicago: Probus Publishing, 1992), 405–420.

Litterman, R. 2005. "Equity duration." *Investments & Pensions Europe* (special report), February.

Modigliani, F., and R. A. Cohn. 1979. "Inflation and the stock market." *Financial Analysts Journal* 35: 24–44.

Nissim, D., and S. H. Penman. 2003. "The association between changes in interest rates, earnings, and equity values." *Contemporary Accounting Research* 20 (4): 775–804.

Vanderhoof, I. T. 1972. "The interest rate assumption and the maturity structure of the assets of a life insurance company." *Transactions of the Society of Actuaries* 24: 157–205.

Viceria, Luis M. 2007. "Bond risk, bond return volatility, and the term structure of interest rates." *Harvard Business School* manuscript, draft February.

Williams, J. B. 1938. *The theory of investment value*. Amsterdam: North-Holland Publishing.

Zeng, Q., S. Galbraith, M. Viviano, D. Norquist, and C. Laine. 2003. *Market valuation model 2.0*. New York: Morgan Stanley Equity Research.

Theoretical and Empirical Stress Betas

Stress Betas and Correlation Tightening

*C*orrelation tightening moves beyond normal times *data to generate higher stress betas and greater levels of downside risk. In particular, if all equity-related correlations actually went to one, the beta risk could increase by as much as 50 percent. Even without this extreme case of "all correlations go to 1," a partial tightening can have a significant impact on downside risk.*

Stress beta effects vary widely across different allocations. Ironically, there would be very little incremental beta risk for the traditional 60/40 funds. The more vulnerable portfolios appear to be those with large percentage allocations to equity classes such as international equity that are initially less-than-fully correlated with the benchmark equity. More reliable diversification benefits would be obtained from asset classes that could maintain stable correlations or, ideally, act as hedges under stress conditions.

Asset classes such as international and emerging market equity that are most subject to short term tightening might provide valuable diversification benefits over the long term. Global decoupling trends could lead to these assets having lower correlations and more divergent returns. The strategic challenge is to incorporate these longer term benefits into the classic short term problem of balancing return prospects versus tolerable risk levels.

PORTFOLIO CONVEXITY EFFECTS

It would be desirable to see hard historical evidence of beta increases from correlation tightening. While truly high stress markets have been (thankfully) rare in recent years, one can find some indication of greater betas under stress. Exhibit 15.1 plots emerging market returns against S&P 500 returns from January 1988 through November 2007. A quadratic regression curve is superimposed on the scatter. The increased downward curvature on the

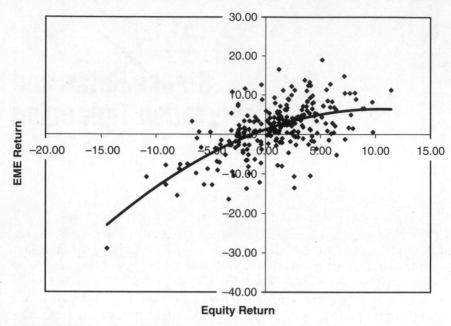

EXHIBIT 15.1　Emerging Market Return versus Equity Return
Source: Morgan Stanley Research

left is an indication of increasing sensitivity to equity movements in adverse markets. Unfortunately, there are too few data points in this region to obtain statistical validity regarding the magnitude of these beta shifts.

Exhibits 15.2, 15.3, and 15.4 provide the historical return scatters and quadratic regression curves for Portfolios A, C, and D from January 1990 through November 2007. The pure equity Portfolio A has a virtually total straight-line response, with the only residuals being due to varying cash returns. However, Portfolios C and D exhibit downward curvature patterns similar to that seen in Exhibit 15.2 for emerging markets. Such curvature is analogous to the convexity patterns within certain fixed income markets.

STRESS CORRELATIONS OF 1

If the correlations were to actually go to 1 for equity-related assets, then the beta values for all three portfolios would be as depicted in Exhibit 15.5. Portfolio A's beta would remain unchanged at 0.60 since its pure equity already has a correlation of 1 with itself. Portfolio C's beta would soar 50 percent from 0.57 to 0.86, and the beta for equity-intensive Portfolio D

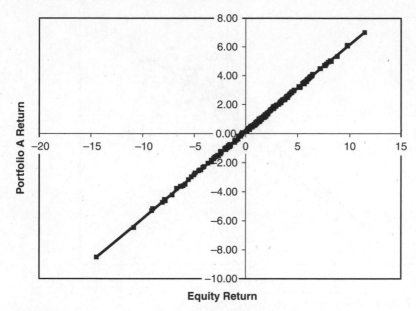

EXHIBIT 15.2   Portfolio A versus Equity Return
Source: Morgan Stanley Research

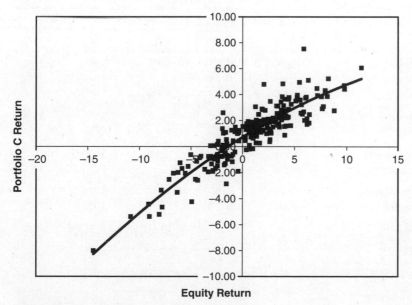

EXHIBIT 15.3   Portfolio C versus Equity Return
Source: Morgan Stanley Research

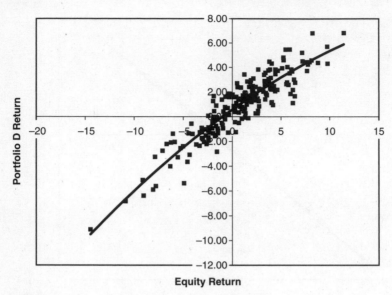

EXHIBIT 15.4 Portfolio D versus Equity Return
Source: Morgan Stanley Research

EXHIBIT 15.5 Effect on Beta of Correlations Going to 1

	Original Beta	Stress Beta	A	C	D
U.S. Equity	1.00	1.00	60%	20%	25%
U.S. Bonds	0.14	0.14		20%	20%
Cash	0.00	0.00	40%		
International Equity	0.77	1.18		15%	25%
Emerging Mkt Equity	0.76	1.70		5%	5%
Venture Capital	0.59	1.68		10%	
Private Equity	0.98	1.39		10%	15%
Absolute Return	0.28	0.56		10%	
Real Estate	0.07	0.07		10%	10%
Normal Beta			0.60	0.57	0.66
Stress Beta			0.60	0.86	0.87
% Beta Increase			0.00	50%	32%
Stress Volatility			9.90	14.89	15.26
Stress Correlation with U.S. Equity			100.0%	95.4%	94.5%

Source: Morgan Stanley Research

would rise 41 percent from 0.66 to 0.87. The total volatilities of C and D would increase accordingly.

It should be noted that these results are not derived from an empirical analysis, but rather from a simple mathematical exercise (as described in the appendix). The overall volatility of equity and the other assets are presumed to remain constant. Under normal covariances, the portfolio volatility is derived primarily from that component of an asset's volatility that is correlated with the dominant equity risk factor. When the correlation goes to one, all of an asset's volatility adds to the fund's volatility in accordance with its percentage weight. Thus, the surge in beta values and in fund volatility arises from the full force of each asset's volatility adding directly to the portfolio volatility, rather than from any increase in the asset volatility.

The results are stated as a beta relative to the benchmark equity. There would be comparable results, however, as long as the selected beta is defined with reference to any dominating risk factor (for example, global equities).

RESIDUAL VOLATILITY CONSTANT

An asset's beta-based co-movement is only one source of its volatility. The remaining volatility is derived from all other factors and idiosyncratic risks that are presumed to be independent of equity movements. For some asset classes, this residual volatility can be quite large and can constitute a large percentage of the asset's total volatility. However, when the asset is embedded as a minority percentage within a portfolio framework, even high residual volatilities become dominated by the portfolio's accumulated beta value (Leibowitz 2004; Leibowitz and Bova 2005; Leibowitz and Bova 2007b).

Correlation tightening can cover a wide range of processes with very different outcomes. One key question is what changes and what stays fixed. One reasonable assumption is that the residual volatility remains roughly constant. The tightening correlation would then have to be focused on increasing only the equity component of the asset's volatility. (The formulas for the beta shifts based on these admittedly simplistic models are presented in the appendix.)

Exhibit 15.6 shows the beta effect of a 25 percent increase in all correlations, given this constant residual assumption. Assets with larger betas at the outset undergo a greater percentage increase than those with lower betas. The net result is that a 25 percent increase in correlation leads to a 36 percent increase in Portfolio C's beta from 0.57 to 0.78, and to a 40 percent increase in Portfolio D's beta from 0.66 to 0.93.

Exhibit 15.6 treats all correlations as increasing uniformly by the same fixed percentage of 25 percent. The equity-related assets undergo the greatest

EXHIBIT 15.6 Effect on Beta of 25 percent Increase in Correlations—Residual Volatility Constant

	Original Beta	Stress Beta	Allocation Percentages		
			A	C	D
U.S. Equity	1.00	1.00	60%	20%	25%
U.S. Bonds	0.14	0.18	40%	20%	20%
International Equity	0.77	1.25		15%	25%
Emerging Mkt Equity	0.76	1.03		5%	5%
Venture Capital	0.59	0.77		10%	
Private Equity	0.98	1.80		10%	15%
Absolute Return	0.28	0.39		10%	
Real Estate	0.07	0.09		10%	10%
Initial Beta			0.60	0.57	0.66
Stress Beta			0.60	0.78	0.93
% Beta Increase			0%	36%	40%
Stress Volatility			9.90	13.61	16.11
Stress Correlation with U.S. Equity			100.0%	94.4%	95.1%

Source: Morgan Stanley Research

increase in stress betas, and have the most significant impact on the overall portfolio. In practice, however, the tightening would neither be uniform across all asset classes nor the same in all market regimes. For example, there are certain historical periods where longer duration bonds exhibited a negative correlation with U.S. equities (Leibowitz and Bova 2007a). For effective risk control under the critical tail conditions, it is important to determine which asset classes would be either resistant to stress tightening or might even be able to act as a hedge.

VARYING RESIDUAL VOLATILITIES

The preceding illustration was based on the assumption that residual volatilities remain constant, so that—with the equity risk staying the same—the tightened correlation is translated directly into higher asset class volatility. A more general analysis would allow all components of asset class volatility as well as the equity volatility to change under adverse conditions.

EXHIBIT 15.7 Effect on Beta of 25 Percent Increase in Correlations—Residual Volatility Varying

	Original Beta	Stress Beta	A	C	D
U.S. Equity	1.00	1.00	60%	20%	25%
U.S. Bonds	0.14	0.17		20%	20%
Cash	0.00	0.00	40%		
International Equity	0.77	0.96		15%	25%
Emerging Mkt Equity	0.76	0.95		5%	5%
Venture Capital	0.59	0.74		10%	
Private Equity	0.98	1.22		10%	15%
Absolute Return	0.28	0.35		10%	
Real Estate	0.07	0.09		10%	10%
Normal Beta			0.60	0.57	0.66
Stress Beta			0.60	0.67	0.76
% Beta Increase			0.00	16%	16%
Stress Volatility			9.90	11.86	13.55
Stress Correlation with U.S. Equity			100.0%	92.6%	93.0%

Source: Morgan Stanley Research

The simplest version is that both asset and equity volatilities increase proportionally so that their ratio remains roughly constant. In such a situation, the residual volatility would be allowed to vary as needed, but a given percentage change in the correlation would always lead to the same percentage change in beta value. The net portfolio effect here would then depend solely on the weight of non-equity (and noncash) assets in the allocation (Exhibit 15.7).

If the asset and equity volatility both remain constant, then the ratio would also be constant. This situation would represent a special case of constant volatility ratios and would have the same outcomes as shown in Exhibit 15.7.

It should be pointed out, however, that this constant volatility ratio case is probably rather optimistic. Consequently, a 25 percent increase in correlation would be more likely to produce beta increases that fell somewhere between Exhibit 15.6 and Exhibit 15.7.

EXHIBIT 15.8 Stress Betas for Different Tightening Conditions

| | Assumed Volatility Characteristics | | | | | |
Level of Tightening	Asset Volatility	Asset Residual	Equity Volatility	A	C	D
0	Normal	Normal	Normal	0.60	0.57	0.66
100%	Constant	Adjusts to Zero	Constant	0.60	0.86	0.87
25%	Variable	Constant	Constant	0.67	0.78	0.93
25%	Adjusts to Keep Volatility Ratio Constant	Variable	Adjusts to Keep Volatility Ratio Constant	0.60	0.67	0.76
25%	Constant	Adjusts Lower	Constant	0.60	0.67	0.76

Source: Morgan Stanley Research

Exhibit 15.8 summarizes the stress beta values for the three funds under each of the tightening conditions described earlier. More complex assumptions regarding the behavior of the different volatility parameters would result in a wider range of beta effects. In particular, while asset class residuals can usually be treated as if they were independent, the residuals themselves could be subject to tightening stress correlations arising from common pressures such as liquidity needs or increasing risk tolerance.

CONCLUSION

The basic message is that, under most volatility assumptions, asset class betas could rise significantly in the face of correlation tightening. Those asset classes with the higher initial betas would incur the greatest beta increase.

These vulnerable assets would include non-U.S. Equity classes such as international equity, emerging market equity, and so forth. These assets may lower the total beta and portfolio volatility under normal times, and that they may well serve as good sources of return and diversification over the long term. However, in short term periods of stress, their vulnerability to tightening correlations could exacerbate a portfolio's downside risk beyond the estimated level on the basis of normal covariances.

Thus, at the portfolio level, the greatest stress beta effects would be experienced for allocations having a sizable diversification into these equity-like assets and having only smaller percentage weights remaining in traditional benchmark equity and fixed income assets.

Correlation tightening causes greater pain for diversified portfolios just when they are already under high levels of stress. The initial betas of most diversified portfolios lie in the same 0.55- to 0.65-range as the traditional 60/40. Thus, with unchanged beta values, both portfolio types should experience roughly comparable price declines. However, with correlation tightening, there could be an even greater increase in the diversified portfolio's total beta. This line of reasoning, ironically, suggests that the typical diversified portfolio might be subject to somewhat greater downside risk than the traditional 60/40.

There are counterpoints to this paradoxical finding. First, diversified portfolios have sources of expected return above and beyond that associated with the beta relationship. Over time, these incremental returns should accumulate and provide a sizable cushion against beta-based risks. Second, the initial correlations embedded in the covariance matrix are based primarily on short-term price changes. Over longer term periods, the correlations may be quite different. For example, the relationship between developed and emerging equity markets may be quite tight for a sudden down move. Over the long term, however, regional de-coupling could lead these two markets to behave much more independently, and an emerging market allocation might serve as a powerful diversifier over the long term.

Nevertheless, in the short run, the most problematic risk for institutional funds is a sudden, severe, and persistent decline in asset value. Such an adverse event is almost sure to entail deterioration in the equity market. To the extent that the feared correlation tightening does indeed occur, then it may well be the more diversified funds that—ironically—will experience higher betas in the short run and greater beta-based pain.

Some investors may view enhanced beta risk as a short-term phenomenon and steel themselves to ride it out. Others may want to consider various forms of tail protection using derivatives, options, or contingent beta overlays. In any case, investors in seemingly well-diversified portfolios should recognize that even a partial version of "correlations going to 1" could drive their downside risks well beyond any projected level based on normal-times covariances.

APPENDIX

For the ith asset that has a correlation ρ_{ie} with equities, the implicit beta value β_i is given by

$$\beta_i = \rho_{ie}\left(\frac{\sigma_i}{\sigma_e}\right)$$

in which σ_i and σ_e are the volatilities for the asset class and the equity market respectively.

In the trivial special case in which σ_i and σ_e remain stable but the equity correlation literally goes to 1, the new beta value $\beta_i{}^*$ just becomes the ratio of the two volatilities,

$$\beta_i{}^* = \left(\frac{\sigma_i}{\sigma_e} \right)$$

The tacit assumption here, however, is that the asset's total volatility remains unchanged by the distress that forces the correlation to 1.

A more realistic case is that the correlation increases by some given percentage that results in a new correlation $\rho_{ie}{}^*$ ($\rho_{ie}{}^* < 1$). This case requires some assumptions about which volatility component changes and which components remain stable.

The asset class residual volatility σ_α is defined by the standard sum-of-squares,

$$\sigma_\alpha^2 = \sigma_i^2 - (\beta_i \sigma_e)^2$$
$$= \sigma_i^2 - \rho_{ie}^2 \sigma_i^2$$
$$= \sigma_i^2 \left(1 - \rho_{ie}^2 \right)$$

The total volatility σ_i can then be expressed as a function of ρ_{ie}, as long as $\rho_{ie} < 1$,

$$\sigma_i = \frac{\sigma_\alpha}{\sqrt{1 - \rho_{ie}^2}}$$

and

$$\beta_i = \rho_{ie} \frac{\sigma_i}{\sigma_e}$$
$$= \left[\frac{\rho_{ie}}{\sqrt{1 - \rho_{ie}^2}} \right] \left(\frac{\sigma_\alpha}{\sigma_e} \right)$$

in which, in general, σ_α could itself be a function of ρ_{ie}.

With the new correlation $\rho_{ie}{}^*$, the revised $\beta_i{}^*$ becomes

$$\beta_i{}^* = \left[\frac{\rho_{ie}{}^*}{\sqrt{1 - \rho_{ie}{}^{*2}}} \right] \left(\frac{\sigma_\alpha}{\sigma_e} \right)$$

Under a further assumption that σ_α and σ_e remain unchanged,

$$\beta_i{}^* = \left[\frac{\rho_{ie}{}^{*'}}{\sqrt{1 - \rho_{ie}{}^{*2}}} \frac{\sqrt{1 - \rho_{ie}^2}}{\rho_{ie}} \right] \beta_i$$

$$= \left[\left(\frac{\rho_{ie}{}^*}{\rho_{ie}} \right) \sqrt{\frac{1 - \rho_{ie}^2}{1 - \rho_{ie}{}^{*2}}} \right] \beta_i$$

One alternative formulation is to assume that both σ_i and σ_e are some function of the correlation $\rho_{ie}{}^*$, but that their ratio remains constant, that is,

$$\left(\frac{\sigma_i}{\sigma_e} \right) = \left(\frac{\sigma_i{}^*}{\sigma_e{}^*} \right)$$

$$\beta_i{}^* = \rho_{ie}{}^* \left(\frac{\sigma_i}{\sigma_e} \right)$$

and

$$\frac{\beta_i{}^*}{\beta_i} = \frac{\rho_{ie}{}^*}{\rho_{ie}}$$

so that the percentage increase in ρ_{ie} generates the same percentage increase in beta values. The situation where both σ_i and σ_e remain unchanged is just a special case of the constant volatility ratio result.

A truly generalized formulation would allow all volatility characteristics to become variable. In seriously distressed markets, one can envision that both the asset volatility σ_i and the equity volatility σ_e might increase, but perhaps by quite different percentages. The residual volatility is also likely to change under stress conditions. Moreover, under stress conditions, the residuals from the various asset classes might become more highly correlated among themselves, resulting in additional adverse factor effects at the portfolio level. It would obviously be difficult to quantify (or even to catalog) the impact of all these moving variables. It is quite certain, however, that stress conditions would lead to a significant surge in the portfolio betas, especially for diversified portfolios with a large allocation to diversifying, but equity-like, assets.

REFERENCES

Leibowitz, Martin L. 2004. "The β-plus measure in asset allocation." *Journal of Portfolio Management* 30 (3): 26–36.

Leibowitz, M. L., and A. Bova. 2005. "Allocation betas." *Financial Analysts Journal* 61: 70–82.

———. 2007a. "P/Es and pension funding ratios." *Financial Analysts Journal* 63 (1): 84–96.

———. 2007b. "Gathering implicit alphas in a beta world." *Journal of Portfolio Management* 33 (3): 10–18.

CHAPTER 16

Stress Risks within Asset and Surplus Frameworks

The most important form of risk for U.S. institutional funds is a decline so severe and persistent as to erode confidence in the fund's current investment policy and ability to fulfill its liabilities without extraordinary sponsor contributions.

At such times of stress, the common expression "all correlations go to 1" may be overstated, but inter-asset correlations are still likely to tighten beyond the levels embedded in standard covariance data. This tightening of correlations with equities creates what might be called stress betas.

Stress betas can exacerbate a fund's downside risk well beyond that estimated from normal covariances. This gap between expected and stress-point risk levels will—ironically—be worse for the more highly diversified funds.

Funds that need to lower their stress risk must reduce the net beta by reallocating to lower beta assets and by some use of overlays. To control surplus risk in stress situations, a balanced combination of liability hedging and beta reduction may be required.

At the same time, funds with long-term liabilities and minimal liquidity needs are particularly well structured for pursuing long-term returns. Concerns about short term beta-driven risks should be balanced against the prospect of a diversified portfolio generating excess returns beyond those from the beta relationship. Over time, these incremental returns can accumulate and provide a sizable cushion against beta-based risks.

RISK LIFE CYCLES

A general principle in fund investment, whether within an asset-only or an asset-liability context, is to deploy the available risk budget so as to maximize expected return. However, there are also times when, for a variety of reasons, a fund may wish to reduce its overall risk on either a short term or even a long term basis.

Indeed, there is a view that most investment funds—institutional as well as individual—have a life cycle that transitions from an early risk-tolerant building period into a lower-risk terminal phase that is primarily focused on liability fulfillment. Many other considerations confound this simplistic model, such as the growing size of the fund in relation to the sponsor's earning power, the need to provide long term inflation protection, the intrinsic structural advantage of being able to focus on long-term horizons, accounting and regulatory constraints, and so forth. However, to the extent that some such life cycle is present, one should not be surprised to see funds move toward risk reduction over the course of time.

STRESS TIMES AS A DETERMINANT OF RISK TOLERANCE

The standard covariance data that project 10- to 11-percent portfolio volatilities are based on performance history that necessarily has a concentration on normal times. A fund's true risk tolerance tends to be more determined by the prospect of a decline in asset (or surplus) value so severe and so persistent as to erode a fund's ability to fulfill its liabilities without extraordinary sponsor contributions. Another facet of this extreme downside risk would be a perceived need to alter the strategic allocation—even when further market deterioration is assessed to have a relatively low probability. It is at precisely these juncture points of maximum stress that standard asset relationships break down and the original risk estimates become invalid.

Such events do happen, but they are insufficiently captured by standard covariance data. Correlation tightening is a problem in an asset-only framework, but it can become even more devastating in asset and liability situations. For example, the funding ratio of defined benefit funds will drop most precipitously when both the equity market and long term interest rates experience sudden, severe declines (Leibowitz and Bova 2007a).

CORRELATION TIGHTENING UNDER STRESS

To be realistic, any risk reduction strategy must address these potential tail events. With equity being the dominant factor even under normal times, it is almost sure to play a crucial role at the points of maximum duress. There are many challenges in trying to estimate the equity movements under such tail events and the inter-asset correlations that may then prevail. In discussions of these prospective events, one often hears the comment that, under such adverse conditions, all correlations go to 1. However, there is rarely any serious analysis of the covariance and volatility effects implied by such extreme extrapolations.

The concept of correlation tightening provides a more measured way to gain some insight into these effects. By assuming varying forms of correlation tightening across asset classes, one can explore how stress conditions might affect different allocations. Any such study would of course be plagued by myriad degrees of freedom. However, with equities as the dominant risk factor, the problem can become more manageable by focusing only on tightening correlations between equities and other asset classes. This approach leads to what might be called *stress betas* for each asset class. For a given allocation, these values will then build to a stress beta for the fund as a whole.

DIVERGENCE UNDER STRESS

With normal times, covariance data and the associated normal beta values, most U.S. funds tend to have roughly the same 10- to 11-percent projected level of volatilities. Unlike this common range for normal times volatility, however, stress betas can affect different allocations very differently. In many cases, it is the more diversified funds that will be severely strained by stress betas that far exceed their normal betas. Naturally, when stress betas are used, the volatility tends to increase markedly.

The traditional 60/40 funds have stress betas that essentially match their normal betas. In a more diversified fund, the lower correlations across the assets tend to moderate volatility under normal times. Under market duress, however, these correlations tighten, resulting in a higher percentage of an asset's volatility being transmitted to the overall fund level. Thus, it is ironic that, in comparison with the traditional 60/40, some diversified allocations may actually experience a much larger gap between the potential losses as estimated under stress times as opposed to normal times.

SHORT TERM RISK REDUCTION
AND LONG-TERM RETURNS

The prospect of such stress events—and the impact of the stress betas that they might induce—clearly deserves serious consideration in any comprehensive risk plan, and especially one that targets beta reduction as a means of risk control.

At the same time, these short term beta-driven risks must be balanced against the prospect of longer term returns from diversification. The initial correlations embedded in the covariance matrix are based primarily on short term price changes. The correlations may be quite different over longer periods. For example, the relationship between developed and emerging market equities may be quite tight under a sudden down move. Over the long term, however, regional decoupling could lead these two markets to behave more independently, and an emerging market allocation might therefore serve as a powerful diversifier over the long term.

It should be noted that, theoretically, pension funds and certain other institutional funds are ideal vehicles for pursuing long-term investment returns. Diversified portfolios can have the potential to provide both passive and active expected returns above and beyond the returns derived from the beta relationship. The most desirable assets for this purpose would be those that combine the prospect of incremental passive returns and positive active returns that are either relatively uncorrelated with equities, or where the equity component can be reliably stripped out. Over time, the accumulation of these incremental returns can provide a sizable cushion against beta-based risks.

NORMAL CORRELATION-BASED BETAS

The preceding points are illustrated by the three hypothetical allocations shown in Exhibit 16.1. The correlations and volatilities are derived from relatively standard covariance data that are intended to be representative of normal times (Leibowitz 2004). Portfolio A is the ultimate in simplicity at 60 percent U.S. equity and 40 percent cash. Since U.S. equities always have a beta of one, Portfolio A will always have a beta of 0.6.

Portfolio C is a diversified portfolio with only 20 percent direct exposure to U.S. equities and with a wide range of other asset classes. The correlation-based betas are derived as a multiple of the correlation and the ratio of the asset to equity volatility (Leibowitz and Bova 2005). These beta values then accumulate on the basis of the allocation weights to form the total portfolio beta. In spite of its small 20 percent direct allocation to equities, the diversifying assets cumulatively contribute enough beta values to bring C's total beta up to 0.57.

Portfolio D is representative of a fund that has diversified out of U.S. equities, but primarily into other forms of equity. The net result is a total fund beta of 0.66.

It can be seen that, based on normal covariance data, all three funds have similar volatilities, similar correlations to U.S. equities, and similar total beta sensitivity to U.S. equities. Moreover, in all three funds, the

EXHIBIT 16.1 Normal Fund Betas and Volatilities

	Correlation with U.S. Equity	Correlation Based-Beta	Portfolio		
			A	C	D
U.S. Equity	1.00	1.00	60%	20%	25%
U.S. Bonds	0.30	0.14		20%	20%
Cash	0.00	0.00	40%		
International Equity	0.65	0.77		15%	25%
Emerging Mkt Equity	0.45	0.76		5%	5%
Venture Capital	0.35	0.59		10%	
Private Equity	0.70	0.98		10%	15%
Absolute Return	0.50	0.28		10%	
Real Estate	0.10	0.07		10%	10%
Correlation-Based Beta			0.60	0.57	0.66
Beta × Equity Volatility (16.5%)			9.90	9.45	10.91
Total Volatility			9.90	10.45	11.99
Correlation with U.S. Equity			100.0%	90.4%	91.0%

Source: Morgan Stanley Research

beta-based volatility accounts for 90 percent or more of the total volatility. While Exhibit 16.1 presents only three idealized allocations, this convergence in volatility characteristics appears to hold true for almost all institutional allocations seen in practice. Moreover, this convergence remains intact across a range of commonly used covariance matrixes.

BETA RESPONSE CURVES

Under certain circumstances, some funds may find even these normal volatilities to be beyond their risk tolerance. The only practical path to significant risk reduction is through lowering the beta value. For Portfolio A with its limited choice of assets, it is very clear that fund volatilities can be brought down only by a lower allocation to equity. If this percentage were to be dropped to 30 percent, both the beta value of 0.6 and the total volatility would be cut in half.

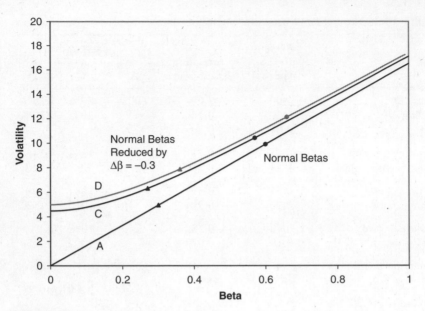

EXHIBIT 16.2   Beta Response Curve
Source: Morgan Stanley Research

For Portfolios C and D, the situation is somewhat more complex. Suppose their basic allocation structure could be kept intact while the fund beta—through an overlay or by some other means—is lowered by 0.30. The nonbeta residual risk of the diversifying assets would then still remain, together with their desirable nonbeta returns. As the fund beta is reduced, these residual risks would loom ever larger as a percentage of the fund's total volatility. At the limit, if the fund beta were to be reduced to zero, the fund volatility would consist solely of these residual risks.

This situation is depicted in Exhibit 16.2 as beta response curves, in which the volatility is plotted against the fund's net beta. At the outset, all three funds have similar betas and similar volatilities, in large part because the beta effect dominates the residual risks. However, as the fund betas are reduced to lower levels, the residual risks in C and D become more relevant, keeping their volatilities above that of the purely beta-driven Portfolio A.

STRESS BETAS

The preceding results were based on covariance data that purports to represent normal market behavior. For many funds, however, it is conditions of potential market duress that determine their short term risk limits. In such situations, the normal asset relationships will be strained, and correlations are likely to tighten.

Correlation tightening can cover a wide range of processes with very different outcomes. One key question is what changes and what stays fixed. A literal interpretation of the expression "all correlations go to 1" would generally lead to an unrealistic covariance matrix. A more coherent interpretation is that each asset class volatility becomes totally loaded on a primary risk factor such as U.S. equities. Exhibit 16.3 displays the beta values that would arise, assuming that all asset classes were to have such a correlation of 1 relative to equities. The net result is dramatic. Portfolio A retains the same 9.9 percent volatility, since U.S. equity already has a correlation of 1 with itself. The fund volatilities for C and D, however, increase by 43 percent and 27 percent, respectively.

A more modest—and probably more reasonable—interpretation will suffice to illustrate the basic concept of stress betas. With the equity movement acting as the driving factor, the simplest approach is to apply a given percentage increase uniformly to both the correlation and beta values of each

EXHIBIT 16.3 Beta Effect from All Correlations Going to 1

	Original Beta	Stress Beta	A	C	D
U.S. Equity	1.00	1.00	60%	20%	25%
U.S. Bonds	0.14	0.14		20%	20%
Cash	0.00	0.00	40%		
International Equity	0.77	1.18		15%	25%
Emerging Mkt Equity	0.76	1.70		5%	5%
Venture Capital	0.59	1.68		10%	
Private Equity	0.98	1.39		10%	15%
Absolute Return	0.28	0.56		10%	
Real Estate	0.07	0.07		10%	10%
Normal Beta			0.60	0.57	0.66
Stress Beta			0.60	0.86	0.87
% Beta Increase			0.00	50%	32%
Stress Volatility			9.90	14.89	15.26
Stress Correlation with U.S. Equity			100.0%	95.4%	94.5%

Source: Morgan Stanley Research

EXHIBIT 16.4 Stress Betas from 25 Percent Increase in Correlations

	Original Beta	Stress Beta	A	C	D
U.S. Equity	1.00	1.00	60%	20%	25%
U.S. Bonds	0.14	0.17		20%	20%
Cash	0.00	0.00	40%		
International Equity	0.77	0.96		15%	25%
Emerging Mkt Equity	0.76	0.95		5%	5%
Venture Capital	0.59	0.74		10%	
Private Equity	0.98	1.22		10%	15%
Absolute Return	0.28	0.35		10%	
Real Estate	0.07	0.09		10%	10%
Normal Beta			0.60	0.57	0.66
Stress Beta			0.60	0.67	0.76
% Beta Increase			0.00	16%	16%
Stress Volatility			9.90	11.86	13.55
Stress Correlation with U.S. Equity			100.0%	92.6%	93.0%

Source: Morgan Stanley Research

asset class. Thus, in Exhibit 16.4, a 25 percent correlation tightening raises the beta for international equity by 25 percent from 0.77 to 0.96. Such tightening has obviously no effect on either U.S. equities itself or cash, so Portfolio A's beta remains unchanged. In contrast, the 25 percent tightening on the 80 percent non-U.S. equity in C raises its beta by 16.3 percent. Similarly, with D's 75 percent non-U.S. equity, the beta increases by 15.5 percent.

One could of course argue about whether the appropriate tightening percentage should be higher or lower. In addition, a more realistic model should probably incorporate tightening factors for each asset class. However, the simple approach in Exhibit 16.4 will suffice to illustrate the key points about the stress beta concept and its role in determining a fund's short term risk.

It is important to distinguish between short term and long term horizons. In the short term, correlation tightening is a key risk that can lead to significantly high stress betas. Some investors may view this enhanced beta risk as just a short term phenomenon and steel themselves to ride it out.

EXHIBIT 16.5 Beta Reduction Effects

	A	C	D
Beta			
Normal	0.60	0.57	0.66
Correlation Tightening	0.60	0.67	0.76
Correlation Tightening $+ \Delta\beta = -.3$	0.30	0.37	0.46
Volatility			
Normal	9.90	10.45	11.99
Correlation Tightening	9.90	11.86	13.55
Correlation Tightening $+ \Delta\beta = -.3$	4.95	7.51	9.13

Source: Morgan Stanley Research

Others may want to consider reallocating to lower beta assets or applying various forms of tail protection, such as derivatives, options, or beta overlays. Exhibit 16.5 shows the effect of applying a beta overlay of –0.3 (for example, a short equity position with futures) to the three portfolios after a 25 percent correlation tightening.

It should be recognized that the cost of any such beta reduction would be a sacrifice in expected long term return.

THE SURPLUS FRAMEWORK

This discussion has focused so far on only the asset side of institutional funds. All institutional funds have objectives (whether or not they are formalized as well-delineated liabilities). For pension funds, the liabilities are becoming even more precisely defined, just as they are becoming ever more onerous in a number of ways. For many funds, risk tolerance is determined primarily within this asset and liability framework.

In basic terms, a fund's surplus is the excess of its asset value over its liabilities. Pension fund liabilities are typically tied to long-duration bond rates, and they can be quite volatile. For example, assuming that long term interest rates have a volatility of 1 percent, a fund with 10-year-duration liabilities would contribute approximately 10 percent to the volatility of the surplus measure. With matched assets and liabilities, an initial zero percent surplus would be subject to variability from both of these liabilities as well as the asset portfolio.

The most stressful situation that has occurred for pension funds is the combination of asset deterioration and falling interest rates. The net result would be a severe deterioration in the surplus funding ratio, because the lower interest rates raised the liabilities at the same time that asset values dropped precipitously.

With 10 percent liability volatility, 10- to 11-percent normal asset volatilities, and only a *bad storm* correlation of +0.3, surplus volatility could still easily reach 16 percent or higher. For deficit situations in which the liabilities exceeded the asset values, the surplus volatilities would be even higher. Even a 1-sigma event at such levels might be well beyond a fund's risk tolerance.

SURPLUS BETA CURVES

This pattern is evident in Exhibit 16.6, where the surplus and asset-based volatilities are both plotted against the fund beta values for the three portfolios. The higher curve represents the surplus volatilities without any liability hedging.

The high level of liability volatility compresses the surplus volatilities for the three funds. In the relevant range for most funds that maintain a performance-seeking asset portfolio, the surplus beta slope remains pretty much the same as in the asset-only case. Even with normal betas, the surplus

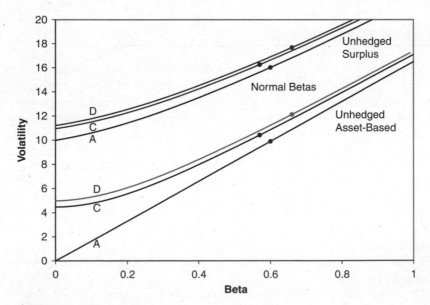

EXHIBIT 16.6   Asset-Based and Surplus Volatilities
Source: Morgan Stanley Research

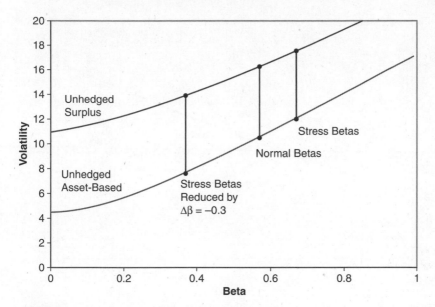

EXHIBIT 16.7   Portfolio D: Unhedged Volatilities
Source: Morgan Stanley Research

volatilities fall into the 16- to 18-percent range. If the goal were to bring the surplus volatility down to a more manageable level of 10 percent, it is clear that this would be very hard to achieve with beta reduction alone.

Exhibit 16.7 exemplifies this situation by focusing on Portfolio D, the allocation with the highest beta. The vertical lines denote the volatilities associated with normal betas, stress betas, and stress betas with a beta-reducing overlay of –0.3. The combination of an unhedged liability and a stress beta results in a surplus volatility of about 19 percent. For any fund that is sensitive to surplus standing at a particular time, this 1-sigma level of risk would not be tolerable. Even with a –0.3 beta reduction, the unhedged surplus volatility would be around 15 percent, a probably still unacceptable level. Thus, pension funds with such surplus sensitivity would have to also consider moving to some degree of liability hedging.

PARTIAL LIABILITY HEDGE

Exhibit 16.8 shows D's beta response curves when a liability hedge is in place against 50 percent of the liabilities. This partial 50 percent hedge leads to a disproportional volatility reduction, bringing the surplus curves

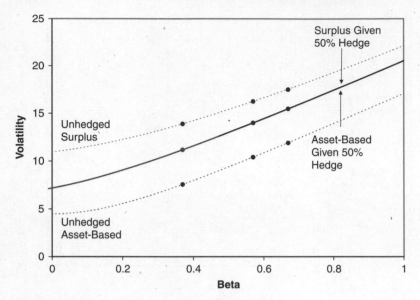

EXHIBIT 16.8   Portfolio D: With a Liability Hedge
Source: Morgan Stanley Research

well below midway between the unhedged and lower asset-based curve. It should be noted that while the partial hedge significantly reduces the surplus volatility, it also introduces an additional—and sizable—interest rate component into the asset-based volatility. For this specific example of a 50 percent hedge, it turns out that—coincidentally—both the asset-based and the surplus volatility have the same value, so that a single beta response curve holds for both frameworks.

However, even with this 50 percent hedge, the net (post-stress) beta must be brought down below the 0.4 level for it to achieve a surplus volatility of 10 percent.

FULL LIABILITY HEDGE

As noted earlier, it is generally impossible to achieve a full liability hedge in practice. There is some theoretical interest, however, in seeing how a hypothetical 100 percent liability hedge would affect our simple asset-liability model.

With full liability hedging, the surplus curves would be purged of interest rate effects. At the same time, the asset-based volatilities would soar, as the

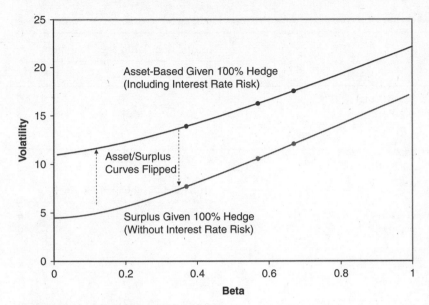

EXHIBIT 16.9 Portfolio D: With a 100 Percent Liability Hedge
Source: Morgan Stanley Research

interest rate effects from the hedge added to the asset-based volatility. As shown in Exhibit 16.9, a full liability hedge would cause the asset-based and the surplus curves to exchange positions, with the asset-based volatility curve ending up much higher than the now-hedged surplus curve.

DE-RISKING AND RE-RISKING

Exhibit 16.10 is a tabular presentation of the relevant asset-based and surplus volatilities under the various stress and hedging scenarios. These entries again demonstrate how asset-based and surplus volatilities coincide under a 50 percent liability hedge. They also show how the two volatilities flip under a 100 percent liability hedge.

It can be seen that beta reduction and liability hedging reduce risk in rather different ways. In contrast to lower volatilities from beta reduction, liability hedging decreases surplus risk but transfers interest rate volatility to the asset-based side. In an asset-and-liability framework, there are strong theoretical arguments that the focus should be solely on the surplus measures. For many funds, however, asset-based performance will still remain a significant consideration. Indeed, in low interest-rate environments, in which

EXHIBIT 16.10 Volatilities under Various Hedging Scenarios

	Normal Beta/Unhedged Liability		
	A	C	D
Asset-Based Volatility	9.9	10.5	12.0
Surplus Volatility	16.0	16.3	17.6
With $\Delta\beta = -.3$			
Asset-Based Volatility	5.0	6.4	7.8
Surplus Volatility	12.4	12.9	4.0
	Stress Beta/Unhedged Liability		
Asset-Based Volatility	9.9	11.9	13.6
Surplus Volatility	16.0	17.5	19.0
With $\Delta\beta = -.3$			
Asset-Based Volatility	5.0	7.5	9.1
Surplus Volatility	12.4	13.9	15.1
	Stress Beta/50% Hedged Liability		
Asset-Based Volatility	12.4	14.1	15.7
Surplus Volatility	12.4	14.1	15.7
With $\wedge\beta = -.3$			
Asset-Based Volatility	8.0	10.0	11.5
Surplus Volatility	8.0	10.0	11.5
	Stress Beta/100% Hedged Liability		
Asset-Based Volatility	16.0	17.5	19.0
Surplus Volatility	9.9	11.9	13.6
With $\Delta\beta = -.3$			
Asset-Based Volatility	12.4	13.9	15.1
Surplus Volatility	5.0	7.5	9.1

Source: Morgan Stanley Research

there is some prospect of sizable future upswings in rates, it would be surprising for many funds not to be concerned with *both* asset-based performance and surplus opportunities. Beta reduction can act as a de-risking agent in both asset-based and surplus terms. However, a liability hedge alone can only be said to transfer or re-risk the interest rate component from surplus to an asset-based framework.

The basic point is that some balanced combination of beta reduction *and* liability hedging may be needed to attain comfortable levels of risk that address a fund's overall concerns.

MAINTAINING A FUND'S RETURN-SEEKING POTENTIAL

Theoretically, surplus volatility could be reduced to a negligible level by eliminating the asset portfolio (and all return prospects) and moving to a full liability hedge. In practice, a total liability hedge may not be feasible because of fundamental uncertainties in the evolving liability structure. Also, as shown in Exhibits 16.9 and 16.10, a full hedge creates a massive asset-based vulnerability to higher rates in the form of asset-based performance. Finally, many funds may find a rigid full-hedging strategy to be unpalatable because of lower available yields, tighter spreads, or asymmetric return prospects. These considerations would loom particularly large in a period of low interest rates, when there is limited potential for significant further declines in interest rates.

In all these examples, the asset portfolios have been treated as remaining intact, with the risk reduction resulting solely from beta overlays. Of course, in theory, a risk-sensitive fund could simply reduce (or even eliminate) the assets deployed into return-seeking functions. Some funds may find that such extreme solutions fit their needs. However, pension funds are characterized by having long term liabilities, minimal near term liquidity requirements, and an organizational and financial sponsorship that can usually accommodate some degree of short term volatility. These features stand in stark contrast to large segments of the financial market that are intrinsically more short term oriented, both in regard to their performance goals and their ability to sustain volatility swings. This intrinsically long term structure should enable pension funds to enjoy certain competitive advantages in pursuing long term investment returns.

DIVERSIFICATION ALPHAS

As shown in these examples, a combination of both beta reduction and partial liability hedging is often needed to bring risk down to acceptable levels. This reduction in portfolio beta comes at the cost of lower returns. There are ways, however, that funds can use their beta dominance and long term horizon to take advantage of certain types of potential return.

The first source is the diversification alphas from asset classes that offer passive expected returns beyond that associated with their equity correlation (Leibowitz and Bova 2007b). As seen in Exhibit 16.1, the residual risks from these assets are swamped by the dominant beta risk, even at normal beta levels. The net result is that very little of the residual risk is transmitted up to the overall fund volatility. Thus, these incremental diversification alphas add to a fund's overall return, while there is only a muted impact on the fund-level volatility from the associated residual risks. (Of course, as the beta levels are reduced, the residual risks play a larger role, as evident in Exhibit 16.2's beta response curve.)

From a risk-and-return point of view, the most desirable diversifying assets are those that can be reliably stripped of the equity relationship and still provide significant excess return. To minimize the stress beta effect, such assets should ideally have either a stable or low equity correlation. With a reliable correlation and a stable beta, the asset beta can be incorporated into a beta reduction strategy.

ACTIVE ALPHAS

A second potential source of incremental returns can be found in the various forms of active management. Asset allocations are usually analyzed in terms of return and volatility characteristics of a passive benchmark that is representative of the asset class as a whole. Active management involves developing customized portfolios and trading specific securities in an attempt to generate relative returns in excess of the respective asset class benchmark.

Active management is fundamentally skill-based and consequently always entails some degree of tracking error relative to the benchmark. The tracking errors that are weakly correlated with a fund's dominant risk factor will have only a minimal impact on a fund's volatility. Consequently, most U.S. pension funds retain a large underused capacity for taking on productive active risk

A fund's experience with active management depends on its ability to identify, access, and monitor successful managers within given asset classes. An ideal alpha-generating process would be one that is uncorrelated in relation to a well-defined benchmark, and when that benchmark itself has either a low beta or reliably low beta variability. A reasonably liquid market for benchmark derivatives would also be desirable.

Of course, positive relative returns cannot be assumed for any active manager or for any fund's selected group of active managers. There are certain management styles, however, that have tracking error patterns that more comfortably fit within a fund's overall program of risk control. For example, all else being equal, a manager with a reasonably stable tracking error pattern is more desirable than one with erratic variation around the specified benchmark. It is also beneficial to have managers whose tracking errors are weakly correlated with each other as well as with the fund's other risk factors. Having said that, the ability to produce consistent active returns—positive active alphas—should always loom largest among all other considerations.

DOUBLE ALPHAS AND PORTABILITY

The ideal situation would be to find an active manager that could generate positive alphas, have the desirable tracking error patterns listed earlier, and lie within an asset class that could also provide a foundation of passive diversification alphas. It would be even more ideal if the asset class provided sufficient liquidity so that the benchmark exposure itself could be reliably controlled using appropriate overlays. The active alphas could then be captured while adjusting the underlying asset class exposure to the desired level. Active alphas that can be generated within the developed equity market or within a high-grade fixed income market would be particularly desirable in these portability terms.

Some funds may be proscribed from using the derivatives needed to avail themselves of alpha portability. Even when portability is theoretically available, the most attractive active alphas may lie within less efficient asset classes in which liquid derivatives may not exist. In such cases of an embedded (as opposed to portable) alpha, the pursuit of active alphas would have to be scaled to the asset's placement within the overall allocation.

REFERENCES

Leibowitz, M. L. 2004. "The β-plus measure in asset allocation." *Journal of Portfolio Management* 30 (3): 26–36.

Leibowitz, M. L., and A. Bova. 2005. "Allocation betas." *Financial Analysts Journal* 61: 70–82.

———. 2007a. "P/Es and pension funding ratios." *Financial Analysts Journal* 63 (1): 84–96.

———. 2007b. "Gathering implicit alphas in a beta world." *Journal of Portfolio Management* 33 (3): 10–18.

CHAPTER 17

Stress Beta Pathways

Stress betas affect diversified portfolios more adversely than traditional 60/40 portfolios. Diversified allocation's greater vulnerability to stress betas suggests that such portfolios may incur more shortfall damage than traditional portfolios under certain types of short term market turmoil.

At times of stress, a common expression is that "all correlations go to 1," which would imply that all residual volatilities fall to zero, a situation that seems highly unlikely. A better model would be based on various degrees of correlation tightening and the associated interaction of asset and residual volatilities. Any such tightening would lead to assets having stress betas that would be higher than the correlation-based betas that apply in more normal periods.

This chapter presents a pathway model for correlation tightening based on specified limit points for an asset's total and residual volatilities. This double-constraint model can then be used to explore how different volatility limits affect the stress betas of individual asset classes and multi-asset portfolios.

For diversified portfolios, stress betas can be quite significant, even for tightening levels well short of having all correlations going to 1. Setting a minimum level for the residual volatility can theoretically lead to higher asset volatilities that exacerbate these stress effects. Under one set of assumptions, a 30 percent tightening raises the total beta of a highly diversified portfolio from a normal 0.57 to a stress level of 0.78.

AN EMPIRICAL EXAMPLE

Emerging market equity (EME) provides a rough indication of the role played by different volatility limits. Exhibit 17.1 is a graph of the 12-month rolling correlation between EME and U.S. equity (USE) versus the 12-month USE returns from 1990 through 2007. During periods of declining USE

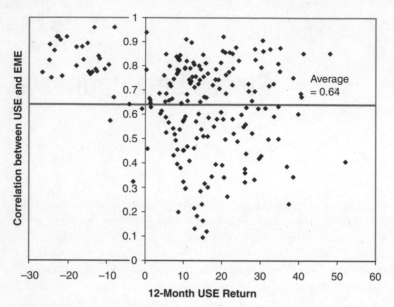

EXHIBIT 17.1 Emerging Market–U.S. Equity Correlation
Source: Morgan Stanley Research

returns, this correlation can be seen to tighten, averaging 0.80 in down equity markets versus an overall average of 0.64. In rising USE markets, the correlation between USE and EME does not exhibit any clear tightening trend.

In Exhibit 17.2, the 12-month rolling EME volatility is plotted against the EME-U.S. correlation for the same 12-month period. Although there is some confounding from the overlap effect, the higher EME volatilities appear to be more associated with the correlations that are higher than their average 0.64 value.

The residual volatility relates to EME returns remaining after extracting that component that the correlation ascribes to EME movements with USE. Exhibit 17.3 plots this residual EME volatility against the EME-U.S. correlation.

For correlations above the 0.64 average, the residual volatility generally declines. For all but a few points, however, these residual volatilities appear to remain above a minimum value of about 8 percent.

A MINIMUM RESIDUAL VOLATILITY MODEL

With this backdrop, our analysis proceeds to assume that under tightening beyond the normal correlation, an asset's total volatility will lie between its

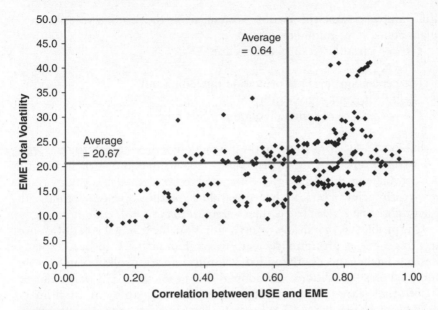

EXHIBIT 17.2 EME Total Volatility versus EME-U.S. Correlation
Source: Morgan Stanley Research

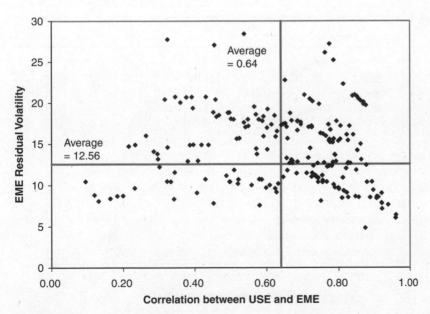

EXHIBIT 17.3 EME Residual Volatility versus EME-U.S. Correlation
Source: Morgan Stanley Research

initial value and some specified maximum, while the residual volatility will remain above some minimum level.

The key variables in this analysis are:

- The percentage level of correlation tightening (m)
- The increase in asset volatility (n)
- The percentage of residual volatility remaining (q)

Exhibit 17.4 is an example of the interaction of these three variables with an illustrative asset having a correlation of 0.6 with equity. For simplicity, the asset and equity volatilities are assumed to both equal 16.5. For a fixed asset volatility, it can be seen that the residual volatility q values decline with higher tightening levels. The q values reach zero at $m = 1/\rho$.

One problem is that in any realistic situation, the residual volatility is not likely to decline as precipitously as shown in Exhibit 17.4. Indeed, in many cases, one might expect both residual volatility and asset volatility to increase under turbulent conditions. To address this problem, a q_{min} value can be specified that places a lower limit on the residual volatility in the primary region of interest. Exhibit 17.5 illustrates this situation for a q_{min} of 0.8.

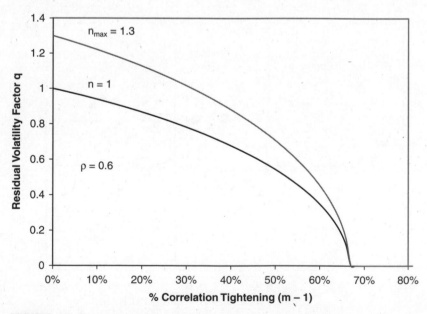

EXHIBIT 17.4   Residual Volatility with Correlation Tightening
Source: Morgan Stanley Research

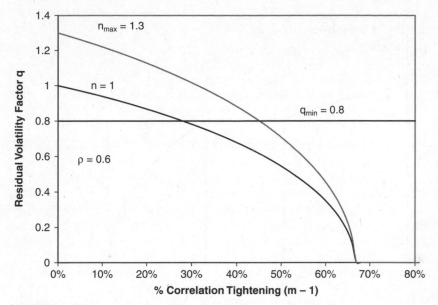

EXHIBIT 17.5 Residual Volatility with Minimum Constraint
Source: Morgan Stanley Research

Note that this q_{min} value requires an ever-higher asset volatility to accommodate the correlation tightening. At some point, the increasing asset volatility will itself reach a specified maximum asset volatility, n_{max}. If we ascribe a higher priority to this n_{max} constraint, further tightening must be accompanied by q values that fall below the preceding q_{min}, ultimately reaching $q = 0$ where $\sigma_r = 0$ and all correlations have indeed gone to 1.

IMPLIED ASSET VOLATILITY

Exhibit 17.6 displays the path of the residual volatility. The asset volatility should not be lower under a stress environment, so that $n \geq 1$. Consequently, the simplest approach is to assume that the initial tightening follows the $n = 1$ curve. When the residual volatility reaches q_{min}, further tightening can only be achieved through increased asset volatility, that is, larger n values. Note that the intersections of $q_{min} = 0.8$ with $n = 1$ and $n = 1.3$ occur at 28 percent and 45 percent, respectively.

As shown in Exhibit 17.7, with the q_{min} of 0.8 in place, one can trace out the corresponding asset volatility to the point at which it attains the specified maximum value, in this case $n_{max} = 1.3$.

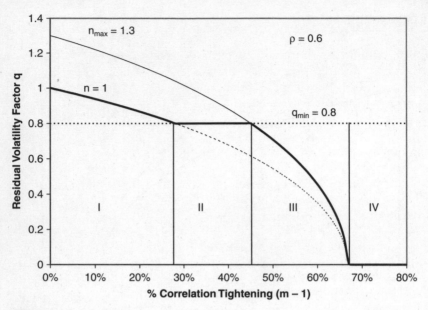

EXHIBIT 17.6 Assumed Path of Tightening
Source: Morgan Stanley Research

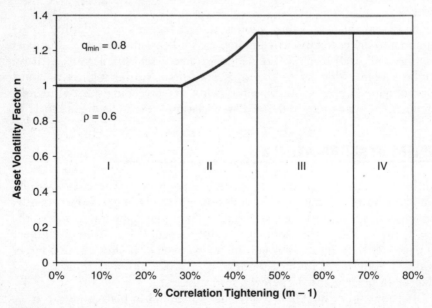

EXHIBIT 17.7 Asset Volatility with Maximum Constraint
Source: Morgan Stanley Research

STRESS BETAS AT THE ASSET LEVEL

The key question is what effect do *m, n,* and *q* values have on the asset beta. In all phases, the stress beta is just the original beta multiplied by (*nm*) for the relevant values of *n* (see the appendix). Exhibit 17.8 displays this four-phase path of beta under assumptions used in Exhibits 17.4 through 17.7. In the first phase, with $n = 1$, beta is a linear function of *m*. In the second phase, with a q_{min} in place, it can be shown that both *m* and *n* increase. When the n_{max} condition is encountered, the third phase begins with beta now growing by ($m*n_{max}$). In the fourth phase, the tightening reaches a level of $m = 1/\rho$, the correlation becomes 1, no further tightening is possible, and beta remains constant.

Apart from these specific results, the general thrust is that stress betas may undergo different growth behaviors at various tightening levels. For modest tightenings that do not press upon the constraints, the betas will increase more or less proportionally with the percentage tightening. At some point, the residual volatility will approach its minimum level, and further tightening will call for some increase in the total volatility that will force the stress betas to rise faster than proportionally. Then, when the maximum

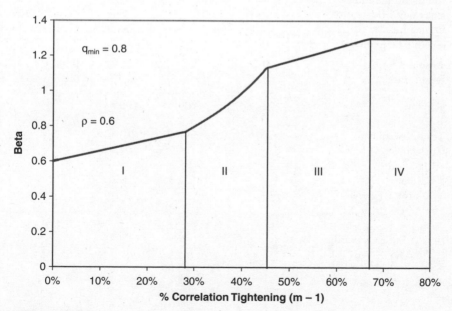

EXHIBIT 17.8 Effect of Correlation Tightening on Asset Beta
Source: Morgan Stanley Research

volatility limit is encountered, the stress betas will again grow linearly until the tightening reaches its own maximum limit and the betas remain constant thereafter.

SHORT TERM VULNERABILITY OF DIVERSIFIED PORTFOLIOS

To put this approach into a fund level context, Exhibit 17.9 presents a traditional 60/40 Portfolio A and a diversified Portfolio C having only a 20 percent direct exposure to U.S. equities. In spite of C's modest direct

EXHIBIT 17.9 Portfolios A and C under Normal Conditions

	Correlation-Based Implicit Beta	A	C	Beta	Alpha
U.S. Equity	1.00	60%	20%	1.00	0.00
U.S. Bonds	0.14	40%	20%	0.14	1.47
				0.00	0.00
International Equity	0.77		15%	0.77	1.33
Emerging Mkt Equity	0.76		5%	0.76	3.36
Private Equity	0.98		10%	0.98	3.14
Venture Capital	0.59		10%	0.59	7.37
Absolute Return	0.28		10%	0.98	3.14
Real Estate	0.07		10%	0.07	3.58
Total		100%	100%		
				0.14	
Total Volatility		11.17	10.45		
Correlation with U.S. Equity		96.7%	90.4%		
Total Beta (Normal Times)		0.65	0.57		
Stress Beta (m = 30%, n_{max} = 1.3, q_{min} = 0.8)		0.67	0.74		
Beta × Equity Volatility (16.5%)		9.90	9.45		
σ_α		0.00	0.01		
% Volatility from Beta		88.6%	90.4%		
		10.67	4.48		

Source: Morgan Stanley Research

EXHIBIT 17.10 Stress Betas for Portfolios A and C

| % Tightening | m | $n_{max} = 1.0$ | | $n_{max} = 1.3$ | | | |
| | | $q_{min} = 1.0$ | | $q_{min} = 0.8$ | | $q_{min} = 1.0$ | |
		A	C	A	C	A	C
0%	1.0	0.65	0.57	0.65	0.57	0.65	0.57
20%	1.2	0.67	0.65	0.67	0.65	0.67	0.72
30%	1.3	0.67	0.68	0.67	0.74	0.67	0.78
50%	1.5	0.68	0.75	0.68	0.85	0.69	0.88
100%	2.0	0.71	0.84	0.71	0.98	0.73	1.02

Source: Morgan Stanley Research

allocation to equities, a standard covariance model would project a value of 0.57 for its normal beta, and 10.45 percent for its volatility, that is, quite close to the respective estimates for Portfolio A.

Using the same methodology as in Exhibit 17.8, Exhibit 17.10 provides beta values for different n_{max} and q_{min} values. For the traditional 60/40 Portfolio A, the actual equity is already fully correlated with itself. Consequently, focusing on the case $q_{min} = 0.8$ and $n_{max} = 1.3$, a 30 percent tightening only affects the 40 percent bond position, with a minuscule effect that raises the total beta from 0.65 to 0.67. In contrast, with the same 30 percent correlation tightening, the highly diversified Portfolio C's total beta rises from 0.57 to 0.74.

Exhibit 17.10 demonstrates that for diversified Portfolio C, stress betas can become quite sizable, even for correlation tightening that falls well short of having all correlations go to 1.

The preceding example leads to the rather ironic finding that, in a period of severe market turmoil, a diversified portfolio might suffer greater damage than a traditional 60/40 allocation. While at first surprising, it can be seen upon further reflection that tightening can only affect allocations where the multi-asset correlations are relevant. From this viewpoint, the greater vulnerability of diversified portfolios should be quite general in nature and not depend on any particular model for the tightening process.

There are counterpoints to this paradoxical finding. First, diversified portfolios have sources of expected return above and beyond that associated with the beta relationship. Over time, these incremental returns should accumulate and provide a sizable cushion against beta-based risks. Second, the initial correlations embedded in the covariance matrix are based primarily on short-term price changes. The correlations may be quite different over longer term periods. For example, the relationship between developed and emerging equity markets may be quite tight for a sudden down move. Over the long term, however, regional decoupling could lead these two markets to behave much more independently, and an emerging market allocation might serve as a powerful diversifier over the long term.

BETA PATHWAYS FOR INDIVIDUAL ASSET CLASSES

Exhibit 17.11 shows the beta pathway for the assets comprising Portfolio C. The individual assets exhibit very different beta patterns: international equity and private equity have the full four-phase path, while emerging market equity and absolute return have only a three-phase path. Assets such as U.S. bonds and real estate with very low correlations remain in the first phase throughout.

The general principle is that at modest tightening levels, assets with higher betas will be more affected than assets with lower betas. These higher beta assets will eventually reach a maximum limit as further tightening

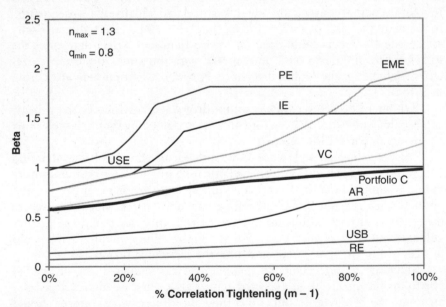

EXHIBIT 17.11   Portfolio C under Correlation Tightening
Source: Morgan Stanley Research

occurs. Higher tightening levels will then continue to affect the lower beta assets.

For funds that have the same total beta, the stress beta effects will depend on the mixture between high and low beta assets and the level of tightening experienced. These results derived from our model appear to make intuitive sense as well.

Since U.S. equity is already fully correlated with itself, it has no vulnerability to the form of correlation tightening described in this chapter. At the same time, it is of course true that equities may themselves provide very dour returns during periods of general market turmoil—and that their intrinsic volatility may even shift dramatically upward. However, the focus here is on nonequity asset class behavior *relative* to the underlying movements in domestic equities. In other words, the stress betas attempt to estimate the degree of additional loss in a nonequity asset beyond what would be anticipated based on its normal beta relationship to equity movements.

Most allocations seen in practice have very similar correlation-based beta values, typically within the range of 0.55 to 0.65. Thus, a higher direct equity allocation implies a lower beta contribution from nonequity assets and hence a lower vulnerability to these stress effects. Conversely, there will be more significant stress vulnerability in highly diversified portfolios in which the fund beta is derived largely from nonequity assets.

Different diversified portfolios, however—even those with similar total betas and similar nonequity betas—may behave somewhat differently, depending on the nature of their nonequity assets. On the basis of our pathway model, diversified portfolios with a concentration of their nonequity in higher-correlation assets will move to higher stress beta levels under only modest tightenings. As the correlation tightening becomes more severe, high-correlation funds will reach a maximum stress beta. At more stringent tightening levels, diversified portfolios even with low-correlation nonequity assets may begin to encounter significant stress effects. While these outcomes are derived from our pathway model, they would also follow—in a more draconian way—from a truly extreme scenario in which all correlations really did go to 1.

APPENDIX

The basic relationship between the correlation with equity ρ, the asset volatility σ, and the residual volatility σ_r is given by

$$\sigma_r = \sigma \sqrt{1 - \rho^2}$$

When the correlation tightens by a factor m to $m\rho$ and the asset volatility increases by a factor n to $n\sigma$, the new residual volatility σ_r' becomes

$$\sigma_r' = n\sigma\sqrt{1 - (m\rho)^2}$$

Reasonability conditions suggest that

$$1 \leq m \leq (1/\rho)$$

and that there be some n_{max} such that

$$1 \leq n \leq n_{max}$$

It is useful to work with the ratio of the residual volatilities,

$$q = \frac{\sigma_r'}{\sigma}$$

With these conditions holding, we can rewrite the ratio q as

$$q = \frac{\sigma_r'}{\sigma}$$

$$= n\sqrt{\frac{1 - (m\rho)^2}{1 - \rho^2}}$$

The initial beta value is given by

$$\beta = \rho\frac{\sigma}{\sigma_e}$$

in which σ_e is the equity volatility.

Under a tightening m, the beta rises to

$$\beta' = (m\rho)\left(\frac{n\sigma}{\sigma_e}\right)$$

$$= mn\beta$$

in the absence of any constraints on m and n.

Our tightening model proceeds, however, in several phases, defined by the points at which the various constraints become operative:

1. In the first phase, the asset volatility remains constant while the higher correlation drains the residual volatility, that is, m rises, and q declines

while $n = 1$. At some point, it does not make sense for the residual volatility to fall below some fraction q_{min} of its initial level.

2. At this point, q becomes fixed at q_{min}, and further tightening must be achieved through rising asset volatility, that is, n grows with m, while $q = q_{min}$. This phase continues until n reaches the specified maximum value, n_{max}.

3. From this point forward, the priority condition is $n = n_{max}$, so that any further tightening requires a falling residual volatility, that is, q declines with m while $n = n_{max}$.

4. Finally, the tightening ultimately reaches the point of $m = 1/\rho$, at which point $(m\rho) = 1$, $\sigma_r' = 0$ and no further tightening is possible. For higher m from this point forward, $n = n_{max}$ and m also remains fixed at its maximum value $1/\rho$.

The beta value follows these phases with the appropriate n and m values.

The following (relatively) compact expression captures this four-phase evolution of the tightening process.

$$\frac{\beta'}{\beta} = \left[\text{Min}\{m, 1/\rho\} \right] * \left[\text{Min}\{n_{max}, \text{Max}[1, n(m)]\} \right]$$

where

$$n(m) = q_{min}\sqrt{\frac{1 - \rho^2}{1 - (m\rho)^2}} \qquad m < \left(\frac{1}{\rho}\right)$$

Computationally, the (generally irrelevant) singularity at $m = 1/\rho$ can be worked around by setting

$$n(m) = q_{min}\sqrt{\frac{1 - \rho^2}{1.001 - [\text{Min}((m\rho), 1)]^2}}$$

CHAPTER 18

The Endowment Model: Theory and Experience

The endowment model does not fit the textbook definition of a diversification that lowers volatility. With U.S. equity acting as the overwhelmingly dominant single risk factor, endowment portfolios may theoretically be even more vulnerable to adverse tail events than implied by the standard volatility estimates.

The largest discrepancy in the 1993 through 2007 experience was in the area of realized returns. Within each of the three five-year subperiods, the alpha returns increased with diversification, but the outperformance was so consistent and so far exceeded the expectations as to raise questions about its probability of persistence.

These results suggest that diversification should not be viewed as smoothing returns and lowering short-term volatility, but rather as a strategy for accumulating incremental returns and achieving more divergent outcomes—over the long term!

THEORETICAL BETA-BASED RISKS

Exhibit 18.1 lists the hypothetical portfolios that will be used throughout this chapter. Portfolio B represents the traditional 60/40 portfolio. Portfolios B1, B2, and C2 have increasing degrees of diversification, moving toward the endowment model Portfolio C.

Exhibit 18.2 summarizes the risk projections for U.S. equity (USE) and for the sample portfolios based on a theoretical return-covariance matrix. It should be noted that this matrix was developed in 2003 and hence does not in any way reflect the actual experience of the subsequent 2003 to 2007 period.

EXHIBIT 18.1 Sample Portfolio Allocations

	Diversification				
	B	B1	B2	C2	C
U.S. Equity	60%	40%	30%	20%	20%
U.S. Bonds	40%	30%	25%	10%	20%
International Equity		20%	20%	20%	15%
Emerging Mkt Equity				5%	5%
Real Estate		10%	10%	10%	10%
Absolute Return			10%	20%	10%
Venture Capital			5%	10%	10%
Private Equity				5%	10%
Total	100%	100%	100%	100%	100%

Source: Morgan Stanley Research

Focusing on these theoretical risk projections, a number of common features can be observed across all the portfolios. The total volatilities all range between 10 and 11 percent, the ratios of portfolio volatility to USE volatility all lie within 60 to 70 percent, and the correlations with USE are all above 90 percent. The ratio of the portfolio to USE volatility and the correlation with USE can be multiplied to derive a portfolio beta, which can be seen

EXHIBIT 18.2 Theoretical Risk Projections

		Diversification				
	U.S. Equity	B	B1	B2	C2	C
Volatility (σ)	16.50%	11.17%	10.65%	10.19%	10.76%	10.45%
Volatility/Equity Volatility	1.00	0.68	0.65	0.62	0.65	0.63
Correlation (ρ)	1.00	0.97	0.93	0.93	0.91	0.90
Beta to U.S. Equity (β)	1.00	0.65	0.60	0.57	0.60	0.57
β-Based Volatility	16.50%	10.73%	9.90%	9.41%	9.83%	9.45%
β-Based Volatility As % of Total Volatility	100.00%	96.00%	93.00%	92.30%	91.40%	90.40%

Source: Morgan Stanley Research

to be around 0.60 for all portfolios. The product of this portfolio beta and USE volatility determines the beta-based volatilities of 9.4 to 10.7 percent. These beta-based volatilities represent more than 90 percent of the total portfolio volatilities, regardless of the level of diversification. Thus, all the sample portfolios are subject to similar domination by the beta volatility.

HISTORICAL RISK CHARACTERISTICS

We now turn to the historical experience for the 1993 to 2007 period and the three 5-year subperiods. These data were based upon the quarterly index values from the sources listed in Exhibit 18.3. The index values were adjusted for the realized inflation to obtain empirical real returns that could be compared with the preceding theoretical real returns.

It can be seen in Exhibit 18.4 that actual portfolio volatilities vary significantly, depending on the period. The primary driver of the level of portfolio volatility is the magnitude of the equity volatility. The higher equity volatility from 1998 to 2002 led to higher portfolio volatilities, while lower portfolio volatilities occurred in the 1993 to 1997 and the 2003 to 2007 periods when equity volatility was much lower.

From 1993 to 1997 and 2003 to 2007, the portfolio volatilities were between 5 and 8 percent, much lower than the expectations of 10 to 11 percent. From 1998 to 2003, the portfolio volatilities were much higher than expectations, ranging from 11 to 14 percent. If we examine the full 15-year period, however, the volatilities were only slightly lower than expectations.

EXHIBIT 18.3 Index Sources: 2003 to 2007 Quarterly Returns

Asset Class	Index Used
U.S. Equity	S&P 500
U.S. Bonds	Lehman U.S. Aggregrate Bond
International Equity	MSCI EAFE
Emerging Mkt Equity	MSCI Emerging
Real Estate	NCREIF Property
Absolute Return	HFR
Venture Capital	Cambridge Associates U.S. Venture Capital
Private Equity	Cambridge Associates U.S. Private Equity
Theoretical Data Based on Cambridge Associates Covariance Matrix	

Source: Morgan Stanley Research

EXHIBIT 18.4 Volatility Characteristics

	Theoretical	1993–1997	1998–2002	2003–2007	1993–2007
U.S. Equity Real Return	7.25%	17.23%	−2.89%	9.42%	7.59%
B	0.65	0.61	0.49	0.61	0.53
B1	0.60	0.56	0.54	0.67	0.57
B2	0.57	0.49	0.51	0.64	0.53
C2	0.60	0.43	0.62	0.67	0.60
C	0.57	0.46	0.59	0.59	0.56

Source: Morgan Stanley Research

It thus appears that over the long term, the volatilities of diversified portfolios (C and C2) are generally close to the theoretical projections, while the behavior in shorter periods can be quite different from projections.

The key point, however, is that diversification does not materially reduce the portfolio volatility within any of these periods. The traditional 60/40 Portfolio B had subperiod volatilities of 6.9 percent, 12.0 percent, and 6.8 percent, while the highly diversified Portfolio C had corresponding subperiod volatilities of 4.9 percent, 14.4 percent, and 6.6 percent. Thus, diversification appeared to have a relatively modest effect on volatility relative to a traditional allocation. Over the entire 15-year period, the traditional and diversified funds had similar volatilities of 9.0 percent and 9.5 percent, respectively.

EXHIBIT 18.5 Ratio of Portfolio Volatility to USE Volatility

	Theoretical	1993–1997	1998–2002	2003–2007	1993–2007
U.S. Equity Real Return	7.25%	17.23%	−2.89%	9.42%	7.59%
B	5.85%	12.17%	0.93%	6.24%	6.35%
B1	6.03%	10.65%	0.82%	9.09%	6.76%
B2	6.15%	11.28%	1.48%	9.99%	7.49%
C2	6.98%	13.28%	2.82%	12.78%	9.52%
C	7.08%	13.21%	4.62%	11.46%	9.70%

Source: Morgan Stanley Research

EXHIBIT 18.6 Correlations with USE

	Theoretical	1993–1997	1998–2002	2003–2007	1993–2007
U.S. Equity Volatility	16.50%	9.16%	21.71%	10.54%	15.08%
B	11.17%	6.87%	12.04%	6.79%	9.01%
B1	10.65%	5.58%	11.95%	7.21%	8.76%
B2	10.19%	5.04%	11.33%	6.90%	8.29%
C2	10.76%	5.09%	14.37%	7.49%	9.87%
C	10.45%	4.93%	14.35%	6.61%	9.52%

Source: Morgan Stanley Research

The volatility effect can be further analyzed in terms of the ratio of portfolio volatility to USE volatility. As shown in Exhibit 18.5, this volatility ratio was generally quite stable across the different subperiods and also across the various allocations. For Portfolio C, this ratio ranged from 54 to 66 percent, in line with expectations of 63 percent. The accuracy and consistency of this ratio has important implications in explaining why the portfolio betas have remained consistent over these periods.

As shown in Exhibit 18.6, the other factor is the high and stable correlation (in most cases 90 percent-plus) that the portfolios have had with USE. As shown in Exhibit 18.2, the portfolio correlation to USE coincides with the percentage of total volatility represented by beta volatility. Thus, these high and stable correlations enable the beta volatility to account for a high proportion of the total volatility. This long term relationship reinforces the idea that USE beta remains the dominant risk factor in virtually all institutional portfolios.

The basically stable beta across all levels of diversification is evident in Exhibit 18.7. Taking the endowment model Portfolio C as an example, the portfolio beta within the 1998 to 2002 and 2003 to 2007 subperiods was 0.59, versus a theoretical projection of 0.57. The strong equity markets from 1993 to 1997 led to a lag that resulted in a lower 0.46 beta for Portfolio C.

The key message from Exhibit 18.7 is that, over longer periods, the covariance-based beta estimate appears to be an appropriate indicator of overall portfolio risk. More generally, the 15-year experience appears to be quite consistent with the theoretical projections from the 2003 covariance matrix.

EXHIBIT 18.7 Portfolio Betas

	Theoretical	1993–1997	1998–2002	2003–2007	1993–2007
U.S. Equity Real Return	7.25%	17.23%	−2.89%	9.42%	7.59%
B	0.68	0.75	0.55	0.64	0.60
B1	0.65	0.61	0.55	0.68	0.58
B2	0.62	0.55	0.52	0.65	0.55
C2	0.65	0.56	0.66	0.71	0.65
C	0.63	0.54	0.66	0.63	0.63

Source: Morgan Stanley Research

ALPHA AND BETA RETURNS

The preceding analysis has been focused on risk factors. The 2003 return-covariance matrix, however, also provided expected real returns for each of the asset classes. As shown in Exhibit 18.8, these assumptions allow projected returns to be calculated for each of the portfolios. Moreover, by using the theoretical beta values, these projected real returns can be partitioned into a beta-component associated with U.S. equity and a residual alpha component. Exhibit 18.9 illustrates how Portfolio C's return can be separated into alpha and beta returns.

Since the portfolios have similar beta values, their beta-based returns are all in the 4.8- to 5.2-percent range. The structural alphas are quite small for Portfolio B but increase with greater levels of diversification. It is these higher

EXHIBIT 18.8 Theoretical Return Projections

		Diversification				
	U.S. Equity	B	B1	B2	C2	C
Total Real Return	7.25%	5.85%	6.03%	6.15%	6.98%	7.08%
Beta	1.00	0.65	0.60	0.57	0.60	0.57
Beta-Based Return	7.25%	5.24%	4.95%	4.78%	4.93%	4.79%
Structural Alpha	0.00%	0.61%	1.08%	1.37%	2.05%	2.29%
Incremental Volatility over Beta-Based Volatility	1.00	1.04	1.08	1.08	1.09	1.11

Source: Morgan Stanley Research

EXHIBIT 18.9 Portfolio C: Alpha and Beta Returns

Equity Real Return	7.25%
Risk-Free Rate	−1.50%
Equity Risk Premium	5.75%
× Portfolio C Beta	×0.57
Beta * Equity Risk Premium	3.29%
Risk-Free Rate	+1.50%
Beta-Based Return	4.79%
Structural Alpha (Passive)	+2.29%
Total Portfolio C Return	7.08%

Source: Morgan Stanley Research

alpha returns that provide diversified portfolios with their return advantages over the traditional 60/40. It is interesting to note, however, that these higher alpha returns lead to only minimal increases in portfolio volatility.

Exhibit 18.10 shows the total portfolio returns realized over the different historical subperiods. There is significant variability in returns across the different periods. As with the portfolio volatility, the dominance of USE plays a major role in determining the portfolio returns. In periods when USE performed well, all the portfolios also did well. In contrast, the weak USE equity market from 1998 to 2002 drove down all the portfolios' returns. At the

EXHIBIT 18.10 Total Portfolio Returns

	Theoretical	1993–1997	1998–2002	2003–2007	1993–2007
U.S. Equity Real Return	7.25%	17.23%	−2.89%	9.42%	7.59%
B	5.26%	11.32%	−0.47%	5.66%	5.39%
B1	4.96%	10.61%	−0.70%	6.30%	5.30%
B2	4.79%	9.50%	−0.56%	5.98%	4.89%
C2	4.93%	8.60%	−1.06%	6.31%	4.53%
C	4.79%	8.99%	−0.91%	5.50%	4.44%

Source: Morgan Stanley Research

EXHIBIT 18.11 Portfolio Beta Returns

	Theoretical	1993–1997	1998–2002	2003–2007	1993–2007
U.S. Equity Real Return	0.00%	0.00%	0.00%	0.00%	0.00%
B	0.59%	0.86%	1.40%	0.58%	0.96%
B1	1.07%	0.04%	1.52%	2.79%	1.46%
B2	1.36%	1.78%	2.04%	4.01%	2.60%
C2	2.05%	4.68%	3.88%	6.47%	4.98%
C	2.29%	4.23%	5.53%	5.96%	5.26%

Source: Morgan Stanley Research

same time, it is worth noting that within each of the periods, the returns generally increased with greater levels of diversification (as predicted).

In Exhibit 18.7, it was shown that the portfolio betas were quite similar, both across allocations and across different periods. However, the beta-based returns clearly depend on the realized USE returns within each period. Exhibit 18.11 depicts how the beta returns were driven by these USE returns. At the same time, it is quite striking how, for the full 15-year period, all the beta returns fell into the 4.4- to 5.4-percent range, that is, very close to the theoretical expectations.

The differences in the total returns are explained, not by their beta exposure, but rather by their alpha returns. The argument for portfolio diversification can be examined by focusing on the realized alpha returns shown in Exhibit 18.12. For Portfolio C, the theoretical alpha return was

EXHIBIT 18.12 Realized Alpha Returns

	Theoretical	1993–1997	1998–2002	2003–2007	1993–2007
U.S. Equity Real Return	7.25%	17.23%	−2.89%	9.42%	7.59%
B	0.97	0.81	0.89	0.94	0.89
B1	0.93	0.93	0.99	0.98	0.97
B2	0.93	0.89	0.98	0.98	0.96
C2	0.91	0.78	0.93	0.95	0.92
C	0.90	0.85	0.89	0.94	0.89

Source: Morgan Stanley Research

2.29 percent. In every subperiod, the actual alpha return was greater than this projection. Moreover, the alpha returns for Portfolio C were roughly stable across the three five-year subperiods. The less diversified portfolios also had positive alphas, but these were smaller and more volatile than for the more diversified funds.

CONCLUSION

The risk estimates from a standard covariance matrix were remarkably accurate in projecting the risk characteristics over the last 15 years. Both the ratio of portfolio volatility to USE volatility and the portfolio correlation to USE have proved consistent, leading to stable betas over the 15-year history.

These theoretical and empirical results demonstrate that the risk characteristics of a traditional 60/40 fund and an endowment-type portfolio are fundamentally similar. The true advantage gained by the typical diversification, therefore, is not risk reduction. Rather, the primary benefit of the endowment model is the accumulation of alpha returns over time.

Finally, over recent history, endowment funds' alpha returns have been far greater and far more stable than projected, which in itself raises a number of intriguing questions.

CHAPTER 19

Diversification Performance: Under Stress (2008) and over the Long Term (1993 through 2007)

*W*hile diversified and traditional portfolios have similar risk character-istics under normal times, diversified portfolios should perform even worse than 60/40 in adverse markets. This stress beta theory is based on the diversified portfolio's having greater vulnerabilities to correlation tighten-ing. Thus, rather than reducing risk in the short term, diversification should be viewed as providing long term benefits in return accumulation and long term divergence of outcomes.

2008 unfortunately provides an opportunity to test these stress effects. The diversified portfolio's 2008 beta was much higher than that of the tradi-tional portfolio. Moreover, 2008 has proved to be the first period in which the diversified portfolio performed materially worse than the traditional 60/40.

A SEMI-DIVERSIFIED PORTFOLIO

The portfolio being examined (referred to as Portfolio D) consists of 30 per-cent U.S. equity (USE), 25 percent U.S. bonds (USB), 25 percent international equity, 10 percent emerging market equity and 10 percent REITS. As a check for consistency between monthly versus quarterly data, Exhibit 19.1 lists the theoretical projections as well as the actual statistics from 1993 through 2007. There is a slight difference in the volatility data but the rest of the characteristics are virtually identical in the two sets of data.

Exhibit 19.2 presents the standard procedure of plotting Portfolio D's monthly returns from 1993 through 2007 versus USE returns. The

EXHIBIT 19.1 Portfolio D Monthly and Quarterly Characteristics

U.S. Equity	30%
U.S. Bonds	25%
International Equity	25%
Emerging Market Equity	10%
REITS	10%

	Theoretical	Monthly 1993–2007	Quarterly 1993–2007
Equity Volatility	16.50	13.76	15.08
Volatility	11.83	9.54	10.50
Volatility/Equity	0.72	0.69	0.70
Correlation	0.91	0.91	0.92
Beta	0.65	0.63	0.64
Beta Volatility	10.74	8.70	9.70
Alpha Volatility	4.96	3.78	4.17
Real Return	6.50	7.29	7.42
Real Beta Return	5.24	5.26	5.33
Real Alpha Return	1.26	2.03	2.09

Source: Morgan Stanley Research

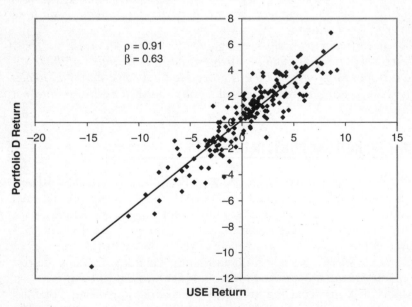

EXHIBIT 19.2 Portfolio D versus USE Returns
Source: Morgan Stanley Research

theoretical beta and correlation with USE of 0.65 and 0.91 closely match the historical results in Exhibit 19.1.

Given this relationship between Portfolio D and USE returns, one would expect to have a high degree of confidence in the beta estimate of the portfolio. There can be significant differences, however, between the beta projections and the actual results over short term periods. A number of factors can cause these short term discrepancies to arise.

VOLATILITIES AND VOLATILITY RATIOS

Exhibit 19.3 graphs the annual volatilities for USE and Portfolio D along with Portfolio B, a mixture of 60 percent USE and 40 percent USB. The volatility of D is usually higher than B, although the two volatilities tend to follow each other quite closely. Thus, as with the earlier findings for diversified portfolios, D's diversification did not lead to a significant reduction in risk versus a traditional 60/40 portfolio.

Another important point from Exhibit 19.3 is that the key determinant of both volatilities is the equity volatility. In any given year, Portfolios D and B had volatilities that were strongly dependent on the equity volatility.

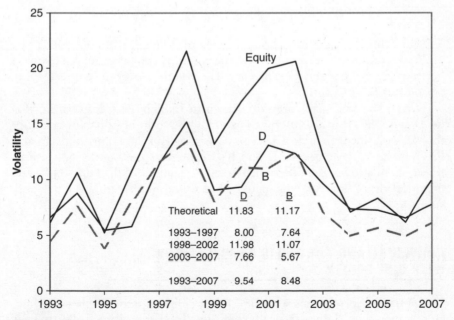

	D	B
Theoretical	11.83	11.17
1993–1997	8.00	7.64
1998–2002	11.98	11.07
2003–2007	7.66	5.67
1993–2007	9.54	8.48

EXHIBIT 19.3   Portfolio D and B: Volatility
Source: Morgan Stanley Research

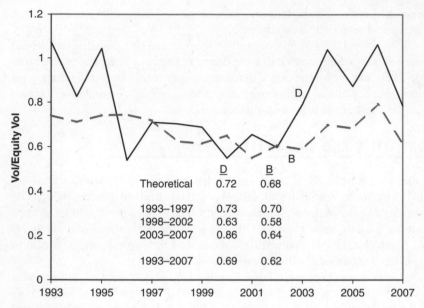

	D	B
Theoretical	0.72	0.68
1993–1997	0.73	0.70
1998–2002	0.63	0.58
2003–2007	0.86	0.64
1993–2007	0.69	0.62

EXHIBIT 19.4   Portfolios D and B: Ratio of Portfolio Volatility to USE Volatility
Source: Morgan Stanley Research

Portfolio D's volatility during a given year ranges from 5.5 percent to 15.2 percent. Over five-year periods, the volatility range becomes narrower, between 7.7 percent and 12.0 percent. The volatility over the entire 15-year period was 9.5 percent.

Given the strong relationship shown in Exhibit 19.2 between Portfolio D and USE, it is also useful to examine the ratio of portfolio volatility to USE volatility. Exhibit 19.4 compares this ratio for Portfolios D and B. Over the 15-year period, D and B's ratios were 0.69 and 0.62, respectively, slightly lower than their theoretical projections of 0.72 and 0.68. The historical ratio, however, fluctuated more significantly within the five-year subperiods.

INDIVIDUAL AND PORTFOLIO CORRELATIONS WITH U.S. EQUITY

The portfolio correlations with USE have remained quite stable over time, closely matching the theoretical projections. Not surprisingly, Portfolio B has generally had a correlation near 100 percent. (See Exhibit 19.5.)

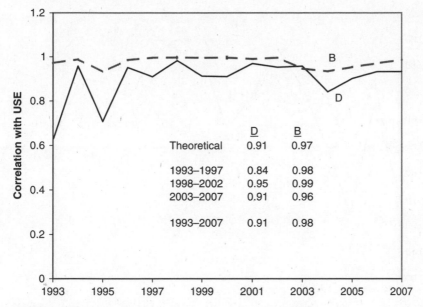

EXHIBIT 19.5 Portfolios D and B: Correlation with USE
Source: Morgan Stanley Research

The stability in the portfolio correlation with USE is even more striking in light of the wide variation in the individual assets' correlations with USE. It is clear from Exhibits 19.6 and 19.7 that all the asset class correlations have had periods of instability.

HISTORICAL BETAS

The actual Portfolio D beta over the 1993 to 2007 period was 0.63 versus the theoretical estimate of 0.65. However, as seen in Exhibit 19.8, the year-by-year portfolio beta was quite volatile, ranging from a low of 0.50 to a high of 0.99.

Exhibits 19.9 and 19.10 examine the individual asset beta components in order to delve deeper into the causes this year-by-year beta variability. With the exception of USB, there is a wide fluctuation in the betas of the component assets.

Exhibit 19.11 graphs the beta contribution of each asset, that is, the asset weight in the portfolio multiplied by the individual asset beta. Not surprisingly, USB has a negligible effect on the overall portfolio beta. Before

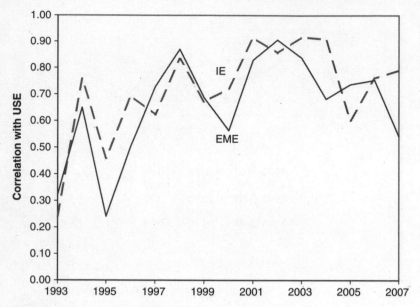

EXHIBIT 19.6 IE and EME Correlations with USE
Source: Morgan Stanley Research

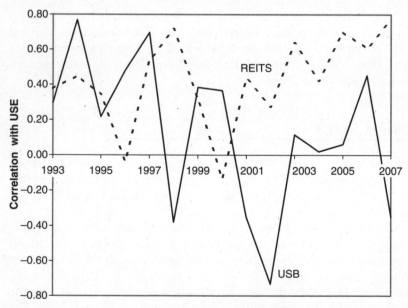

EXHIBIT 19.7 USB and REITS Correlations with USE
Source: Morgan Stanley Research

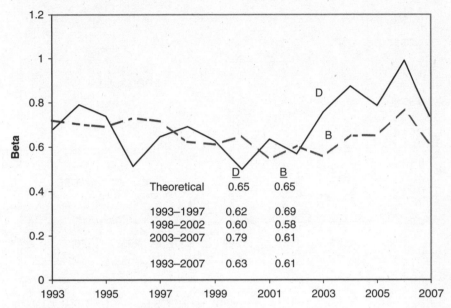

EXHIBIT 19.8 1993 to 2007 Portfolio Betas
Source: Morgan Stanley Research

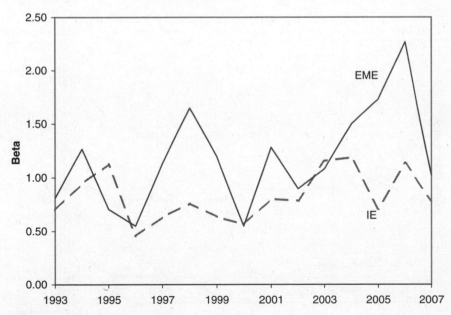

EXHIBIT 19.9 IE and EME Betas
Source: Morgan Stanley Research

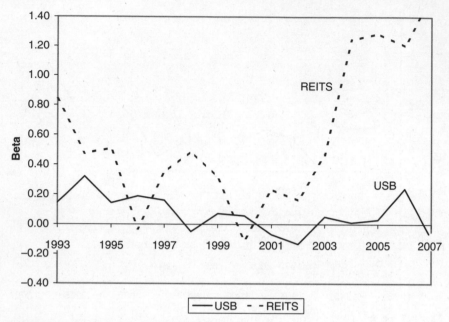

EXHIBIT 19.10   USB and REITS Betas
Source: Morgan Stanley Research

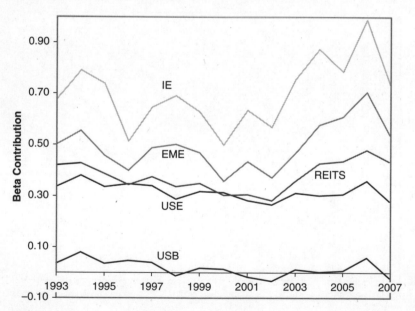

EXHIBIT 19.11   Portfolio D Beta Contributions
Source: Morgan Stanley Research

2003, REITS also did not have a significant impact on the portfolio beta, but this has changed in recent years. The 2003 to 2007 period witnessed a particularly large beta contribution from the 35 percent weight in IE and EME, which may be partially due to the weaker dollar over this time frame. In any case, it appears that the higher IE and EME betas from 2003 through 2007 may be the fundamental cause of the surge in D's beta over this period.

BETA-BASED AND ALPHA RETURNS

The 2003 covariance analysis projected theoretical returns of 6.50 percent for D and 5.85 percent for B, an advantage of 0.65 percent for D. Over the 15-year period, the real return was actually 7.29 percent for D and 6.35 percent for B, a difference of 0.94 percent, that is, very close to the theoretical increment!

Exhibit 19.12 plots Portfolio D's return versus Portfolio B's returns. Since Portfolios D and B share similar risk characteristics, this scattergram should not be surprising. The correlation between Portfolios B and D is 91 percent while the beta between the two portfolios is 1.02.

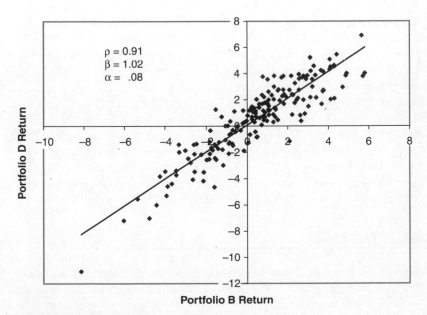

Portfolio B Return

EXHIBIT 19.12 Portfolio D versus Portfolio B Returns
Source: Morgan Stanley Research

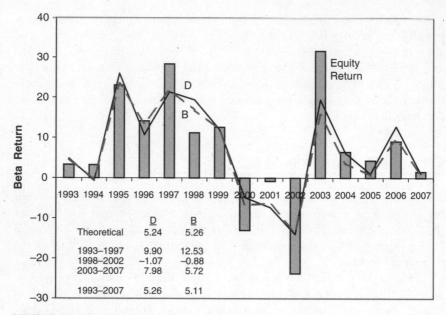

EXHIBIT 19.13 Portfolios D and B Beta Returns
Source: Morgan Stanley Research

The intercept in Exhibit 19.12 of 0.08 represents the monthly alpha (around 1 percent annually) that Portfolio D generates versus Portfolio B. This alpha can be thought of as the return remaining after the beta return is removed from the portfolios. This higher alpha return from Portfolio D is one motivation for diversification over the long term.

Exhibits 19.13 and 19.14 show the beta and alpha returns for Portfolios D and B over time. The bars in Exhibit 19.13 represent USE returns. The beta returns for Portfolio D have been slightly higher when compared with Portfolio B, but both have been driven by the underlying equity return.

The alpha returns for Portfolio D have experienced significantly higher volatility than Portfolio B over the earlier years. However, over the last five years, the alpha returns for D have been consistently higher than Portfolio B.

STRESS BETA THEORY

A common saying is that in a serious market decline, "all correlations go to 1." This statement generally refers to the correlation across various equity-like asset classes, such as USE, IE, EME, PE, and so on (that is, not necessarily fixed income assets).

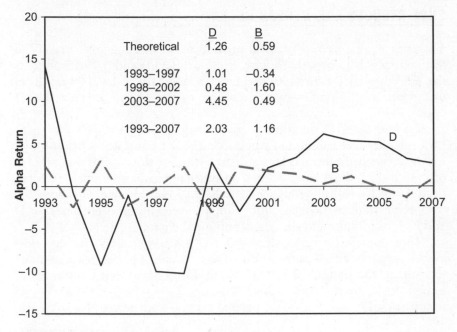

EXHIBIT 19.14 Portfolios D and B Alpha Returns
Source: Morgan Stanley Research

In actuality, all such correlations cannot literally move to 1, but under stress, they can tighten to higher than their normal levels. Within a USE-based beta framework, such correlation tightening would lead to higher than normal beta values, that is, what might be called *stress betas*.

Under normal times, virtually all allocations would exhibit roughly the same beta and volatility levels. In adverse markets, however, any correlation tightening would have little impact on the 60/40 while the diversified portfolios—with its multiple asset classes—would become much more vulnerable to stress betas. Putting these results together, we then conjectured that diversified portfolios would actually be more vulnerable to severe adverse markets than the traditional 60/40. This conjecture was quite at odds with the standard intuition that viewed diversification as a protection against such risks.

The initial betas of most diversified portfolios lie in the same 0.55- to 0.65-range as the traditional 60/40. With unchanged beta values, both portfolio types should experience roughly comparable price declines. With correlation tightening, however, there should be an even greater increase in the diversified portfolio's total beta.

2008 RESULTS AND STRESS BETAS

The weak equity markets of 2008 provide an (unwelcome) opportunity to test the stress beta hypothesis with empirical data. Exhibit 19.15 presents the 1993 through 2007 results along with a summary of the 2008 results in of the form of the various risk characteristics and returns for Portfolios D and B.

For both B and D, the correlations and the ratio of portfolio volatility to USE volatility rose substantially in 2008. The net result was a beta of 0.95 for the diversified portfolio D, significantly higher than its 15-year average of 0.64 and B's 2008 beta of 0.64. At other points in time, such as 2006, both D and B's beta were higher than their 15-year average. However, the truly horrendous markets in 2008 led to a divergence in beta values for D and B of magnitude not seen at any point in the past.

These high stress betas account for D's 9 percent 2008 underperformance versus B. This was the first period in which D performed materially worse than the traditional 60/40. (It should be noted that the returns in Exhibit 19.15 are real returns after deducting 2008 inflation. On a nominal return basis, D came in at −31.3 percent versus −22.3 percent for B.)

EXHIBIT 19.15 1993 through 2007 and 2008 Risk-and-Return Results

	B	D
U.S. Equity	60%	30%
U.S. Bonds	40%	25%
International Equity		25%
Emerging Mkt Equity		10%
REITS		10%

	Monthly 1993–2007			Monthly 2008		
	B	D	D vs B	B	D	D vs B
Beta	0.61	0.63	0.02	0.64	0.95	0.31
Real Return	9.12	10.17	1.05	−22.07	−31.06	−8.99

Source: Morgan Stanley Research

CONCLUSION

During normal times, theory suggests that diversified and traditional portfolios should share similar portfolio betas. The actual betas from 1993 through 2007 verify this assessment, with D and B matching each other as well as their theoretical projections.

While diversified and traditional portfolios have similar risks in normal times, the beta-based theory also suggests that the diversified portfolio should be more vulnerable to stress betas in highly extreme markets. The weak equity markets of 2008 provide an opportunity to test this hypothesis with empirical data. In 2008, the diversified portfolio's beta of 0.95 did indeed turn out to be far higher than B's beta of 0.64. As a consequence, D's 2008 return was 9 percent worse than B's.

Under normal times, international equity and emerging market equity may lower the total beta and portfolio volatility and serve as sources of return accumulation and outcome divergence over the long term. However, in short term periods of stress such as 2008, their vulnerability to tightening correlations increases their betas, leading to higher stress beta and more severe losses for the diversified portfolio.

Asset Allocation and Return Thresholds

Asset Allocation and Return Thresholds in a Beta World

A *minimum objective for any risk-taking portfolio is to surpass the return available from a (nearly) risk-free alternative. For a given equity risk-and-return ratio, the characteristic probability of surpassing this minimal objective is the same for every equity and cash mixture and every risk-free rate and it is surprisingly low (for example, 60 percent) over a one-year horizon. Higher return targets require accepting a minimum level of beta risk even for success probabilities that fall below the characteristic probability.*

Longer term horizons are the key to generating significant probabilities of achieving even modest return targets. But there is a natural tension between long-horizon investing, which may increase the required minimum beta risk, and shorter term volatility limits, which call for a maximum beta risk on a year-by-year basis.

We can use this combination of a risk maximum and a return minimum to define a range of feasible beta values. (Under some specifications, this beta range may be tight or nonexistent!) In this chapter, the feasible beta values (for example, 0.53) closely approximate the equity sensitivity of most individual and institutional portfolios, even those with the highest level of diversification.

These findings and, more generally, the results reported in this book have important implications for the endowment model and, more broadly, for asset allocation. They provide support for allocations that incorporate a return-seeking core that is long-term oriented and can accommodate a relatively high level of short term risk. Far from simply embracing alternative, nonstandard assets as return generators, or eschewing them as risk injectors in stressful times, investors can gain attractive advantages, but must be able to evaluate their use in light of feasible risk limits.

PERCENTILES IN RETURN AND BETA SPACE

Following our studies of empirical betas, we return to hypothetical assets. We first consider a basic cash-equity model with hypothetical rates of 5 percent for risk-free cash, 4 percent for the equity premium over cash, and a normal distribution of equity returns, where the volatility is 16 percent (we will expand this model later on to include other assets). A 60 percent equity–40 percent cash portfolio would then have an expected one-year return of 7.4 percent and a volatility of 9.6 percent. Exhibit 20.1 depicts the distribution of outcomes for this 0.60 beta portfolio.

This 60 percent equity portfolio has an 80 percent probability of surpassing a return level of –0.67 percent. Since our focus is on the probability of exceeding various thresholds, it is useful to express percentiles in an inverted fashion, for example, the –0.67 percent level will be referred to as the 80th percentile.

Exhibit 20.2 plots the beta market line of expected returns against beta values for different equity and cash mixtures. The equity market line begins at the risk-free rate of 5 percent and extends to 9 percent for a 100 percent equity portfolio with a beta = 1.

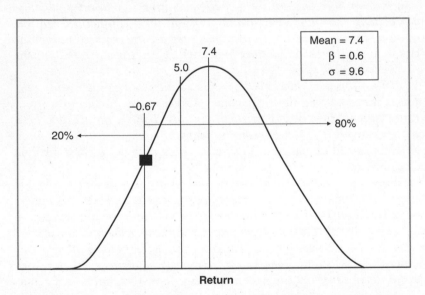

EXHIBIT 20.1   Probability Distribution for 60/40 Portfolio (Beta = 0.6)
Source: Morgan Stanley Research

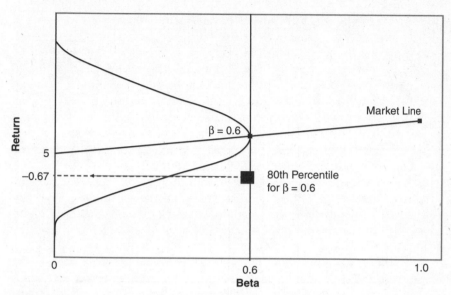

EXHIBIT 20.2   80th Percentile in Return-Beta Space (Beta = 0.6)
Source: Morgan Stanley Research

This distribution in Exhibit 20.1 can be rotated and plotted against the 0.60 beta point on this equity market line. This distribution centers on the 7.4 percent expected return of the 0.6 beta portfolio. Using our revised definition, the 80th percentile is located at –0.67 percent.

A 40/60 portfolio with a lower 0.4 beta will naturally have a lower volatility (6.4 percent) and a reduced expected return (6.6 percent). With this narrower distribution, the 80th percentile now falls at the higher line of 1.2 percent.

Once again, the distribution can be rotated and plotted against the equity market line (Exhibit 20.4).

THE PERCENTILE FAN

Exhibits 20.1 through 20.4 depict the 80th percentiles for two specific portfolios of stock and cash mixes of 60/40 and 40/60, respectively. In Exhibit 20.5, a straight line is drawn between these two points. It is demonstrated in the appendix how any point on this line can be interpreted as the 80th percentile for every return distribution defined by a beta value along the

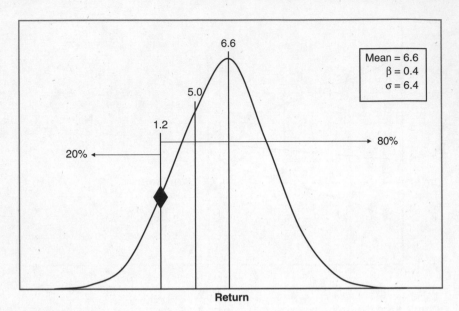

EXHIBIT 20.3 Probability Distribution for 40/60 Portfolio (Beta = 0.4)
Source: Morgan Stanley Research

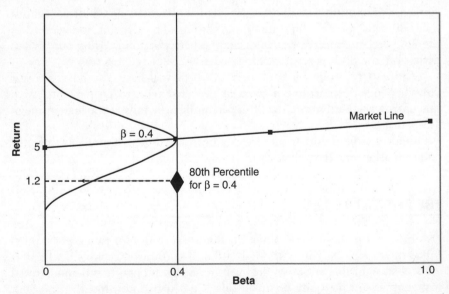

EXHIBIT 20.4 80th Percentile in Return-Beta Space (Beta = 0.4)
Source: Morgan Stanley Research

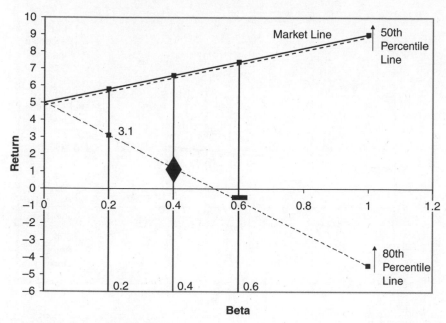

EXHIBIT 20.5 The 80th Percentile Line
Source: Morgan Stanley Research

horizontal axis. Thus, a beta of 0.2 corresponds to a return of 3.1 percent on this line, indicating that a 20/80 portfolio would have this value as its 80th percentile.

Exhibit 20.5 also indicates how the market line itself can be interpreted as the 50th percentile line. The 50th and 80th percentile lines both intersect the 0-beta axis at the 5 percent cash rate. At 0-beta, the portfolio consists of 100 percent cash, so there is a 100 percent probability of realizing the cash rate and all the percentiles collapse into a single point.

Exhibit 20.6 now adds percentile lines of 20 percent, 40 percent, and 70 percent. Focusing on a beta = 0.6, there is a 20 percent chance of exceeding 15.5 percent and a 40 percent chance of exceeding 9.8 percent. Not surprisingly, these percentile fans are symmetric around the market line, that is, the angle from the market line to 20th percentile is the same as the angle to the 80th percentile line. This underscores the point that these percentile fans are associated with a specific set of market assumptions and the corresponding market line. Risk premiums that are greater than our assumed 4 percent would rotate this entire percentile fan upward in a counterclockwise situation.

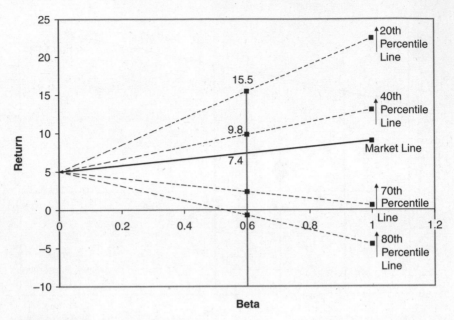

EXHIBIT 20.6   The Percentile Fan
Source: Morgan Stanley Research

    The wide spread of the percentile lines in Exhibit 20.6 dominates the modest upward slope of the market line. It should also be emphasized that the fan structure depicted in Exhibit 20.6 represents a one-year time horizon. It should be no surprise that, over such a short time, the expected returns derived from the 4 percent equity premium are overshadowed by the much larger 16 percent volatility, especially at the higher beta values.

    With our definition of percentiles and our adoption of a normal distribution, percentiles higher than 50 percent imply thresholds below the expected return. Consequently, all greater-than-50th percentile lines fall below the market line in Exhibit 20.6, while all lower-than-50th percentile lines lie above the market line.

MINIMUM AND MAXIMUM BETAS
FOR RETURN TARGETS

The percentile fans can be useful for an investor seeking a specific return target. For example, suppose an investor targets an 8 percent return with a

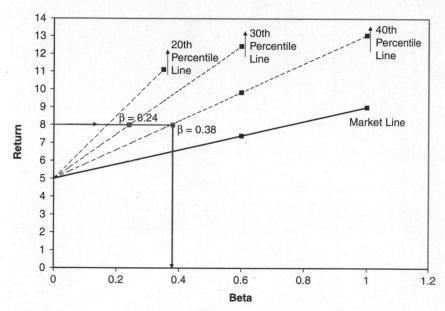

EXHIBIT 20.7   The Minimum Beta for an 8 Percent Target with 40 Percent Probability
Source: Morgan Stanley Research

probability of at least 40 percent. In Exhibit 20.7, the beta must be extended beyond the 20th and 30th percentile lines until it reaches the 40th percentile line at a beta of 0.38. Lower portfolio betas would lead to lower probabilities of achieving the 8 percent target. Thus, to achieve the stated target of an 8 percent return with a 40 percent probability, a minimum beta of 0.38 is required.

In the preceding example, the 8 percent target return was above the 5 percent risk-free rate. In contrast, risk constraints typically specify both a threshold well below the cash rate, together with a high probability that returns do not fall below this shortfall limit. For example, in Exhibit 20.8, the specified shortfall limit is set at a zero percent return with at least an 80 percent probability. As the beta extends along this zero percent horizontal threshold, it proceeds through the overly stringent 90th percentile line to reach the last acceptable 80th percentile line at a beta of 0.53. Higher betas would lead to unacceptably low probabilities. This suggests that 0.53 is the maximum beta that will allow for an 80 percent probability of positive returns.

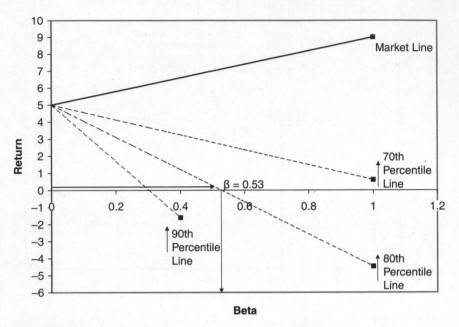

EXHIBIT 20.8 The Maximum Beta for Zero Percent Shortfall Limit with 80 percent Probability
Source: Morgan Stanley Research

THE CHARACTERISTIC PROBABILITY OF EXCEEDING THE RISK-FREE RATE

Since the 5 percent risk-free rate can be achieved with 100 percent assurance, a key reason for accepting beta risk is to improve upon this cash rate. Every line in the return-beta space that emanates from the cash-rate point can be interpreted as reflecting some percentile value. This interpretation specifically includes the horizontal line that starts at 5 percent.

In Exhibit 20.9, this horizontal line is shown as being equal to a 60th percentile line. This suggests that for a return minimum of 5 percent, the probability remains constant at 60 percent for all positive beta values. In other words, for this particular set of market parameters, every portfolio mixture has this same 60 percent chance of exceeding the 5 percent cash rate.

As depicted schematically in Exhibit 20.10, a 0-beta portfolio (that is, 100 percent cash) provides 100 percent assurance of achieving the 5 percent rate. Any move off this solid cash pedestal into the more turbulent region

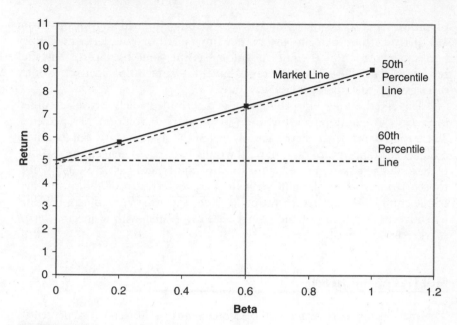

EXHIBIT 20.9 The Characteristic Probability
Source: Morgan Stanley Research

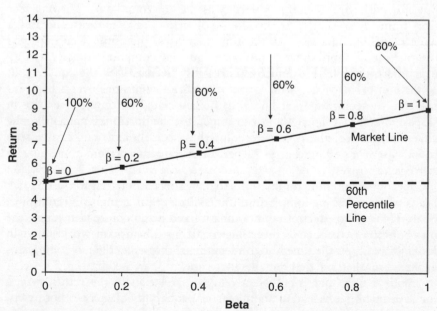

EXHIBIT 20.10 Probability of Matching or Exceeding 5 Percent Risk-Free Rate
Source: Morgan Stanley Research

of positive betas, however, and the probability immediately drops from 100 percent to 60 percent—no matter how small or how large the equity percentage! Any $\beta > 0$ equity position has the same balance of risk and return, so that all equity percentages have this same 60 percent probability of exceeding the 5 percent risk-free rate.

This fixed 60 percent probability is determined solely by our assumed 0.25 ratio of equity return premium (4 percent) to volatility (16 percent). There is no dependence on the actual level of the risk-free rate. For example, a higher risk-and-return ratio of 0.40 would lead to a 65 percent probability of beating the risk-free rate, again for any equity and cash mixture. Thus, this horizontal percentile value serves as a characteristic probability attached to the equity risk-and-return ratio. As such, it can be viewed as a baseline incentive to incur any of the equity risk associated with a specific set of market assumptions.

MULTIYEAR HORIZONS

The analysis has thus far focused on a one-year time horizon. The percentile lines can also be useful when looking at multiyear periods, however. Exhibit 20.11 plots the risk-and-return percentile fans for one- and five-year periods, but now with the annualized volatility as the horizontal axis. The one-year time frame is subject to tremendous volatility and therefore generates a wide range of outcomes. As the time increases, the annualized expected return remains approximately the same (ignoring compounding or volatility drag effects), while the annualized volatility decreases by the square root of the number of years. With lower annualized volatilities over a five-year horizon, the equity market line and the associated percentile lines rise in slope and contract in length. For example, for the horizontal percentile, the characteristic probability for exceeding the 5 percent cash rate can be seen to increase from 60 percent to 71 percent as one moves from a one-year to a five-year horizon.

It is not uncommon for investors to have shorter horizons for setting risk limits while accepting longer time frames for return generation (Leibowitz et al., 1996). The effect of maintaining a fixed beta posture year after year may be better envisioned by reverting to the return-beta framework shown in Exhibit 20.12. As the time horizon lengthens, the percentile fan compresses around a market line that remains invariant.

With a beta that is sufficiently high in relation to the return target, longer time horizons lead to an increasing probability of success. For example, in Exhibit 20.13 we can see that, for a fixed beta of 0.6, the probability of returns above zero percent increases from 78 percent for 1 year to

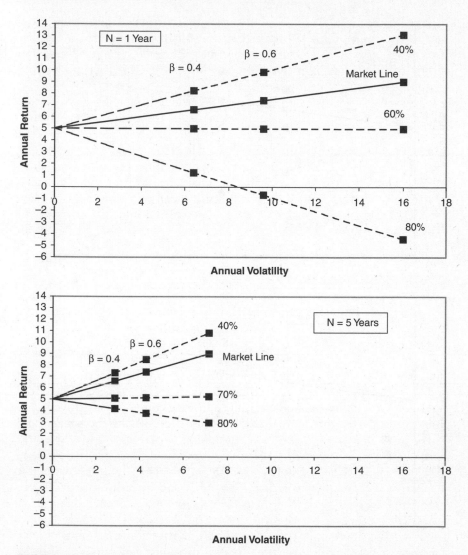

EXHIBIT 20.11 Horizon Effects in Return-Volatility Space: One and Five Years
Source: Morgan Stanley Research

96 percent for 5 years, and 99 percent for 10 years. Similarly, the probability of surpassing the 5 percent risk-free rate is 60 percent, 71 percent, and 79 percent for 1, 5, and 10-year horizons. However, the expected returns for a 0.6 beta portfolio is 7.4 percent, and the probability of exceeding this value is 50 percent for one year—and remains right at 50 percent for ever

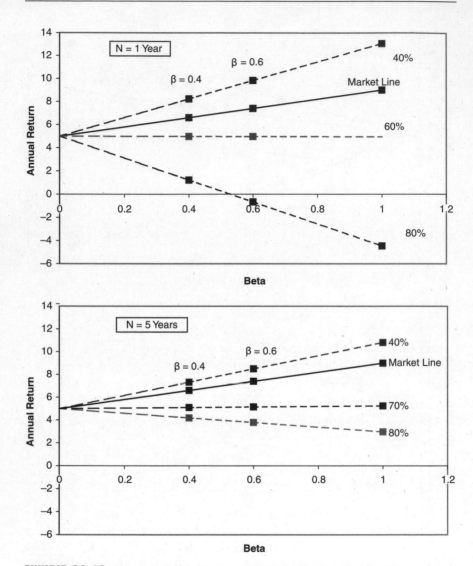

EXHIBIT 20.12 Horizon Effects in Return-Beta Space: One and Five Years
Source: Morgan Stanley Research

longer time horizons as well. As illustrated in Exhibit 20.13, once we move to return targets above the 7.4 percent expected return, the success probability actually declines with time. Thus, for a 10 percent target, a 0.6 beta portfolio leads to declining success probabilities of 39 percent, 27 percent, and 20 percent for 1, 5, and 10 years, respectively.

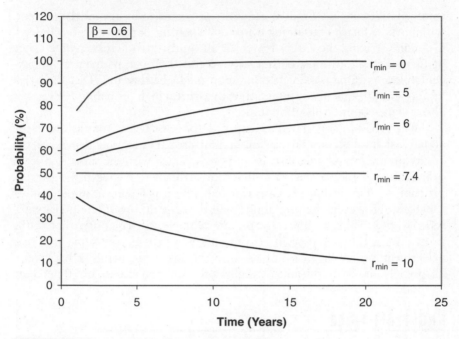

EXHIBIT 20.13   Success Probabilities over Time
Source: Morgan Stanley Research

All these results follow from the tightening of the theoretical distribution of annualized returns over longer time horizons.

BETA REGIMES

A related effect of the fan compression with longer horizons is that low minimum betas may need to be increased. For example, in Exhibit 20.7, it was shown that a minimum beta of 0.38 was needed for a 40 percent probability of obtaining an 8 percent target return. If the horizon is stretched to five years, the same 40 percent probability would now require a minimum beta of 0.52. Together with Exhibit 20.8's risk-based maximum beta of 0.53 for a positive return over one year, this five-year minimum beta implies an extremely narrow beta range—from a minimum of 0.52 to a maximum of 0.53.

Although this example is strictly hypothetical, it is interesting to note that the typical beta value for U.S. institutional portfolios actually does lie in the 0.55- to 0.65-range (Leibowitz and Bova 2005, 2007). Moreover, the total volatility of such funds is generally projected to be around 10 percent, with the beta factor accounting for over 90 percent of this volatility. Indeed, it is quite striking the extent to which all funds, even across a wide range of diversified allocations, cluster around this 0.60 beta value and 10 percent volatility. One possible explanation might be that funds set their risk limits—either explicitly or implicitly—to assure a high probability of returns above some common shortfall limit.

When the target is stated as a spread above or below the cash rate, the actual cash level becomes irrelevant and the probabilities only depend on the equity premium and volatility assumptions. Thus, with the same 4 percent premium and 16 percent volatility, one will always have a 60 percent probability of exceeding the cash rate, whether it is 5 percent, 6 percent, or 2 percent. However, the probability will be different for different risk-and-return ratios. Thus, an 8 percent premium/32 percent volatility (that is, the same 0.25 ratio as 4 percent/16 percent) will provide the same one-year 60 percent probability of returns over the cash rate, while a 6 percent/16 percent ratio would lead to a higher one-year probability of 70 percent.

SHORTFALL LINES

Thus far, we have focused on the percentile lines that essentially describe the probability distribution for a given beta portfolio. As repeatedly emphasized, these percentile fans are derived from a specific set of market assumptions. An alternative approach is to specify a minimum return with a given probability and ask what combinations of expected return and volatility satisfy this constraint. We can refer to the results as a *shortfall line*.

As shown in the appendix, one can draw such a shortfall line where all risk-and-return combinations above the line satisfy the constraint, while all combinations below the line do not. The specified minimum return acts as the shortfall line's point of origin on the vertical axis. The slope is determined by the required probability. It should be noted that a given shortfall line applies to all combinations of expected return and volatility, that is, unlike the line in the percentile fan, a shortfall line is not tied to a given market line.

Returning to the one-year horizon, Exhibit 20.14 shows a 40 percent shortfall line for an 8 percent return. This shortfall line intersects the equity market line at the same beta of 0.38 that was seen earlier in Exhibit 20.7.

While Exhibit 20.14 demonstrates the consistency between the shortfall and the percentile approach, it should again be emphasized that unlike the percentiles, which rotate around the assumed market line, the shortfall line is independent of the market model.

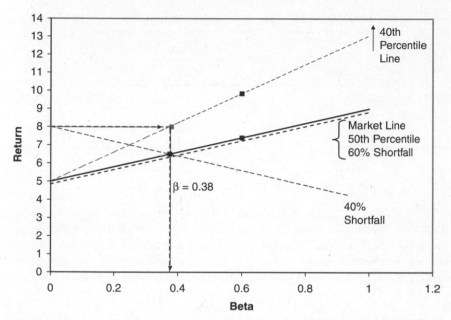

EXHIBIT 20.14 40th Percentile and 40 Percent Shortfall Lines
Source: Morgan Stanley Research

Every straight line in the expected risk-and-return space represents a shortfall line for some probability of achieving some minimum threshold. And the market line itself represents a shortfall line at which the risk-free rate is taken as the minimum threshold. As with all shortfall lines, the associated probability is determined by the line's slope. For our market model (for example, in Exhibit 20.9), the associated shortfall probability is 60 percent—the same characteristic 60 percent probability given by the horizontal percentile line. In other words, the market line's shortfall interpretation and the horizontal percentile line reflect the same 60 percent characteristic probability that any equity and cash mixture will be able to exceed the risk-free rate.

For our example of a 4 percent risk premium and 16 percent volatility, the Sharpe ratio is 0.25, which corresponds to a shortfall probability of 60 percent. Thus, all risky portfolios on the market line (those with $\beta > 0$), will have the same 60 percent probability of surpassing the 5 percent risk-free rate. (It should be noted that this shortfall probability depends only on the Sharpe ratio, that is, not on the specific level of the risk-free rate.)

In Exhibit 20.15, the Sharpe ratio and associated shortfall probabilities are shown for various risk premiums, assuming that the 16 percent volatility

EXHIBIT 20.15 Characteristic Probabilities

Risk Premium	Sharpe Ratio	Shortfall Probabilities	
		1 Year	5 Year
0%	0	50%	50%
2%	0.125	55%	61%
4%	0.25	60%	71%
6%	0.375	65%	80%
8%	0.5	69%	87%

Source: Morgan Stanley Research

is kept constant. In contrast to the 60 percent probability for our basic example of a 4 percent risk premium over a one-year period, one can see that a 6 percent premium over a five-year period would lead to a much greater Sharpe ratio of 0.375 and a significantly higher 80 percent probability.

ALPHA CORES AND STRESS BETAS

In practice, portfolios are more complex than our two-asset model. A typical institutional fund will have multiple sources of risk and return that may include a variety of diversifying asset classes, more granularities within the equity component itself, a better yielding structure for the lower-risk alternatives than just cash, a whole spectrum of active management and hedging strategies, and so forth. Each such component will contribute some (hopefully positive) measure of expected return, risk, and a correlation with all the other components.

However, most asset classes and most active strategies have some degree of correlation with equities, and their resulting betas (which is the product of the correlation and the ratio of the volatilities) are additive in nature. The net result is that at the fund level, the beta sensitivity to domestic equities remains the overwhelmingly dominant source of risk, even for highly diversified allocations with minimal direct equity exposure. Commonly used return estimates (and certain historical evidence) suggest that the benefit from a typical diversification is to be found, not in lower short-term volatility, but in higher expected return (Leibowitz and Bova 2009). Indeed, as noted earlier, most diversified funds seen in practice appear to have the same fund-level 0.55- to 0.65-betas as the more traditional 60/40 funds.

As we have shown in previous chapters, beta dominance allows allocations to be approximately modeled as having only two key sources of risk and return: the fund-level beta sensitivity, and a theoretical alpha core that provides an expected return—and a source of volatility risk—beyond that which can be directly ascribed to the benchmark equity. However, we must modify our current analysis to account for the effects of the alpha core on the portfolio.

First, inclusion of an alpha core would materially alter the shape of the percentile fan. The addition of an increment of expected return would raise the market line (now a market curve) above the earlier risk-free rate. At the same time, the total portfolio volatility would now depend on the alpha volatility as well as the beta-based volatility. Since these two volatility sources combine as sum-of-squares, the portfolio's total volatility would no longer be linear in beta. Instead of a straight line, a fixed-percentile value would now lead to a fan of percentile curves as the beta is varied.

Exhibit 20.16 depicts this one-year percentile fan for portfolios that incorporate an alpha core with an assumed incremental return of 2 percent and a beta-independent volatility of 5 percent. In contrast to the basic equity-cash model, the 60th percentile curve now lies above the risk-free rate. At a beta of 0.6, the alpha portfolio provides returns that exceed the risk-free rate with a probability of 66 percent for one-year and 82 percent for five-year

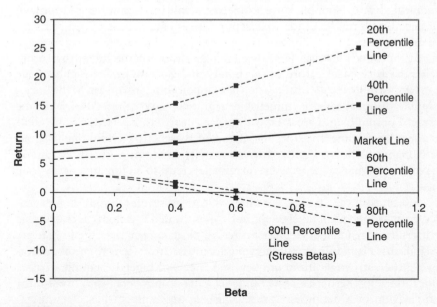

EXHIBIT 20.16 An Alpha Core Percentile Fan
Source: Morgan Stanley Research

horizons, compared with the equity and cash model's 60 percent and 71 percent for the corresponding time periods.

Second, the multi-asset structure of an alpha core can present special problems, especially during periods of market stress. In normal times, the 60/40 fund and diversified allocations both have similar fund-level betas. However, in severe market declines, correlations generally tighten. In the multi-asset structure of an alpha portfolio, these increasing correlations can raise the beta sensitivity to stress levels—at just the wrong time! Because of these stress beta effects, it is ironic that it is the diversified portfolios that turn out to be more vulnerable to seriously adverse markets than simple two-asset funds. Exhibit 20.16 illustrates this stress beta effect as a more stringent (that is, lower return) 80th percentile curve that would result from a 25 percent correlation tightening.

Thus, while a productive alpha core may offer the prospect of improved return targets (and more divergent outcomes over the long term), it comes at the potential cost of more severe short term risk under extreme markets.

CONCLUSION

The results reported in this chapter and throughout this book support the argument that reasonable return objectives call for a long term approach combined with the fortitude to accept relatively high levels of year-by-year volatility risk.

At the same time, these strong findings should be tempered by recognizing the very basic nature of our equity-and-cash models, which exclude many important considerations such as compounding, reversion to the mean, volatility drag, fat tails, asymmetric distributions, and so on. Also, while the assumed premium and volatility values are close to those used in many allocation studies, some investors may feel that these values should be dramatically higher (or lower) under various market conditions. Finally, it should be recognized that all expected return models tend to be fundamentally long term in nature.

Subject to these caveats, our analysis leads to several key guiding principles. First, a long term investment horizon is needed to achieve a reasonable probability of reaching even modest return targets. Even over the long term, a significant probability for achieving decent return targets requires accepting a sufficiently high minimum beta risk. Second, when designing an asset allocation, short term risk constraints set a maximum beta limit. In turn, the combination of a maximum risk-based beta and a target-based minimum beta defines a beta regime, which can be quite tight (or sometimes even nonexistent!).

APPENDIX

The market model consists of a risk-free rate y, an equity risk premium r_e, and an equity volatility σ_e. The equity-and-cash portfolio with an equity fraction β then has an expected return R,

$$R = y + \beta r_e \qquad \beta \geq 0$$

and a volatility σ,

$$\sigma_\beta = \beta \sigma_e$$

For a given distribution of returns (assumed to be normal in this paper), the pth percentile can be expressed as k_p units of standard deviation to the left of the mean. For a given beta value β, this would imply a pth percentile return r_p,

$$
\begin{aligned}
r_p &= R - k_p \sigma_\beta \\
&= y + \beta r_e - k_p \beta \sigma_e \\
&= y + \beta \left(r_e - k_p \sigma_e \right) \\
&= y + \beta \sigma_e \left(SR_e - k_p \right)
\end{aligned}
$$

where SR_e is the Sharpe ratio $\left(\frac{r_e}{\sigma_e} \right)$ for the equity market line.

The percentile fan consists of the percentile lines traced out in return-beta space as β varies.

Alternatively, percentiles can be plotted against the volatility σ_β

$$r_p = y + \sigma_\beta \left(SR_e - k_p \right)$$

in which σ_β ranges from $0 \leq \sigma_\beta \leq \sigma_e$.

The case in which $k_p = SR_e$ for $\beta > 0$ deserves special mention. This condition defines a horizontal line $r_p = 4$ emanating from the cash rate y. For a given market model with its assumed Sharpe ratio, SR_e, there will be one probability p derived from the $k_p = SR_e$ relationship. This p value can be interpreted as the probability that a portfolio with a positive equity fraction β will be able to exceed the risk-free rate. Moreover, this same probability p will apply to all beta values ($\beta > 0$) along the entire market line. In other words, each set of market assumptions has a characteristic probability p that any equity portfolio—regardless of the exact mixture—will provide returns above the risk-free rate.

From this equation, one can see that this characteristic probability p is determined only by the Sharpe ratio. Thus, as long as the risk premium and the volatility lead to the same Sharpe ratio, one will have the same characteristic probability of besting the cash rate—whatever that cash rate may be.

Multiyear horizons can be simplistically modeled (ignoring compounding and volatility drag) by treating all returns as annualized and reducing the annualized volatility by a factor of $\left(1/\sqrt{N}\right)$ where N is the number of years. The percentile lines then take the form,

$$r_p = y + \beta \left[r_e - k_p \frac{\sigma_e}{\sqrt{N}} \right]$$

$$= y + \beta \left(\frac{\sigma_e}{\sqrt{N}} \right) \left[(SR_e) \sqrt{N} - k_p \right]$$

In this case, the characteristic probability p is defined by

$$k_p = \sqrt{N}\,(SR_e)$$

so that this probability rises with a lengthening investment horizon.

The expression

$$k_p \left(\frac{\sigma_e}{\sqrt{N}} \right)$$

becomes smaller as N increases, which leads to a compression of the percentile fan around the basic market line, which remains invariant. In the limit, for very long horizons (where this simple model surely does not hold), all percentile lines will converge on the market line itself. Thus, the return for a given beta portfolio should theoretically converge toward the expected return associated with its beta position. In other words, over the long term, a given return target will be hypothetically achievable only by beta values having expected returns that match or exceed the target level.

An alternative approach to the multiyear horizon is to view percentiles using the annualized volatility as the horizontal axis. The annualized volatility $\sigma\,(\beta, N)$ corresponding to a β portfolio over N years is

$$\sigma\,(\beta, N) = \frac{(\beta\sigma_e)}{\sqrt{N}}$$

so that

$$r_p = y + \beta \left[r_e - k_p \left(\frac{\sigma_e}{\sqrt{N}} \right) \right]$$

$$= y + \frac{\sqrt{N}\sigma\,(\beta, N)}{\sigma_e} \left[r_e - k_p \left(\frac{\sigma_e}{\sqrt{N}} \right) \right]$$

$$= y + \sigma\,(\beta, N) \left[\sqrt{N}\,(SR_e) - k_p \right]$$

Where $\sigma\,(\beta, N)$ now has the more limited range,

$$0 \le \sigma\,(\beta, N) \le \left(\sigma_e / \sqrt{N} \right)$$

In this formulation, the larger Sharpe ratio term increases the slope of the market line while the tightened $\sigma\,(\beta, N)$ range comprises the percentile fan around the higher market line. This framework has the advantage that multiple horizons can be plotted on the same diagram, providing a view of both the rising market line and the associated fan compression.

Shortfall lines are a related concept. Unlike the percentile lines described earlier, a shortfall line only specifies a minimum return threshold T that is to be achieved with a desired probability p. For a given σ_β, the expected return R that will achieve T with probability p is

$$R = T + k_p \sigma_\beta$$

$$= T + k_p \beta \sigma_e$$

Shortfall lines can be generated for any threshold T and any required probability p

A given market line,

$$R = y + \beta r_e$$

$$= y + \sigma_\beta\,(SR_e)$$

will have an intersection with a shortfall line at a point at which the beta portfolio can satisfy the shortfall constraint. This intersection point may also serve as a maximum beta for threshold risks (below the risk-free rate) or a minimum beta for return targets (above the risk-free rate).

For a threshold T, this intersection can be found by setting

$$R = y + \beta r_e$$

$$= T + k_p \beta \sigma_e$$

or

$$T = y + \beta \left[r_e - k_p \sigma_e \right]$$

which has the same value as the pth percentile line at the beta value β, that is,

$$r_p = y + \beta \left[r_e - k_p \sigma_e \right]$$

from the earlier expression for the pth percentile lines. Thus, a shortfall line's intersection with the market line coincides with the pth percentile line for a target return T.

One particular shortfall line is especially notable—the market line itself—in which

$$T = y$$

and so

$$R = T + \beta r_e \qquad \text{(market line)}$$
$$= T + k_p \beta \sigma_e \qquad (p\text{th shortfall line at } T = y)$$

This equality implies that

$$k_p \beta \sigma_e = \beta r_e$$

or for all $\beta > 0$

$$k_p = \left(\frac{r_e}{\sigma_e} \right)$$
$$= SR_e$$

Thus, from viewing the market line as a shortfall line, every equity mixture, that is, $(\beta > 0)$ turns out to have the same pth probability of exceeding the risk-free rate $T = y$.

This finding is also consistent with the horizontal percentile line described earlier, in which

$$r_p = y$$

and again

$$k_p = SR_e$$

In other words, the horizontal percentile lines and the market line's shortfall interpretation both describe the characteristic probability of exceeding the risk-free rate for any equity mixture having a given Sharpe ratio.

REFERENCES

Leibowitz, M. L., L. N. Bader, and S. Kogelman. 1996. *Return targets and shortfall risks*. New York: Irwin Professional Publishing.

Leibowitz, M. L., and A. Bova. 2005. "Allocation betas." *Financial Analysts Journal* 61 (4): 70–82.

———. 2007. "Gathering implicit alphas in a beta world." *Journal of Portfolio Management* 33 (3): 10–18.

———. 2009. "Diversification performance and stress-betas." *Journal of Portfolio Management* 45 (3): 41–47.

CHAPTER 21

Key Takeaways

This book suggests the following fundamental takeaways:

Portfolio Similarity: Using structural measures of beta and alpha, it is apparent that many institutional portfolios that appear quite different on the surface in fact share common risk-and-return characteristics. For example, our sensible hypothetical portfolios from previous chapters, as well as the portfolio risk band result (0.52–0.53 beta range) from the current chapter, roughly approximate the 0.55–0.65 beta values widely seen in practice.

Portfolio Construction: Identifying and using structural alphas to design portfolios that combine an alpha core of nonstandard alternative assets with more traditional swing assets can help in structuring portfolios for the desired balance of risk and expected return.

Return versus Risk: Adoption of the modern endowment model, with its reliance on nonstandard alternative assets, seems more designed to enhance returns than control risk.

Stress Betas: During periods of market stress, correlations, and volatility ratios, betas can and do rise, thereby reducing the benefits of shortfall risk protection.

Excess Return: Even in normal times, the probability of achieving a return that exceeds the risk-free rate over one year is surprisingly low, regardless of how much beta risk is taken.

Alpha Core: To achieve reasonable return targets within the framework of a standard market model, allocations may need to incorporate a return-seeking core that is seriously long term oriented, and yet able to accommodate relatively high levels of year-by-year volatility.

Short versus Long Horizon Investing: Positive alpha returns from diversifying assets, better-yielding low risk alternatives, and active strategies can also help achieve reasonable return targets over the long run, but with a potentially greater vulnerability to stress risks in severely adverse markets.

Finally, what are the implications for the endowment model? In the first chapter, we noted the challenges posed by extreme market volatility for institutional portfolios that rely on nonstandard assets for return generation. We have seen that the effects on correlations, betas, and returns can and have been severe. This course of events has surprised many who thought that the endowment model would be good in all kinds of weather. Some have called for abandoning or reforming the endowment model by reducing the commitment to alternatives or even returning to the traditional 60/40 asset mix.

By revealing the underlying sources of risk and return in modern portfolios, this book has shown that having an endowment portfolio exceed the volatility of traditional portfolios should be an entirely expected phenomenon during periods of market stress.

Because stress betas can temporarily reduce the effects of portfolio diversification, we might think that the lesson here is to eliminate reliance on alternative assets for return generation. We might also think that, because it is very hard to exceed the risk-free rate in the short run, we should reduce risk-taking altogether. Rather, the critical lesson is that the endowment model needs to include a clear analysis of the role of short term risk in the pursuit of long term return. In short, the modern endowment model is not a magic potion that will smooth returns and lower short term volatility, but rather a strategy for accumulating incremental returns and achieving more divergent outcomes—*over the long term*. And, in the final analysis, one of the most powerful defenses against portfolio risk is the accumulation of incremental return over the long term.

About the Authors

MARTIN L. LEIBOWITZ

Martin L. Leibowitz is a managing director with Morgan Stanley Research Department's global strategy team. Over the past four years, he and his associates have produced a series of studies on such topics as beta-based asset allocation, active extension 130/30 strategies, asset and liability management, stress betas, and the need for greater fluidity in policy portfolios.

Before joining Morgan Stanley, Mr. Leibowitz was vice chairman and chief investment officer of TIAA-CREF from 1995 to 2004, with responsibility for the management of more than $300 billion in equity, fixed income, and real estate assets. He previously had a 26-year association with Salomon Brothers, where he became director of global research, covering both fixed income and equities, and was a member of that firm's Executive Committee.

Mr. Leibowitz received both A.B. and M.S. degrees from the University of Chicago and a Ph.D. in mathematics from the Courant Institute of New York University.

He has written more 150 articles on various financial and investment analysis topics, and has been the most frequent author published in both the *Financial Analysts Journal* (FAJ) and the *Journal of Portfolio Management* (JPM). Ten of his FAJ articles have received the Graham and Dodd Award for excellence in financial writing. In February 2008, an article written by Mr. Leibowitz and his associate Anthony Bova was voted Best Article in the ninth annual Bernstein Fabozzi/Jacobs Levy Awards by the readers of JPM.

In 1992, *Investing*, a volume of his collected writings, was published with a foreword by William F. Sharpe, the 1990 Nobel Laureate in Economics. In 1996, his book *Return Targets and Shortfall Risks* was issued by Irwin Co. In 2004, two of his books were published: a compilation of studies on equity valuation, titled *Franchise Value* (John Wiley & Co.), and a revised edition of his study on bond investment, *Inside the Yield Book* (Bloomberg Press). The first edition of *Inside the Yield Book* was published in 1972, went through 21 reprintings, and remains a standard in the field. The new edition includes a foreword by noted economist Henry Kaufman.

In 2009, Mr. Leibowitz co-authored *Modern Portfolio Management: Active Long/Short 130/30 Equity Strategies.*

The CFA Institute presented him with three of its highest awards: the Nicholas Molodowsky Award in 1995, the James R. Vertin Award in 1998, and the Award for Professional Excellence in 2005. In October 1995, he received the Distinguished Public Service Award from the Public Securities Association, and in November 1995 he became the first inductee into the Fixed Income Analyst Society's Hall of Fame. He has received special Alumni Achievement Awards from the University of Chicago and New York University, and in 2003 was elected a Fellow of the American Academy of Arts and Sciences.

Mr. Leibowitz is the chairman of the Institute for Advanced Study at Princeton. He is also a member of the Rockefeller University Council and the Board of Overseers of New York University's Stern School of Business. Mr. Leibowitz serves on the investment advisory committee for the Harvard Management Corporation, the University of Chicago, the Carnegie Corporation, and the Rockefeller Foundation. He is a past chairman of the board of the New York Academy of Sciences and a former vice chairman of the Carnegie Corporation.

ANTHONY BOVA

Anthony is a vice president with Morgan Stanley Equity Research's Global Strategy team, focusing on institutional portfolio strategy. Before his current role, he spent four years covering commodity chemicals at Morgan Stanley. Mr. Bova received a B.S. in economics with a minor in mathematics from Duke University and holds the CFA designation. In 2008, Mr. Bova won Best Article in the ninth annual Bernstein Fabozzi/Jacobs Levy Awards presented by the *Journal of Portfolio Management* for his co-authoring of "Gathering Implicit Alphas in a Beta World" which ran in the Spring 2007 issue. In 2009, Mr. Bova co-authored *Modern Portfolio Management: Active Long/Short 130/30 Equity Strategies.*

P. BRETT HAMMOND

Brett Hammond is a managing director and chief investment strategist for TIAA-CREF, with nearly $400 billion under management. In his 16 years at the company, he has worked on the creation of and studies of inflation-linked bonds, target-date asset allocation products, individual financial advice, an international nonprofit pension investment consortium, models of market behavior, and Social Security reform. He also serves as TIAA-CREF's ambassador on issues relating to the macro economy, financial markets, and long-term investing, working to advise TIAA-CREF's institutional and individual clients across the country.

Before joining TIAA-CREF, Mr. Hammond spent nearly 10 years in Washington, D.C., principally at the National Academies (the National Research Council), where he was a member of the senior management team, with specific responsibility for behavioral and social sciences studies, including policy-related books and reports on population, education, human factors in design, national statistics, employment, and a major study of African-Americans. He also worked at the National Academy of Public Administration and oversaw completion of studies on congressional organization and emissions trading.

Before his time in Washington, Mr. Hammond was a member of the faculty of the University of California (Berkeley and Los Angeles) from 1979 to 1984.

Mr. Hammond received B.A. degrees in economics and political science from the University of California at Santa Cruz and a Ph.D. from the Massachusetts Institute of Technology.

He has published more than 30 articles and books in the areas of finance, higher education, and public policy. In finance, his work has covered inflation-linked bonds, savings and investment adequacy, individual and institutional asset allocation, pension design, and Social Security trust fund investment. His work in higher education focuses on faculty retirement policy. His public policy writings include environmental health risk, Medicaid, science and technology, and energy.

Mr. Hammond is an adjunct professor at the Wharton School of the University of Pennsylvania and executive chair of the Research Council on Global Investment, an organization of senior leaders in pension and investment management. He is also program chair and member of the board of the Institute for Research in Quantitative Finance (Q Group) and a member of the advisory board of the Wharton School's Pension Research Council. He is a past president of the Society of Quantitative Analysts.

Index

A
active alphas, 139–140, 187–199, 254–255
  allocation alphas, comparison with, 190–191
  bound-active alphas, 192
  characteristics, 193
  expanding sources of, 196–197
  integration, 192–194
  overweighting, 206–207
  versus passive alphas, 201–202
  portable alphas, 191
  without reweighting, 206, 207
active weightings effect, 203
allocation
  across the frontier, 63
  dual-alpha, 115–116
  process, 47
  and stress beta, 227, 267
allocation alphas, 180–181, 187–189, 201
  active alphas, comparison with, 190–191
  integration, 192–194
alpha and beta returns, 276–279
alpha-based volatility, 77, 102
alpha-beta framework, 47, 49, 68, 95–98, 201, 203, 206
  components, 188
  frontiers, 122
alpha core, 16, 47, 49–51, 52, 68, 69, 187, 312–314, 321
  analysis, 86–90
  building, 103, 119

decay and beta domination, 144–145
expansion of, 101–117, 109–112, 117
fixed, 51, 53, 54
  and efficient frontiers, 154–155
generality of, 54–56
increasing the percentage of, 125–129
maximum exposure limits, 116
structure of, 77
varying the parameters, 56–58
alpha effect, 82, 93–95
alpha independence, 69–71
alpha return effect, 56
alpha space, efficient frontier in, 120–125, 189
alpha uplift model, 65, 90, 91
alpha volatility, 122
alpha volatility effect, 56, 57
alphas
  diversification, 253–254
  dual active-allocation, 115–116
  sequential erosion, 150
alternative assets, 3, 322
  inherent constraints on, 101–102
  and investment manager relationship, 4
  and societal efficient frontier, 135–136
annualized efficient frontiers, 164
annualized expected returns, 154
Asness, Cliff, 39–40